THE SOCIALIST ORIENTATION OF JAWAHARLAL NEHRU

THE SOCIALIST ORIENTATION OF JAWAHARLAL NEHRU

NEELAM MISHRA

With a Foreword by

Dr. Shankar Dayal Sharma
Vice-President
India

GIAN PUBLISHING HOUSE
New Delhi-110002

GIAN PUBLISHING HOUSE
4-C Ansari Road, Daryaganj
New Delhi 110002.

ISBN 81-212-0285-X

Consultant: Dr. S.Gopal

This publication is financially supported by the ICSSR. The responsibility for the facts stated, opinions expressed or conclusions reached, is entirely that of the author and that the ICSSR accepts no responsibility for them.

Published by Mrs. Gayatri Garg for Gian Publishing House
4-C Ansari Road New Delhi 110002.
Laser Typeset by Shiva Shakti Laser Printers
4379/4B Ansari Road Daryaganj New Delhi
Printed at Goyal Offset Works A-60, G.T. Karnal Road, Delhi.

Dedicated to

my loving

Ma, Babuji and Chacha

Foreword

Jawaharlal Nehru was a towering figure of this century, a transcendental personality.

One of the facets of Jawaharlalji's multi-dimensional personality was his attachment to Socialism. In 1936, while delivering his Presidential Address at the Congress Session held in Lucknow on April 12, that year, Panditji had said: "I am convinced that the only key to the solution of the world's problems and India's problems lies in socialism, and when I use this word I do so not in a vague humanitarian way but in the scientific, economic sense. Socialism is, however, something even more than an economic doctrine; it is a philosophy of life and as such also it appeals to me".

Jawaharlalji's ideas about socialism were influenced by many streams of thought. His concept of socialism was moulded to suit conditions prevailing in India. The principle of secular democratic socialism became an integral part of his thinking.

I am happy that through her study of "Socialist Orientation of Jawaharlal Nehru", Smt. Neelam Mishra has sought to trace various forces which influenced formation of Nehruvian socialism. I hope readers would find her exposition rewarding.

Vice - President
India
New Delhi
August 30, 1989

S.D. Sharma

Preface

There is no dearth of reading material on Nehru. In fact, a considerable volume of literature has grown up around him - *Nehruana,* as it may be called. Still, studies continue to pour on the grand personality of Jawaharlal Nehru and will go on, because he had a breadth of vision of the world which is of vital importance even today. His idealism, unorthodoxy, socialism, secularism, humanism, internationalism, scientific spirit and the sense of history spilled over the frontiers of India and time itself to cover tomorrow's world no less than today's.

The worth of Jawaharlal Nehru cannot be gauged by any mundane standards. We are creatures of one generation; he belongs to history, we walk the beaten track of custom and traditions; he blazed new trails, striding forward like the law of historical development itself. The study of Nehru is also a study of history, for the forces that influenced his mind were also influencing other parts of the world. Nehru truly symbolises the mind of Asia and Africa which is renascent, on the voyage of discovery and towards the goal of fulfilment. Moreover, an analysis of personalities like Nehru would provide us some values with which we could identify, especially when the very edifice of society and systems is in a state of convulsion. India is being ripped apart by the destructive forces of communalism, casteism, regionalism, abuse of money power and the most dangerous of all, terrorism. It is during these traumatic times when Jawaharlal Nehru's wisdom, thought, endeavour and statesmanship should work as a sanitizing force. The year of his centenary presents us a good opportunity to re-examine his ideas, views and experiments towards finding out an amicable solution for various ills affecting our body-politic.

A study of Socialist Orientation of Jawaharlal Nehru is the focal point of the present study. The objective has been to identify and locate the forces which helped shape it, to delineate the zig-zags in its evolution under the cross-currents of national and international developments in the absence of a clear-cut class analysis of the situation, and finally to make a critical evaluation of his contribution to socialist thinking and movement in India.

Socialism has to be defined more by what it is not, than by what it is. On the one side, stands liberal capitalism, with its distrust of the state and its emphasis on competition and the liberation of the individual from any, if not all, social principles of obligations. On the other, stands communism, with its totalitarian identification of liberty with the realisation by the individual of a collective social purpose. Socialists have sought the *via media*.

Socialism, then is best defined as a self-conscious middle way. Its original doctrine was opposition to capitalism, its later doctrine opposition to communism. For many years communism and socialism were synonymous; after Marx they were regarded by some, as separate successive historical stages, but the socialist movement was not yet split clearly from communism. The split came when Bernstein and other thinkers differed from the majority of Marxists on the nature of revolution and the direction of the bourgeois state. For Bernstein, as for Fabians, the state was a mechanism for social improvement and for the gradual achievement of socialism; for the Bolsheviks it was an instrument of the bourgeois, with no possibility of any other use. After the Bolshevik seized power in Russia the division between socialists and communists attained an objective basis. Political and economic actions by the Soviet Government showed clearly that the Bolsheviks were not liberals, were no gradualists, and that they were apostles of violent revolution throughout the world. On the other hand, Socialists were parliamentarians.

It is difficult to relate socialist practice directly to socialist philosophy, or to relate it either to political or economic reality, since socialist practice has for the greater part been directed by short-term parliamentary considerations, and socialist philosophy has been like the shadows of Plato's cane, reflected and refracted from capitalist societies to communism and back to socialism, and then hastily related to what the socialist parties were doing. To attempt to make socialist policies and principles consistent is self-evidently an impossible task, for both philosphical response and political urgency have led to innumerable accretions of policy and philosophy which are often incompatible with one another.

How then is socialism to be defined? This was precisely the question that confronted Nehru. Abhorrence of dogma induced him to examine every theory with scepticism. At the same time he was also aware that no ideology could be grafted on India. This resulted in a quest on his part for search of an all comprehensive philosophy. A study of history, practical testimony of the socialist revolution in Soviet Russia, and an objective assessment of the Indian condition led him to have firm conviction in socialism as the panacea for the solution of problems of Indian poverty, feudalism and social backwardness. He was perhaps the foremost leader of the anti-colonialist movement to declare with clarity, and forcefulness that socialism is the objective need of the developing countries. Throughout this endeavour Nehru kept in mind that socialism to be effective and successful in India would have to appear in the Indian garb and mingle with the spirit of India. Precisely, this objective reality led him to combine scientific socialism with what Nehru called the 'Indian genius'.

The objective has been to examine Nehru's orientation towards scientific socialism, to identify the spheres where he differed from classical socialism and make an evaluation of his contribution towards evolving a kind of socialism which would suit the Indian objective conditions. Nehru recognised the objective necessity for the radical reorganisation of Indian society on socialist lines, though he held his own views on how the process, forms and methods of these changes should be understood. Nehru is not a dogmatic socialist. He does not follow any particular ideology, rather builds an ideology for himself. He takes much from orthodox socialism but does not stop at that, goes beyond and formulates his own brand of socialistic ideology. Marxian socialism had its validity but with changes of time and conditions many of its concepts proved outdated. Therefore, Nehru starts with Marx but goes much farther and adds to it new dimensions to make it relevant for the present, though he retains his orientation towards scientific socialism. In fact, by adding to it, he frees Marxism of its rigidity and dogma and thereby makes socialism a progressive ideology.

Here it would not be out of place to discuss as to what exactly I understand by Nehru's socialist orientation.

The word orientation implies that Nehru was oriented towards scientific socialism or the principles of Marxian socialism. The study of Marx convinced him of the inevitability of socialism. According to marxian theory of materialistic interpretation of history, the progress of history and institution through development of economic system, one system replacing another which had turned obsolete would inevitably lead to the advent of socialism. Capitalism when it had run its full course would be a dead- weight on the existing society and it would be replaced by another, which was more scientific and more rationally solved the problems of society. The Marxian economic interpretation of history by emphasising the inevitability of class struggle paved the way for Nehru's socialist thought. It provided the rationale for justifying the advent of socialism.

Nehru believed that dialectical materialism, the historic contribution made by Marx represented a scientific methodology for understanding the history, historic forces, historic development and various economic and social forces that shaped the course of history. He himself used dialectical materialism, with positive modification, for the purpose of understanding history, he analysed Indian history, world history and tried to understand how the forces of fascism could grow in Spain, Italy and in Germany and even long before some could envisage the growth of this phenomenon.

Nehru accepted the objective of Marx's Socialism, of equality and social justice, but preferred to adopt different techniques for achieving the same. He presented his own theory of class-struggle, progress of history, the position of the individual vis-a-vis the state, the form of Government appropriate for India as well as the goals that India would pursue according to her cultural heritage and civilization.

Nehru accepts the presence of class-struggle in society, but refuses to accept class- war and violence as the only solution. Particulary in the later years he proceeded from the thesis that class contradiction could be resolved through class-cooperation in a cooperative way rather than threatening or through the concept of war. Automatically according to

Nehru, bloody revolution and the dictatorship of the proletariat becomes superfluous. Here Nehru clearly differs from Marx, for the dictatorship of the proletariat is one of the basic tenet of Marxian philosophy. Therefore, it can be observed that Nehru is oriented and not committed towards Scientific Socialism. His commitment lies elsewhere.

Like the Revisionists of Germany, France and Britain, he viewed that in a democratic framework Marx's violent solution had become redundant. He felt that inner contradicitions of capitalism, the accumulation on the one hand and poverty on the other, had been significantly resolved by the scientific and technological revolution in industry and the economy. Due to the extension of franchise, growth of working class movements, extension of the power of the Trade Unions and comprehensive Social Security measures, prosperity had come within the reach of all. Instead of concentration of wealth and economic power there had been cosiderable diffusion of the same through spread of education and technical knowledge etc. Besides the problem posed by the advent of nuclear weapons had made the concept of class-struggle and class -war an outdated philosophy.

From these views of Nehru it is clear that though he turned to Marxist philosophy to understand the process of history and accepted the important concept of social justice from Marxism and the basic economic theory and the Russian social structure, he did not accept Marxism in its totality nor he insisted on emulating Russian system completely to bring about structural changes in the social and economic field in India. Thus his concept of Socialism or socialist orientation cannot reasonably be quoted with Marxism in the strict sense nor it can be callously subsumed to communism in the Russian way of life.

It was precisely for this reason that he never defined socialism in exact words when he talked of socialism, it may be remembered that he had used various expressions both in his speeches as well as in his writings such as "Economic Democracy", "Socialist Democracy", "Socialist State" and "Socialistic pattern of Society". When he used these expressions, he used them as synonymous with one another and not as distinct expressions. Nevertheless, he deliberately refrained from giving a definition.

Nehru visualised a modern democratic socialist India, achieved with as much importance attached to the means as to the end. Nehru's hope was for a society where decisions would be made on the basis of popular will and rational discourse by education and social progress promoted by general consent. He was convinced that socialism required the discarding of liberal values. His strategies both political and economic arose coherently out of his fundamental belief in liberty. Nehru had a harmonic conception of society, and India finding her own peaceful path to modernity without suppressing her individuality. He tried to evolve a Modern Socialist State within the Indian culture, which he called the Indian genius.

A human democratic socialism is Jawaharlal Nehru's specific brand of socialism. It is above all a humanistic creed, placing its major emphasis on the fulfilment of the individual. By linking socialism with democracy Nehru made socialism a more respectable creed, thereby liberating it from dogma and rigidity for Marxian socialism condemns democracy as the weapon of the bourgeois and for the perpetuation of an unjust society. Instead it reçommends dictatorship of the proletariat, class-war and withering away of the state, whereas Nehru's idea of socialism encompassed at every stage a large and irreducible measure of civil liberty. One could have neither democracy nor socialism without the other, in fact each thrived on the other. Socialism is inherent in Democracy and Democracy is the womb of socialism. Nehru asserts that condemnation of democracy should come not from the side of socialism, rather democracy stands condemned in a capitalist society. Freedom of the individual and equality of opportunity can be attained only in a democratic socialist society.

A sufficient amount of meaningful work has been done to unravel the many ideas and versatile mind of Jawaharlal Nehru which have contributed towards understanding of the Nehru phenomenon. No doubt exhaustive studies will continue to be taken up for a still better understanding of his thoughts, ideas and actions. However, a careful analysis reveals that his idea of socialism has been mostly dealt with rather lightly. An indepth study of his socialism has in our opinion not been carried out. Almost all the works give a good account of his failures and success as an administrator, but none attempts to analyse the basic concepts on which Nehru's socialism rests. The present book is an attempt in this direction.

An understanding of the subjects, academic interest in the problem of search of an adequate system for the country, led me to a study of Jawaharlal Nehru's socialist orientation in the Indian perspective. I felt that it was essential that a study of Nehru's intellectual and psychological mind-set had to be made to enable one to understand the forces which are shaping the present and future course of modern India, for no aspect of Indian life is immune to the impact of the ideas of Nehru.

A humble attempt has been made and it is hoped that the proposed work would shed more light on the unfoldment of the socialist ideas of Jawaharlal Nehru and contribute further towards a proper assessment of his personality, thereby taking the debate forward.

NEELAM MISHRA

Acknowledgements

I take this opportunity first and foremost to express my sincere thanks to the Vice-President of India, Dr. Shankar Dayal Sharma for being kind enough to write the foreword for my book, despite his immensely busy schedule. His words are a blessing for an amateur like myself, and will help greatly in my future academic pursuits.

The present book is a revised version of my doctoral dissertation, which owes its inception to late professor Manoranjan Jha, under whose able guidance and inspiration the contours of this book was drafted. I imbibed many a human value from him, that will stand me in good stead throughout life.

I am indebted to my supervisor Prof. H.N. Tripathi who has been instrumental in the completion of my thesis. I benefited immensely from scholarly discussions I had with him. He took the trouble in spite of his busy schedule to guide me and clarify many concepts which were hazy in my mind. I am also grateful to Prof. Sharan and Mr. Priyankar Upadhyaya, Department of Political Science, B.H.U. for their kind cooperation. The staff of the department has been extremely cooperative. I must mention also the assistance that I received from the staff of the Central Library, B.H.U. and Institute of Gandhian Studies, Rajghat, Varanasi.

The suggestions of Prof. Iqbal Narain and Prof. K.P. Mishra who were examiners of my thesis, have proved of immense value in my academic pursuits. I am grateful to Prof. S. Gopal who was the expert for examining the thesis for the award of grant-in-aid by the Indian Council of Social Science Research, New Delhi. I thank also Shri L.P. Shahi (Minister of State for Education) for his cooperation.

I take this opportunity to express my respect and love for my mother who has been a constant source of inspiration. She bore patiently my long absence from home. My father, uncle, brothers, sisters, brother-in-law and parents-in-law helped greatly with their affection and inspiration. Lastly, I cannot find adequate words to express my love and feelings for my husband Ratnesh, who has been my moral support, companion and friend throughout this academic endeavour. I also acknowledge with gratitude friendly help and cooperation from my numerous friends and acquaintances in completing this work. My friends, especially boosted my spirit whenever I fell in depressive moods due to various handicaps and difficulties that cropped up in course of my studies.

The Nehru Memorial Museum and Library, New Delhi occupies an important place in the completion of this book. The staff has been very cordial and the systematic functioning of the library speeded up my work. I am grateful to Prof. A.N. Pandya of the Department of Humanities, I.I.T., New Delhi, Sq. Leader Vikram Dheesh, Prof. Shanti Swaroop, Dr. Bakshi and Dr. A.K. Gupta, whom I had the opportunity to meet at the Library and discuss my work in detail. Their suggestions have proved valuable. My mental horizon was very much widened by the scholarly ambience of the library. The press Information Bureau, New Delhi, as well as the National Archives, New Delhi and the Indian Institute of Public Administration, New Delhi were extremely cordial and helpful.

In the end, I must mention the financial help that was rendered to me by the Indian Council of Social Science Research, New Delhi, in form of award of Short Term Doctoral Fellowship and a grant-in-aid for the publication of this book.

CONTENTS

CHAPTER 1

THE MAKING OF JAWAHARLAL NEHRU

Of immense importance and interest is the study of the forces, the factors and the circumstances that led Jawaharlal Nehru to hold socialist convictions. The study of multifaceted life of Nehru is a subject of absorbing interest for many. With his complex personality he often presented himself as a paradox and still continues to be an enigmatic figure. From the sheltered shell of aristocratic life given to luxury, pomp and ceremony, drift to politics is not unnatural and is quite in tune with the political climate of the first quarter of the present century. Nehru's conversion to socialism, however, with a high middle class background is certainly a long leap.

The complex and many-sided personality of Nehru has baffled many people, friends and opponents alike. Contrary epithets have been advanced to measure his exact stature. Some have styled him 'fellow traveller', others a 'bourgeois reformist'. He would better style himself a 'repentant bourgeois'. Gandhiji was unhappy that Nehru was moving "too fast and too far". A Khadi clad and Gandhi-capped critic of Nehru once wrote "... you are a grand paradox, a strange enigma".[1] Indeed he was a paradox but for a different reason. Born and brought up in bourgeois surroundings with all the vices and inhibitions of a sheltered life, his subsequent unfoldment as the doyen of Indian Socialism really makes him an enigmatic figure.

Before we start to analyse systematically Jawaharlal Nehru's socialist ideals, it should be remembered that he cannot and should not be judged from a dogmatic point of view or from any particular angle because he allowed himself to be influenced by various streams of thought, never completely succumbing to anyone in particular. He was receptive to change throughout his life and since he displayed an allergy to rigidity, his ideas and acts can be examined only historically or chronologically. As he came across new ideas or as new situations confronted him, he made what he considered to be necessary adjustments to these changes. To study these changes and adjustments it becomes necessary to follow the story of his life as it unfolded amidst various influences.

Nehru, like many other outstanding historical personalities, but perhaps more than most others, was less a product of his environment than one who influenced and shaped it. In fact, he steered the thought of the entire nation to his own way of thinking. And yet, the environment, especially in the early formative years of his life has inevitably an influence, which no individual can forsake altogether. So it was with Nehru, with his receptivity to new ideas and sensitiveness he continued to imbibe new influences all his life.

Family Heritage

Kashmir holds a unique place in India. Due to its strategic location it has been the meeting ground of various cultures and has borne the impact of diverse civilisations and thoughts. Yet, traditions are deep rooted in the land. In spite of various impacts and cosmopolitan interaction it has retained its indigenous entity and culture. Therein lies its uniqueness. Also, despite deep rooted traditions and ancient culture, the character of Kashmir has been dynamic, eclectic and progressive.

The Brahamins of Kashmir are one of the most aristocratic sub-castes in Hindu social system.[2] They have long been associated with high education, learning and culture and praised for their sharp intellect and indomitable spirit. Krishna Hutheesing, the younger sister of

Jawaharlal Nehru has aptly evaluated their position thus, "Brahmins were thus highest order of Indian society. Because learning was more honoured than war, they were above the kings, who always belonged to the warrior caste. Throughout our history a Brahamin has been Prime Minister to the greatest of kings, but the kings themselves bow to the Brahamin. He stands bold upright and blesses them, but he will not bow. The Kashmiri Brahamins go beyond that. Though in other parts of India it is customary for younger people to bow and touch the feet of their elders as a sign of respect, we Kashmiris bow only to God". [3] This evaluation reflects the proud, fearless and aristocratic character of the Kashmiri Brahamin community. They have always been inclined towards power based thought. The high and envied position that this community occupies in Indian society is the result of this inherent trait of their character.

Jawaharlal Nehru belonged to this coveted community. Being the son of an illustrious, aristocratic and intelligent man like Motilal Nehru, Jawaharlal Nehru was born with a unique heritage which made him out a unique personality of the Indian political scene. His consequent unfoldment as the Prime Minister of India and one of the leading statesmen of the world was the flowering of the seed which had been sown in his inheritance.

From his father Nehru acquired an intense pride, the root of his resentment against British rule–for his initial response to politics was emotional, not intellectual.[4] Many years later, on the ninety-fifth anniversary of his father's birth, he referred to him as 'something like a Renaissance Prince'... [5]

Still another legacy of his home in Allahabad was a broad secular outlook. Three cultural strands pervaded Anand Bhavan during his formative years: Hindu, Moghul and British. The impact of cosmopolitan cultures remained throughout his life and sustained his immense faith in secularism.

The young Nehru lived in comfortable surroundings throughout the formative period of his life. However, apart from the period of infancy, he lived amongst Europeans until the age of twenty-two, first in Allahabad, then at Harrow, Cambridge and in London. And even at home the atmosphere was more European than Indian. In his early education, too, the young Nehru was subjected to European influences. From the pre-school age until he left for England at the age of fifteen he was trained at home by private tutors, most of them British.

Early Influences

An important influence on Nehru during his childhood was his acquaintance with F. Brooks, who on Mrs. Annie Besant's recommendation was appointed to teach him. He has noted in his *Autobiography,* the tremendous influence Brooks had on his young sensitive mind.[6] It was through this keen theosophist that Nehru acquired the taste for reading and a quest for knowledge which made him one of the most well informed scholar-statesmen of the world. Brooks also kinded in him an enquiry into the mysteries of science. And this spirit of scientific enquiry was to remain the most consistent strand of his thought.

While at Harrow Nehru remained a mere observer of happenings in and outside India. Harrow reflected the leisure world outside with its predilections and prejudices.

There were a few Jews in the school including some in Nehru's House and he detected an undercurrent of antisemitic feeling. Although he had no opinion on the matter, he confesses he was influenced by the atmosphere sufficiently " to think that it was the proper thing to have this feeling".[7] His regard for the artificial proprieties which were part and parcel of his environment momentarily overcame his innate sense of social justice. He was maturing fast, but the social conscience of later years had still to develop.

During this period he read voraciously and came across a book which intensified this feeling, one of G.M. Trevelyan's three volumes on Garibaldi and his struggle for Italian freedom and unification. In his mind, already politically conscious as far as his own country was concerned, he equated Italy with India. Why, he asked should India not wage a similar struggle? It is interesting to see how this parallel between India and Italy burned itself in his mind and stayed in his memory. Many years later in his *Autobiography* he was to return to the theme..[8] His Asian consciousness was aroused by the Russo-Japanese war (1904-1905). Nehru had followed political events at home which in turn had been influenced by developments in and outside of Asia.

Nehru, read and thought on the intellectual developments of his day but his interest in them, he admits, was superficial, and although his mind was stirred by some of their manifestations, the observation was not sufficiently deep. At Cambridge his nationalism, which was stirred as a boy by the Russo-Japanese war found emotional vent in the happenings in India. But his political convictions, had as yet no firm foundations.

Few events during the war excited India more than the developments in Ireland. As a student, Nehru while on visit to Ireland had watched with interest the first faint beginnings of Sinn-Fein which Arthur Griffith had founded in 1900. Now the Easter Rebellion of 1916 stirred his heart and mind. He was moved by Roger Casement's speech from the dock, and marvelled at the invincible spirit which animated it.

Nehru traces the beginnings of his interest in socialism to his Cambridge days when the Fabianism of Bernard Shaw and H.G. Wells attracted him. The three years which he spent at Cambridge coincided with an intellectual ferment in England and other parts of Europe. Europe was gradually but certainly moving towards the darkness of a global war. The Puritan values of the Victorian age were yielding place to an era of challenge and interrogation. Powerful critics came to dominate the scene at the turn of the century. H.G. Wells, Bernard Shaw, Ibsen, Tolstoy, Nietzsche and Anatole France where challenging the old social and economic values by appealing to wider audiences.[9]

More than anyone else, Shaw, Wells and Bertrand Russel, John Mynard Keynes, Lowes Jackinson and Meredith Townsend stimulated Nehru's thought and left their mark on him. While Wells rejected the static Victorian conception of permanence of institutions, Shaw was foremost among the heralds of change. While as an undergraduate at Cambridge, Nehru had not only read Shaw, but had also heard his lecture on 'Socialism and the University Man'.[10] But he confesses that his interest was academic. Recording his own feelings at the time in his *Autobiography,* he wrote, "It was all nationalism and patriotism and I was a pure nationalist, my vague socialist ideas of college days having sunk into the background".[11] A little later he adds, "And yet fresh reading was again stirring the embers of socialistic ideas in my head. They were vague ideas more humanitarian and utopian than scientific.

A favourite writer of mine during the war years and after was Bertrand Russel,..."[12]

However, the impact of Fabianism was substantial in the formation of Nehru's personality and policies. Emphasis on reformism, constitutionalism and gradualism which came to constitute the hall-marks of the Nehruvian socialist approach, were essentially Fabian. The much more significant Marxist formulation of the socialist philosophy was still rather remote both in England and in India to which he returned. It needed the revolution in Russia and the dramatic impact of Lenin's ideas on both the organisation of state after revolution and quite separately, the inevitable relationship between capitalism in the home country of imperialism, and the exploitation in the colonies to make Jawaharlal Nehru a little more aware of the hard realities and complexities of international politics.

The British Political Heritage

Nehru's patriotic urge received its form and content from the humanist liberal tradition. His attachment and indebtedness to the humanist liberal tradition is clearly expressed in his writings and utterances. "My roots", Nehru confessed, "are still perhaps partly in the nineteenth century, and I have been too much influenced by the humanist liberal tradition to get out of it".[13] Without any commitment, Nehru unconsciously imbibed the values and ideals of the British hamanist liberal tradition, the social and ideological foundation that gave 'life and consistency' to that tradition, as it stood in the late Victorian era.[14]

The formative years of his life were spent in Edwardian and Victorian England. His resilient mind imbibed the very spirit of the British humanist liberal tradition in the best centres of liberal education during the hey -day of liberal civilization. The tradition included gradualism, adaptability, adjustability, peaceful progress, resilience and eclecticism. These qualities went to constitute his intellectual make-up, his habits of mind, his likes and dislikes, and his personality.

As a liberal humanist, Nehru was also an individualist from the behavioural as well as philosophical standpoint and looked upon social problems also from an individualistic angle. Respect for the individual, his dignity, creativity and personality formed the kernel of his thought and outlook.

As a thinker the real problems for him were those of individual and social life, of harmonious living, of a proper balancing of an individual's inner and outer life, of an adjustment of the relations between individuals and between groups, of a continuous becoming something better and higher, and of social development."[15] The *Laissez-faire*, which the nineteenth century liberalism, especially the British brand, had adopted as its ideal, was inadequate to the task. Its failure as also of the capitalist order, had become quite evident to Nehru and other progressive thinkers even before the depression of 1929-31. These problems, together with their passion for seeing the individual became 'something better and higher' and gain freedom for his development, led him and many other progressives to the acceptance of the socialist ideal.

Replying to Subhas Bose's doubt about the success of socialism through his (Nehru's) individualistic stand, he confessed: "I suppose I am temperamentally and by training an individualist and intellectually a socialist....I hope that socialism does not kill or suppress individuality; indeed I am attracted to it because it will release innumerable individuals from economic and cultural bondage."[16] A still more explicit statement was made about the same time: "I do not see why under socialism there should not be a great deal of freedom for the individual; indeed far greater freedom of conscience and mind, freedom for enterprise, and even the possession of private property on a restricted scale. Above all he will have the freedom which comes from economic security, which only a small number possess today."[17]

Evidently Nehru gravitated towards socialism, because he saw in it a far greater possibility than under the capitalist system of the fulfilment of the liberal ideals and values--freedom of conscience, mind, enterprise, private property--though on a restricted scale, and above all, of developing individuality. A Marxist humanist will not hesitate to employ violence and regimentation to reach the stage where perfect and positive freedom, that is knowledge of necessity becomes possible. Nehru the liberal humanist, abjured both capitalistic and Marxist creeds and stood for the preservation and enlargement of liberal freedom.

The source of origin of democratic thought the most important stand of Nehru's political philosophy can also be traced to the British liberal political tradition. He did not 'discover' western political democracy as he did the socialism of Karl Marx. He grew up in an intellectual environment which assumed it. His father, steeped in the principles of British constitutional law, presupposed parliamentary democracy as the natural structure of government. As a law student in England, Nehru's thinking developed within the same framework of generally accepted ideas. In India too the rationalism of the new elite made them aspire for parliamentary democracy. Already the English had imparted the political institution and practices of their island home into India to manage their own affairs. In the process a skeleton of the liberal-cum-democratic institutions had come into existence. The nationalist elite pleaded and struggled for adding flesh and blood to that skeleton.[18]

'In his books Nehru quotes Montesque's *Espirit des Lois*, Rousseau's *Des Contract Social*, and John Stuart Mill's *On Liberty*, all of which apparently made a considerable impression on his mind. But it is probable that Nehru's reading of these and other political philosophers did little more than confirm, clarify, and intensify ideas which he already had.[19] Nehru's democratic thought is more the product of this broad tradition, the humanist liberal tradition, than of specific sources. The faith in the dignity and individuality of man found its logical manifestation in the ideas of democracy.

A natural corollary to democratic thinking was establishment of representative institutions. Nehru believed in the efficacy of parliament and its power to invite popular participation. The frail machinery of cabinet-government had to be set in the wider context of parliamentary authority. Building on the familiarization with politics brought about by the national movement, Nehru defied conventional wisdom and introduced adult suffrage. Much as he disliked the sordid rivalry implicit in election to legislative assemblies, Nehru gave life and zest to the campaigns, and between elections he nurtured the prestige and vitality of the parliament. He took seriously his duties as leader of the Lok Sabha. By transferring some of his personal command to the institution of Parliament, he helped the parliamentary system take root.[20] Nehru's belief in parliament stemmed from the practical testimony of the smooth functioning of parliamentary democracy, coupled with the freedom of Press in the formation of public opinion in Great-Britain.

Thus, some of the most important postulates of Nehru's thought emanated from the humanist liberal tradition. Belief in the dignity and creativity of the individual, application of reason in place of dogma in thought and practice, faith in democracy and the introduction of parliamentary system in India with its representative institutions were the hall-marks of his political philosophy, which has roots in the resulting essentially from the Humanist liberal tradition.

Impact of the National Movement

Jawaharlal Nehru returned to India in 1912. Seven long years of absence wrought many changes in him. Away from home in a distant land, he had outgrown his lonely boyhood to that of an independent but largely isolated existence. He had come to terms with himself, and his sense of independence, combined with his introspective nature, gave an edge to his personality. He lived in a peculiar atmosphere wherein he could feel at home neither in the East nor in the West. His western education, having studied in the best centres of learning in the world and having imbibed the manners and habits of an English nobleman was superimposed on what he had learnt as a boy from his elders about the ancient past of India, and her glorious history. He wrote about himself on his return to India that "I was a bit of a prig with little to commend me".[21] Nehru had gone to England in spirit of adventure and discovery. However, he returned to his homeland to discover India.

From 1912 to 1916, he was merely a passive observer of happenings in the country. His early venture into politics were not spectacular. About this time he was drawn towards the Servants of India Society founded by Gopal Krishna Gokhale in 1905. He had great respect for Gokhale's serious and earnest approach to politics and public affairs and was much impressed by his sense of dedication and seriousness of purpose. In spite of admiration for the Society he did not entertain any idea of joining it, partly because he did not want to give up the lucrative and prestigious legal profession.[22]

It was in 1915 that he plunged in active politics for the first time, becoming secretary of fund drive for Indians in South Africa, initiated by Gokhale. It was not until 1915 that he made his first public speech to express opposition to a new Act which curtailed the freedom of the press. Also during this period he actively participated in the agitation against the system of indentured labour for Indians in Fiji. However, all these activities were peripheral to his fundamental interest in politics.

The political events of 1917 genuinely moved Nehru. For the first time Home Rule League was established by Tilak and Mrs. Annie Besant, which was a point of departure from the passive and loyalist outlook of the Congress. "The atmosphere became electric and most of us young men felt exhilarated and expected big things in the near future".[23] During the war period, the internment of Annie Besant on 16 June, 1917 created a stir in Nehru's mind. This was seen as another link in the chain of the conspiracy to stifle Indian political aspirations leading to countrywide agitation. The Allahabad branch of the League was formed with Nehru as its joint secretary. This meant that politics in the U.P. was hotting up and undergoing radical transformation. For the first time since Nehru's return to India, there was a glaring issue and an atmosphere was created for political action. Reason as well as passion was on the side of Nehru when he decided to cast his lot with the nationalists. The internment of Mrs. Besant seemed to him a sign of madness which had befallen the bureaucracy and presaged its fall: "Home-Rule has come and we have but to take it if we stand up like men and falter not". Mere protest meetings and representations were the politics of cowards and opium-eaters: what was needed was non-cooperation with the government till they reversed their folly.[24] In the context of erstwhile Indian politics, he was in sympathy with the more extreme wing of it as represented by Tilak.

Nationalism

Certain landmarks were deeply rooted in Nehru's memory. The first to be mentioned was Jallianwalla Bagh --The Amritsar Tragedy in 1919--the effect of which has been feelingly described in his *Autobiography*. The Rowlatt Bills and the Amritsar Tragedy mark important steps in Nehru's deeper involvement in the nationalist movement. For the first time he came in personal contact with the darker side of British rule and with the sufferings, privations and humiliating condition of his own countrymen as a result of British callousness and brutality, as he viewed the whole episode as a profound insult to national honour, pride and self-respect. This provoked an instinctive response in him. The behaviour of the British in India violated his sense of justice and liberal idealism which he had imbibed during his long stay in England.

Of this period Nehru wrote: "I was a pure nationalist, my vague socialist ideas of college days having sunk into the background..".[25] Throughout his adult life these two ideologies, nationalism and socialism, were to vie for primacy in his thought and action. Nationalism was invariably to be the more compelling drive, though he maintained his allegiance to both.[26]

Impact of Gandhi

1916 can be considered a year of supreme importance because this was the time when he first met Gandhiji at the Lucknow Congress of 1916. Nehru and the young men admired him for his great struggle in South Africa, but still to most of them he seemed very distant and different and impolitical.[27] But in later years Gandhi made a profound impact on Nehru, which remained until his death. The echo of Gandhi's influence could be heard throughout his life.

In India, from the early beginnings of modern political and social action we have witnessed repeated attempts to unravel the Indian reality. It was part of the inner struggle of sensitive, enlightened men to find communion with their people from whom they were separated by an almost unbridgable spiritual and physical gulf. The unchanging village societies of a subcontinent seemed to defy understanding. Raja Ram Mohan Roy, Swami Vivekananda, Bipin Chandra, Gopal Krishan Gokhale, were among the giants who launched upon the building of a bridge, but the effort was largely incomplete. Failing to achieve an equation with the people, these outstanding men sought in comparative alienation the introspective world of personal salvation. Over the decade the gulf widened.

When young Nehru returned to his country, he was already in the throes of this inner struggle. A love of the country and its people was not enough, nor was the nationalism by the British Colonial presence. Indeed, circumstances almost pushed him into the Civil-Service and later into the lucrative legal profession of his father. This had been the fate of most of the elite. Nehru's search for the means with which to expel imperialism from India should be seen in the context of his struggle to link with his peoples so as to be able to understand their hopes and fears and to lead them to their dreams. Like so many before him, this modern, rational, impatient individual was aware that alone as an individual, he would become irrelevant in the enormous vastness and complexity of India. Someone would have to help him belong.

And that individual had arrived on the Indian scene, that rare individual who at last possessed the key to the ethos of the people--Gandhiji. Nehru's almost immediate alliance with Gandhi was not accidental. Gandhi was lifting the freedom of the individual responses to the place of mass action. He was also evolving the technique of non-violent disciplined Statyagrah which held out the hope that mass action would not end in chaos. Here was an intensely practical man consciously applying his theories to the Indian reality, testing and retesting them, determined to make the village his base. The bridge at least seemed complete.

It appears that two processes were at work simultaneously in India --the process of reform within tradition to suit the needs of the modern age on the one hand, and the re-interpretation of modernity to suit India's needs and conditions on the other. While Gandhi was at the lead of the first type of movement, Nehru played an outstanding role in the second type. Both were, therefore, the great bridge-builders between tradition and modernity in India.

Nehru introduced clearer thinking on the question of modernity versus tradition and made some fundamental points which deserve special attention. He reiterated the deep inner crises of western liberalism and emphasised that problems of the twentieth century could not be tackled with the tools provided by the ninteenth century liberal thought. He tirelessly showed how liberalism failed to either explain or resolve the major social contradictions of western civilization. The first was the gap between its profession of equality and its practice of inequality. Though committed to equality between nations and between individuals and groups within nations, in practice it tolerated colonial domination over non-white peoples and social and class inequality within.[28]

On the other hand, without Gandhi's impact Nehru would have been as unaware of the permanent elements of Indian civilization and as much of a stranger to India's village dwelling peasant masses, as were rootless modernists and radicals from the urban intelligentsia. It was Gandhi's impact which set Nehru on the path of the *Discovery of India* through an exploration of Indian history and tradition and through direct contact with the Indian peoples in different parts of India. Nehru's later writings and speeches are marked by a synthesizing quality,a catholicity and a deep love and respect for the Indian people. Here is a Nehru qualitatively different from the Nehru of the *Autobiography* with his pronounced romanticism and deep individualism.. One can discern in Nehru's inner transformation quiet, profound and persuasive influence of Gandhi who was mainly responsible for Nehru's psychological transformation from an ivory-tower intellectual into a mass leader. The credit for Nehru's de-westernization or his Indianisation in the best sense of the term should go to no other than Gandhi. Nehru's thinking on economic and social questions became less theoretical and more conscious of the concrete situation, as a result of interaction with Gandhi and Tagore.

The Mahatma's personal influence was remarkable. Nehru gave up smoking and took to vegetarianism. He began reading the *Bhagvad Gita* afresh, with its emphasis on right action, caring less for consequences. His faith in the importance of means dates from this period, as does his stress on the ethical side of politics.[29] As a true representative of Gandhian ideals he believed that a right cause should succeed only if the right path was pursued, Nehru was a part of the high moral traditions which Gandhi has laid down for his followers by forging a method of political action that was ethical. In the broadest sense, his life was simplified and spiritualised. The political and spiritual heritage of Gandhi left a lasting influence on him, who in his later life steadfastly followed the straight path, though it may not have brought immediate advantages to the country.

The agrarian bias of Jawaharlal Nehru's socialism, which is a distinctive feature of Indian and Asian Socialism also, is attributable to Gandhian influence. When Gandhi talked of the underdogs and the downtrodden masses, he used to make special mention of the peasants of India. His experiments in non-violent and peaceful revolution to stave off exploitation by the bourgeoisie, started with the organisation of agricultural labourers in Bihar and Gujarat. Hence Gandhi was the doyen of agricultural as against industrial proletariat. From him Nehru, imbibed this concern for the peasants. "So our thinking became more and more conditioned to the peasantry of India, not so much to the industrial workers though to some extent to them too."[30]

Finally, Nehru needs to be remembered for his attempt to make creative use of Gandhi's critique of modern civilization. He did not reject modernization as Gandhi had done, but incorporated some of the latter's thoughts to evolve an Indian variant of the modern industrial society. For instance, Nehru rejected Gandhi's backward looking revivalism, but recognized the role of rural development, of labour intensive technology and of small and cottage industries in village based, labour surplus and mass, poor, Indian economy. Nehru also shared Gandhi's revulsion against elitist affluence without rejecting the concept of economic progress. Nehru sought to interpret economic progress as war on mass poverty.

Thus, each of these personalities provided a corrective to the other, for instance, Gandhi's intensely religious tone, his reliance on his inner-voice, his anti-westernism, his consistent appeal to Indian tradition and his numerous idiosyncracies carried to their logical conclusion, without the powerful corrective from someone like Tagore or Nehru, this ideology would have led to the emergence of the cult of the *messiah* and to Gandhi's elevation into a miracle--working saint reminiscent of the Middle-Ages. But for the sharp intellectual thrust from Nehru, these ideas would also have given free play to forces of mysticism and irrationalism in Indian politics. If Gandhism had been left to the interpretation of lesser men claiming to be true followers of Gandhi's thought and practice, Gandhi would have acquired exaggerated prominence and might have been used on an extensive scale to rationalize hypocrisy, empty moralizing, sectarianism and blind anti-westernism. And here Nehru provides a powerful corrective.[31]

Especially noteworthy, however, was his insistence on an intellectual rather than a mystical approach to social problems; his distinction between the universal elements of western civilization and its aberration, and his plea to look ahead rather than behind us. It redounds to Nehru's credit that he re-interpreted the vital elements of Gandhi's message to India and the world in terms of concepts and categories which could be understood by the modern intelligentsia in India and outside. Without Nehru Gandhi's message may have run the risk of being distorted and even vulgarized by ardent adherents eager to create a Gandhi-cult. Without Nehru, Gandhi would have had no interpreter of his message in the modern idiom to the modern world.

Thus Gandhi and Nehru changed the axis of the renaissance thinking. The one appealed to the noble in man, the other to the rational. The one put emphasis on purity of means, the other on the promise of the end too. The one raised the level of public life and morals, the other that of national thinking and debate. Gandhi spiritualised politics, Nehru rationalised it. And yet neither made a complete break with the immediate past. Nehru tried to synthesise the spiritual quintessence of Gandhism, the rationalism of the liberal nationalists and the radicalism of the socialist youth. He was a liberal science tripos putting on the gown of Gandhism and the hood of socialism. In fact, Nehru was the chief vehicle of Gandhism.[32]

Nehru fought the battle against the medieval ideology of Gandhi, taking of its various aspects and subjecting them to a radical critique.[33] But this did not prevent him from seeing Gandhi's role in the anti-imperialist struggle as having wrought revolutionary changes.

On his total relationship with Gandhi by this time one could say that Nehru had worked out the basic assumption of his relationship as those of unity and struggle - consistent ideological struggle while maintaining not only overall political but also organisational unity against imperialism. It was in this sense that in the eyes of Nehru Gandhi was "greater" than all his "little books".[34] Nehru presumed there would be considerable ground for common action.

Contact with the Peasants

1920--these were the years of World War I, also of Nehru's first contact with Indian politics, but his contact with the people had not yet begun. Ideas on socialism yet were framed mainly from the books, and not from practical experience. As a result, "they were vague ideas, more humanitarian and utopian than scientific."[35] In later years, his study of socialistic theories as well as his observation of the real condition of the people led to development of concrete ideas on the subject. Though, he wrote, that in 1920 he was totally ignorant of labour condition in factories or fields and his political outlook was entirely bourgeois.

Yet the year 1920 was a turning point in his life as also the growth to maturity. This was the year when he discovered the peasants by coming into direct contact with them. This land mark in his life was to occur by accident. He writes, "Just then a new interest developed in my life which was to play an important part in later years. I was thrown almost without any will of my own, into contact with the peasantry." 'This came about in curious way.".[36]

At Allahabad he met a delegation of the *Kisans.* The picture of peasants clad in rags, half naked and emaciated suffering from hunger and poverty, was a new and overwhelming experience. The peasants told him of humiliation and oppression, the cruelty of the land owners, the greediness of the money-lenders, and frequent ejectment from their lands. He was appalled and touched by the dumb misery of the credulous peasant. 'To understand *Kisan* is to understand India', goes an ancient saying and Jawaharlal Nehru wanted to understand his native country and comprehend it through the soul of the peasant. This was an educational experience. Not only did it broaden his horizon, it also aroused his sympathy for the underdogs, one of the key motives of his subsequent behaviour in politics.[37]

In 1921, *The Independent* began to publish a series of articles under the general heading of "The Rai - Bareli Tragedy". One of them said, "...And what of *Kisans* ? Poor, miserable, downtrodden men and women, ever in want, ever suffering, seldom complaining. What of them? Their blood lies on the bank of the Sone river, their bodies under a thin layer of sand or in the open, prey to the beasts who feast on the dead. And the living have a worst fate reserved for them. They have the Police and the minions of the *Taluqdars*, torturing them, beating them and inspiring them ".[38]

The articles, exposing ruthlessly the new crimes of the colonial regime, were written by Nehru. The deep insight which he got into the nature and meaning of poverty provided him with the emotional basis for his later attachment to socialism. From that time onwards his conception of a good society always involved the socio-economic transformation of the conditions in the rural areas. To him, socialism was the potent to eradicate poverty, to which he developed an aversion.

Nehru's realization of this momentous truth, the most important single basic truth of contemporary Indian history, namely the awakening of the Indian peasant as an active social force, is projected in his desire to have his mortal remains showered over the Indian earth where the peasants toil.[39]

The poverty and misery everywhere, with which he became acquainted during the earlv twenties of the century, created in him a strange urge to work in a socialist direction. In the late twenties of the century he was seen busy in directing people's attention to social and economic changes. The experience with *Kisans* and their plight led him to realise that political freedom would be meaningless unless it involved economic freedom also. It was from that time that he started to define clearly the objective of the national freedom struggle.

Crucial to Nehru's development was his involvement in the peasant unrest in the United Provinces. The importance of bringing the peasants, with their tradition of agitation, into the national movement had been underlined by Gandhi's successful organization of resistance to the indigo planters in Champaran in Bihar in 1917, and towards the end of that year Malviya and a few others in Allahabad established the United Province Kisan Sabha. What, in fact, Nehru hoped for was to link *Kisan* discontent with nationalist politics. He had made no study of economic and land problems and he had no clear ideas about peasant participation. It was still not his intention to provide a revolutionary dimension to Indian nationalism. But this contact with the *Kisan* was satisfying psychologically, for he felt that this was the first step to his Indianization and closeness to the problems of the country. Politically it was important for it provided an opportunity to do this in this own province what Gandhiji had done elsewhere, harnessing peasant struggle in the interest of the Congress.[40]

The awareness of rural India became an inalienable part of Nehru's being. For the first time he realized what the peasants were and what they meant to India. "This realization came to me during these Pratapgarh visits and ever since then my mental picture of India always contains the naked, hungry mass. Perhaps there was some kind of electricity in the air, perhaps it was in a receptive frame of mind and the pictures I saw and the impression I gathered were indelibly impressed on my mind.''[41] So to Nehru, the humanist, the Pratapgarh peasantry was a great school--as great as Harrow or Gandhi's company. The Nehru of school and college days was quite unused to the heat and dust of India, but the Pratapgarh peasants brought him the experience of the real tropical heat. India was unveiled to him and the urge to speak out grew increasingly strong. The picture of this real India was to fashion his nationalism in later years.

Impact of the World Socialist Order

The October Revolution --The Russian Revolution of 1917 dealt a major blow to the western capitalist system and the imperialist order which the colonial powers had established over the larger part of the world. The Russian Revolution was a milestone in the history of the human race, which ushered in a new era of hope, a new civilization and a new relationship between man and man. Above all it marked the point of transition from the era of capitalism to the era of socialism on a world scale.

The most powerful writing in support of the October Revolution, however, came from the *Independent,* a daily started in 1919 from Allahabad by Motilal Nehru. The daily in its short timed existence of merely three years, wrote a series of editorials, presenting the most objective assessment of the development taking place in Soviet Russia in the wake of the Revolution. In an editorial on June 14, 1920 under the caption ''The Red Menace?'' it gave an unequivocal analysis of the Russian Revolution. It said, ''From the time Bolshevism first raised its head uptil now, it has steadily grown in power and prestige... The leaders of the Bolshevik cult are not fools or mere idealists. They are richly endowed men with many qualities that make for success....Bolshevism has been a success because it has kindled hope and a mighty hope in the minds of the masses. It is the hope of a better future and more rational conditions of life that has rallied round the red banner the millions of oppressed in Russia... The resurrection of the masses that followed on, was the remarking of a giant--a phenomenon unique in the history of the world''.[42]

The only revolution with which the world was familiar then was the French Revolution and though it set out its ideals as *liberty, equality* and *fraternity,* it soon ended in an empire with a kind of elected monarchy. Political thinkers of the time had condemned the French Revolution for its terror and excesses. *The Independent* compared the French and Russian revolutions and noted that, "The French Revolution had its limits--no common objective, disorganized, not honest and insecure. The leaders of the Russian Revolution have not the personal ambition that was characteristic of the French revolutionary leaders. They are to establish their ideals and have taken good care to impress on the adherents the justice of their cause. The French Revolution brought no necessary hope to proletariat" *The Independent* was not convinced that the Russian Revolution was also another variant of terror. It underlined, "If Bolshevism had been a reign of terror pure and simple (as made out by the British) it would have died a natural death by the time... The soundness of some of the Bolshevik principles have been generally recognized and a new policy is being introduced".[43]

In another editorial on March 26, 1920, it explained why the British were opposed to Soviet Russia. It pointed out that the basic tenet of British foreign policy since the late 19th century was of opposition to Russia. The editorial went to analyse the fundamentals of Bolshevism and said that its major aim was to secure, "the elimination of the wage system in economies and the annihilation of centralised class - ruled state in politics", it said that "the economic programme of the Bolsheviks is the destruction of modern capitalism. . . Bolshevism demands that the instruments of production shall not be owned and controlled by private capital and worked for private profit, but still go to coffers of the state and shall be applied for securing the general advancement of the whole community."

The Independent thus provided a much clearer analysis of the political and economic objectives of the Bolsheviks. It is of course difficult to say as to who actually wrote editorials in *The Independent,* but in thought, diction and word, the stamp of Jawaharlal Nehru was unmistakable. During the sheltered existence of the daily Nehru was its virtual editor, albeit not openly. The editorials reflect a deep knowledge of European politics, which neither Motilal Nehru nor anybody else in the nationalist circle, except Jawaharlal Nehru could have possessed in those days. During his stay abroad and as a result of his vast readings he learnt how British imperialism functioned. There is indeed no doubt that of all of the Indian leaders, who were exposed to the Russian Revolution, Nehru alone had a better understanding of the historical process which brought about this momentous development in history. His anti-imperialist orientation naturally drew him to the Russian Revolution. He confessed that the social aspects of the Russian Revolution appealed to him more than anything else and made him think of politics in terms of social change.''[44]

To him, the Revolution ended the age-old domination of the upper classes, and so it was natural, he said, that those who enjoyed power and privileges in society should oppose and malign the Russian Revolution. "It is difficult to imagine how millions of human beings should prefer this tyranny and degradation and should voluntarily labour to bring it into existence", he argued. The revolution appealed to him all the more as he saw its great relevance to India and its various problems.[45] Therefore, as early as 1919, he wrote that a dispassionate and critical study of the ideas underlying the October Revolution should be made, which would be of help to us in solving the problems, which affect our own country.

Brussels Congress

Another landmark in the evolution of Nehru's socialist thought was the year 1926--1927 during which he came in contact with the main currents of radical thought and movement in Europe, particularly through his participation in the Brussels Congress of oppressed Nationalities and visit to the Soviet-Union after the 10th anniversary of the October Revolution. Nehru studied and analysed India and international situation, cultivated contacts with some revolutionary intellectual and young socialists. He met eminent people like Roman Rolland, the young German poet Ernst Toller, Roger-Baldwin, Ellen Wilkinson, Harry Pocllilt- Madam Sun-yat-Sen, labour leaders like George Lamsbury, Fenner Brockway, Madam Cama as well as some other members of the British parliament. He also met a number of Indian revolutionaries like Baraktullah, Raja Mahendra Pratap, Shyamji Verma, M.N. Roy and V. Chattopadhyay. He was particularly drawn to the last two.[46]

These personal contacts with revolutionary leaders and men of thought, who were all engaged in the struggle against imperialism and colonialism in their own way, helped Nehru to formulate his own views on various issues particularly of politics and economics. He began to reformulate his ideas about the need for both economic and political reforms within India. They sharpened his understanding of world developments and shaped his outlook. Nehru was indeed growing more mature and stable in his thoughts. It was also during this period that he began to look at problems from a global perspective. It indeed, was to remain a major characteristic of his approach in later life.[47]

It has been said that the Brussels Congress was Nehru's first baptism in internationalism. The Brussels days had an important place in his career. He came in contact with the Marxists, avidly studied Marxist-Leninist Literature and had a glimpse of the new civilization that was being built in Soviet Russia. His class prejudices against communism and the Soviet system were shaken to a considerable extent. He was de-prejudiced, consequently, he could see the world in a clearer perspective.

Clearly, at such a conference where the prime target was British imperialism, the official representative of the Indian National Congress would be an important figure and Nehru was appointed one of the members of the Presidium. He arrived at Brussels on 6th February, took part in all the important meetings, presided over one of the formal session and played a leading role in the drafting of many of the resolutions.

The resolution on India drafted by Nehru accorded the warm support of the conference to the liberation of India from foreign domination and all kinds of exploitation as an essential step in the full emancipation of the people of the world. The peoples should cooperate fully in this task and in particular take effective steps to prevent the dispatch of foreign troops to India and the retention of an army of occupation on India.[48] This was really meant by Nehru for his audience in India, to weaken the extraordinary mentality which clings on to the British connection in spite of everything and took the presence of British troops for granted. Similarly, to goad the Indian National Congress into looking beyond political freedom, Nehru in the last paragraph of the resolution, expressed the hope of the conference that the Indian National movement would base its programme on the full emancipation of the peasants and workers of India, "without which there can be no real freedom'' and would cooperate with the movements for emancipation in other parts of the world.[49]

According to Prof. S.Gopal, for the first time instead of merely condemning British imperialism, Nehru had tried to understand the motives, manner and method of its functioning. His mind had taken a big step forward.[50]

Nehru's sojourn in Europe during 1926-27 and his contact with progressive thinking in that continent gave him a firmer grasp of socialist theories and ideas. As he reflected a few years later, men move in different ideological grooves and it is difficult to cross the boundaries. ''They constitute different philosophies of life, and we grow into them gradually and unconsciously... Socialism involves a certain psychological outlook of life and its problems. It is more than mere logic... only life itself with its bitter lessons forces us along new paths and ultimately, which is far harder, makes us think differently.''[51] With his stay in Europe, Nehru had definitely crossed into the 'ideological groove' of socialism. He wrote, ''I was returning from Europe in good physical and mental condition. I felt full of energy and vitality, and the sense of inner conflict and frustration that had oppressed me so often previously was, for the time being absent. My outlook was wider, and nationalism by itself seemed to me definitely a narrow and insufficient creed. Political freedom and independence were no doubt essential, but they were steps only in the right direction without social freedom and a socialist structure of society and the state neither the individual nor the country could develop much''.[52]

Impact of the Soviet Union

However, it was the Soviet Union where the developments of far reaching consequences were taking place that now dominated Nehru's mind, just as it had, an unseen presence, dominated the Brussels conference. He read all that he could lay bands on books both by partisans and by critics about developments and conditions in that country and found much to admire. He believed that whatever the tradition of hostility between Britain and Russia, to a free India she would be no threat; and even if India were wholly opposed to communism she could have friendly relations with Russia. Nehru, farseeing as ever, recognised that as she grew in power Soviet Russia might develop a new type of imperialism, but he thought that there was little chance of this for a long time to come and for the moment, for reasons of self-interest, Russia was befriending all oppressed nationalities.[53]

It seemed logical, therefore, that he should visit the Soviet Union before returning to India; and the opportunity came, after Motilal Nehru's arrival when both were invited to the decennial celebration of the 1917 revolution.

Jawaharlal Nehru's earlier views regarding Socialism were vague. The Brussels Congress strengthened his conviction about socialism, and his brief visit to Russia in 1927 further deepened his conviction. Though there were some features in the Soviet Union which he disliked—"Violence, ruthless suppression and wholesale regimentation", he was still very appreciative of the Socialist revolution which was taking place in the Soviet Union. "Soviet Russia, despite certain unpleasant aspects, attracted me greatly and seemed to hold forth a message of hope to the world".[54] He wrote that, "it lighted many a dark corner of my mind" and felt that Soviet Russia had shown light in the dark and dismal world of imperialism and colonialism. On his return, he wrote, several articles in appreciation of the Soviet experiment. His *Soviet Russia* which contained his impression revealed his overall acceptance of the 'good society' although it was punctuated by occasional reservations. Nehru wrote, "Nations have, in the past, concentrated all their efforts on the accomplishments of one great task, but this is in times of war only. During the world war, Germany and England and France lived for one purpose only, to win the war. To that purpose everything else was subordinated. Soviet Russia for the first time in history, concentrated the whole strength of the nation in a peaceful effort to build, and not to destroy, to rouse a backward country industrially and within a framework of socialism".[55]

Nehru's commendation of the Soviet Society was due to composite factors. He was deeply impressed by the attitude and efforts of the new rulers to bring about magnificent transformations in the Soviet economic and social structure. The educational pattern had been changed. The lot of the tiller had been improved. The principles of the prison were "certainly far in advance of anything we had known elsewhere in practice", and that, "to be in a Russian prison is far more preferable than to be a worker in an Indian factory".[56] There had taken rapid progress in agriculture and, "the progress is remarkable when the manifold difficulties and the lack of aid from outside are considered".[57]

The problems of Russia and India were considered identical in many respects: both were predominantly agricultural countries with only the beginning of industrialization and both had to face poverty and illiteracy.[58] Russia interested him because he himself was a prominent actor in the mighty drama of India with the ultimate design of introducing social and economic liberation. He was convinced that the Russian experiments would help India in finding out a solution for her own problems."If Russia finds a satisfactory solution for these, our work in India is made easier".[59]

Not only did the soviet system point out a solution for India's basic problem–education, agrarian reforms and the National question–the Indian nationalists had noted that the new Russian government had sent a note to President Wilson pungently criticising his fourteen points. It said: You demand the independence of Poland, Siberia, Belgium and freedom for the people of Austria, Hungary but strangely, we do not notice in your demands any mention of freedom for Ireland, Egypt and India or even the Phillipine island".[60] This definitely attracted him towards Russia and communism. Moreover, the blend of orient and the occident in Russia had a definite attraction for Nehru. The Asian part of Russia was also going ahead. It swelled his pride as an Asian.[61]

But the basic consideration influencing Nehru's commendation of the Soviet system was the egalitarian society which it conceived. "The real change one notices in Moscow and which grows with every day's stay, is in the atmosphere and the very aim of the place. The contrast between extreme luxury and poverty are not visible nor does one notice the hierarchy of class and caste".[62]

Moreover, conscious of growing Hindu-Muslim strife in India, he was particularly interested in the Soviet treatment of minorities.

Thus, the Soviet Union which Nehru saw, was in the last days of its first, halcyon period. The grounding in Marxism, which he had received at the Brussels Conference and after, was followed by a near-conversion to communism by practical testimony. Lenin's leadership, particularly impressed him, by his realism and resilience, and above all by his insistence on professional, full-time revolutionaries. Nehru felt, the need for such workers in India was obviously even greater and it was one such that he now doubtless saw himself. 'He who had sailed from India as a dedicated disciple of Gandhi returned a self-conscious revolutionary radical'. Although always to be deeply influenced by Gandhi he was never again to be wholly a prisoner in the Gandhian mould. But it is significant that the change was wrought not by the revolutionary situation in India but by what he saw and heard and read in Europe.[63]

Nehru's 'discovery of Russia' was without doubt a step towards the evolution of his political and economic thoughts. It did influence his thinking. Indeed, it would be surprising if it did not influence a sensitive, open-minded person like Nehru, but he showed no signs of "infatuations with the Soviets"[64] as Michael Brecher thought he did. His socialist thoughts were yet to take concrete shape and join issues with his nationalistic emotions in an inner struggle which he has described so well in great detail in the many pages of his *Autobiography*.

For the present, his sojourn in Europe, rounded up with his brief visit to the Soviet Union, gave his mind the breath of fresh air he longed for. It provided a window on the progressive forces of the world. It gave him ideas not dogmas, which he tried to apply in his own country. In doing so, he came up against the realities of the nationalist movement to which he had already dedicated himself.

Influence of Marx

The study of Marx convinced Nehru of the inevitability of socialism. The Marxian theory of materialistic interpretation of history, the progress of history and institutions through development of economic system, one system replacing another which had turned obsolete inevitably led to the advent of socialism. The Marxian economic interpretation of history by emphasising the inevitability of class-struggle paved the way for Nehru's socialistic thought. It provided the rationale for justifying the advent of socialism.

While Gandhian ethics and particularly its emphasis on purity of means, enamoured Nehru, Marxian analysis of history gradually exercised a spell on him. His initial response to socialism, germinated during the Cambridge days and maintained at London, was purely aesthetic, humanitarian and ethical in nature. It was utopian and vague.[65] It was mainly bred out of sympathy for the misery of the underdog. But after his study of Marx and Marxian literature and his visit to Russia, a country then busy experimenting with Marxian socialism, Nehru's approach became more systematic and panoramic. Summing up the Marxian impact on him, he wrote:"A study of Marx and Lenin, produced a powerful effect on my mind and helped me to see history and current affairs in a new light. The long chain of history and social development appeared to have some meaning, some sequence and the future lost some of its obscurity."[66] At another place he wrote, "Marxism is an attempt at reducing human history, past, present and the future, to a rigid logical system with something of the inevitability of fate, or 'Kismat' about it."[67] One social order must necessarily yield place to another social order, more in conformity with the present stage of history. The coming of socialism was inherent in the Marxian evolutionary unfoldment of history.

Marx conceived an ever changing and advancing society where one social order shall be replaced by another. Yet a social order only disappeared after it had run its course, and grown to its full extent. He viewed that all previous stages of social development had already passed and the last stage for the emergence of socialism was only imminent. Nehru also viewed that the last stage had arrived and socialism was in sight, "The last class-struggle between the capitalist bourgeois society and the working class was now taking place".[68] In conformity with the Marxian analysis, Nehru was of the opinion, "The capitalist system of industry whatever its services in the past may have been is no longer suited to the present methods of production."[69]

The pull of Marxism was potent for Nehru not merely because it was a theory of inevitability of socialism. The prime attraction for him was the scientific method he adopted in analysing history. Starting with his college days, this pull of scientific method was the primary magnetic force for Nehru and he attributed his attraction for Marxism to the belief that "Marx surveyed past history as a scientist and drew certain conclusion from it."[70]

Speaking about *Das Capital*, Nehru, pointed that in this book Marx analysed and criticised the existing theories of economics and explained at length his own socialist theory. But the outstanding feature of the book according to him was that, "It was purely scientific work. He (Marx) dealt with the development of history and economics dispassionately and scientifically, avoiding all vagueness and idealism."[71]

Marx had discussed the advent of the industrial civilization of the big machine, and development of class-interests leading to class-antagonisms, which inevitably occasioned advent of socialism. Nehru's appreciation of Marx emanated from the fact that Marx started without any bias or mental predilection. That according to Nehru, was the speciality of Marx which gave him a distinct status in the realm of socialist thought.

Nehru drew abundantly upon Marxism and Leninism for his critique of the basic premises of classical liberalism. He drew especially upon Marx's conception of historical materialism and class-struggle and on Lenin's conception of imperialism, to reveal the inner contradictions of liberal thought and the capitalist structure of Indian society. From the vantage point of Marxism, Nehru was able to look beyond 19th century liberalism in general and capitalism in particular. He thus saw very clearly the futility of repeating the course of western history in the Third-World. He emphasised the need for a new ideological basis for the changing societies in Asia[72]. He interpreted the Soviet civilization as a clear break from 19th century liberalism, and a part of the search for a new type of social order based on economic and social justice. At the same time Nehru could not identify himself with violence, civil war and severe restriction on liberty which became associated with the Stalinist alternative to western Liberalism.[73]

Nehru's approach is thus marked by a clear demarcation both from 19th century liberalism with negation of equality and the early twentieth century Russian experiment in socialism with its association with violence and denial of liberty. The historical significance of Nehru's vision for India lies in his bold attempt to overcome the schism characterizing western civilization and to harmonize liberty with justice on the one hand and social revolution with non-violence on the other. A synthesis of the vital elements of liberalism with those of Marxism thus embodied an important appeal of Nehru's creative approach to modernity.

Marxism sharpened his senses of scientific enquiry and pragmatism, and gave him insight to view things in proper perspective.

Speaking about the advisability of gaining some knowledge about Marxism, Nehru said, "It is well to know these theories because they are moving vast masses of men and women today and they may be of help to us in our own country".[74]

Influence of Indian Thought

Nehru was greatly influenced and inspired by the ancient Hindu culture. He read liberal assumptions namely, individualism and rationalism, in ancient Indian society and philosophy. He saw intense individualism, exclusiveness and metaphysical democracy in the Indo-Aryan civilization.[75] For philosophical truths, he naturally turned to the *Upanishads,* which indicated the existence of 'an old and wise civilization with inexhaustible mental reserves.' 'There was' no totalitarianism in religion or culture. 'He appreciated' the vigour of thought, the questioning, the rationalistic background of these philosophical works. A profound impact was left on his mind by "the vigour of the thought, the clarity of the language and the richness of mind that lay behind" ancient Indian literature.[76]

An important stream of thought which influenced Nehru's ideas of socialism was the Vedanta Philosophy in Indian thought, the message of Vivekananda, which influenced him in his interpretation of the Indian ideal of service and his skilful sense of socialism as an instrument of diagnosis and therapy. But this also implied a constant quest for an Indian expression of socialist thought. The so-called Marxist *mantras* would not suffice, for socialism to be meaningful to India, ought to be related to some fundamental ideals of Indian life. This relation Nehru found in the Vedantic tradition of service, in the spurning of the profit motive as a value, which ranked very low in the scale of India's social values. He was aware of this influence and considered it to be one of the most important elements of his thought. Like Gokhale, who once admitted that Vivekananda had voiced his own feelings, Nehru was inspired by Vivekananda's vision of India's unity, by his emphasis on 'Karma yoga' as a means of redeeming the poverty stricken people of India, and by his self-assessed approach to the west. In fact both were the spokesmen of the Renaissance humanism of their times. Both stood for the liberation of the individual from ignorance and slavery. If Vivekananda was a Vedantist on horseback, Nehru was one in a fighter plane.[77] Nehru's study of Indian philosophy during the long imprisonment in Ahmednagar fort had brought him round to the view that the essential basis of ancient Indian thought was in accordance with the scientific temper and approach. As the years passed Nehru came closer to the teaching of Vedanta, the Gita and Buddhism.

Conclusion

It is not possible to categorise Nehru: for he was a Marxist who rejected regimentation, a Socialist who was wholly committed to civil liberties, a radical with a preference for non-violence, and a world citizen who combined his international obligation with a total involvement in India, saw the necessity of self-reliance even in a shrinking world and stressed the need to adapt every ideology to the Indian objective condition. Indian by birth yet western by education, modern in outlook yet influenced by the heritage of his native land, a staunch patriot with an international vision, he was the symbol of a new society--liberal, humanist and equalitarian.

The rare appeal of Jawaharlal Nehru arose from his combination of contradictory elements. As one of his admirers remarked in 1940,"He is explosive in speech, disciplined in action, impulsive in gestures, deliberate in judgement, revolutionary in aim, conservative in loyalty, reckless of personal safety, cautious about matters affecting Indian welfare". The same writer, Krishna Kripalani observed:"An aristocrat in love with the masses, a nationalist who represents the culture of the foreigner, an intellectual caught up in the maelstrom of an emotional upheaval--the very paradox of his personality has surrounded it with a halo".[78]

Almost all the ideological currents of the past half a century appealed to his keen and receptive mind : first in line was classical liberalism with its emphasis on individual rights; then at Cambridge, he was drawn to Fabian Socialism with its emphasis on reformism, constitutionalism and gradualism, thereafter. He was influenced by the Gandhian stress on purity of means and the message of non-violence; and in the late twenties and thirties by Marxist theory and the gospel of a classless society.He was also attracted to the ethical norms of western humanism, and later during his long war-time imprisonment to the precepts of the Vedanta, the ancient system of Hindu philosophy, but stripped of its purely metaphysical and religious beliefs. Underlying all was a passionate devotion to the ideas of nationalism and racial equality. None of these, however, dominated his outlook; all of them influenced his thought. Indeed, the key to his thinking was scepticism about all claims to absolute truth and virtue. But the two influences that left a lasting mark were that of Gandhi and Marx. Gandhi appealed to his heart whereas Marx stimulated his mind.

References

1. D.F. Karka, *Nehru : The Lotus Eater from Kashmir*, London, Richard Clay and Co. Ltd. London, 1953, p-87.
2. Michael Brecher, *Nehru : A Political Biography,* Abridged Edition, London, Oxford University Press, 1959, p.1.
3. Krishna Hutheesing, *We Nehrus,* Bombay, Pearl Publication, 1967 p.14.
4. MichaelBrecher, *Nehru: A Political Biography,* p-2-3.
5. *Ibid.,* p-27.
6. J. Nehru, *An Autobiography* Delhi, Oxford University Press, 1980, p-14-15.
7. *Ibid* p-18.
8. *Ibid* p-19.
9. V.T. Patil, *Nehru and the Freedom Movement,* Delhi, Sterling Publishers,1977. p-17.
10. *Ibid.*
11. J. Nehru, *An Autobiography,* p.35.
12. *Ibid.*
13. *Ibid,* p.591.
14. Ganesh Prasad, *Nehru : A Study in Colonial Liberation* (New Delhi, Sterling Publishers, 1976), p-43.
15. Nehru, *The Discovery of India,* Bombay, Asia Publishing House, 1961,p.-17.
16. Dorothy Norman, *Nehru : The First Sixty Years,* Vol. II, Bombay, Asia Publishing House, 1965, p-621.
17. J. Nehru, *The Unity of India,* (London, 1948), p-134.
18. Ganesh Prasad, *Nehru : A Study in Colonial Liberation.* pp-30-31.
19. *Op.cit.*
   "My roots are still. . . to get out of it completely". J. Nehru, *An Autobiography,* p-591.
20. S. Gopal, *Jawaharlal Nehru: A Biography,* vol.-II,Delhi, Oxford University Press, 1975 p-304.
21. J. Nehru *An Autobiography,* p.-26.
22. *Ibid.* p-30.
23. *Ibid,* P-31.
24. Letter to the Editor, *The Leader,* 21 June, 1917 (NMML).
25. J. Nehru, *An Autobiography,* p-35.
26. Michael Brecher, *Nehru : A Political Biography,* Abridged Edition, London, Oxford University Press, 1961, p.-33.
27. Frank Moraes, *Jawaharlal Nehru* pp.-51-52.
28. P.C. Joshi, "*Gandhi and Nehru: The Challenge of a New Society*" in *Gandhi and Nehru* (ed.), Bombay, Oxford University Press, 1979 pp.- 45-47.
29. J. Nehru *An Autobiography,* p.-73.
30. Tibor Mende, *Conversations with Nehru,* London, Secker and Warburg, 1956, p.-18.

31. P.C. Joshi, *Gandhi and Nehru:*."The challenge of a New Society" in *Gandhi and Nehru,* pp. 38-39.
32. Ganesh Prasad, *Nehru: : A Study in Colonial Liberation,* p. 191.
33. *Selected Works,* vol. 3, p.-284.
34. Letters to Gandhi, *Selected Works,* vol. 3, p-13.
35. J. Nehru, *An Autobiography,* p-25.
36. *Ibid.,* p-49.
37. Michael Brecher, *Nehru: A Political Biography,* p-40.
38. Gorev. V. Zimyanin, *Jawaharlal Nehru* (Moscow, Progress Publishers, 1982), pp.-76-77.
39. *The Will of Jawaharlal Nehru.*"
40. S. Gopal, *Jawaharlal Nehru: A Biography,* vol.1, Oxford University Press, 1975, p-48.
41. J. Nehru, *An Autobiography,* p. 57.
42. *The Independent,* Jan. 14, 1920, (NMML).
43. *Ibid.*
44. Dorothy Norman, *Nehru: The First Sixty Years* - vol. 1, from Conversation WithTibor Mende, Asia Publishing House, Bombay, 1965, pp-57-58.
45. Dorothy Norman, *Nehru: The First Sixty Years, vol.1,* "Impressions from Soviet Russia", pp.-128-137.
46. J. Nehru, *An Autobiography,* pp.-161-165.
47. *Ibid.*

    "The Brussels Congress, as well as the subsequent committee meetings of the League, which were held in various places from time to time, helped me to understand some of the problems of the colonial and dependent countries..."
48. S. Gopal, (ed.), *Selected works,* vol. 3, p-54.
49. *Ibid.*
50. S. Gopal, *Jawaharlal Nehru: A Biography,* vol. 1, p 101.
51. *Ibid.* pp.-368-9.
52. J. Nehru,*Towards Freedom,* p 128.
53. "A note on Foreign Policy for India, 13 September, 1927", *Selected Works,* Vol. 2, pp. 348-64.
54. J. Nehru, *An Autobiography,* p. 166.
55. J. Nehru, *Glimpses of World History,* Allahabad, Kitabistan, 1935 vol. 1, p 886,
56. J. Nehru, *Soviet Russia,* (Allahabad, Kitabistan, 1963) pp 85-87.
57. *Ibid.,* p 72.
58. *Ibid.* p 16.
59. *Ibid.* p 16
60. J. Nehru, *Glimpses of World History,* p-655.
61. Benudhar Pradhan, *The Socialist Thought of Jawaharlal Nehru,* p 14.
62. J. Nehru, *Soviet Russia,* p 16.
63. S. Gopal, *Jawaharlal Nehru : A Biography,* Vol. 1, Dolhi, Oxford University Press, 1975), pp 108-9.
64. Michael Brecher, *Nehru : A Political Biography,* p 57.
65. J. Nehru, *An Autobiography,* p 35.
66. J. Nehru, *Discovery of India,* p 29.
67. J. Nehru *Glimpses of World History,* p 565.
68. *Ibid.* p 547.

69. J. Nehru, *India's Freedom*, p 26.
70. J. Nehru, *Glimpses of World History*, p 544.
71. *Ibid.*
72. *Jawaharlal Nehru's Speeches*, vol.-4, p. 123.
73. J. Nehru, *An Autobiography*, p-163.
74. R.K. Karanjia, *Mind of Mr. Nehru*. London, 1960, p. 28.
75. J. Nehru, *Discovery of India*, pp.-80-84, 134 and 519.
76. *Ibid.*, p.-39.
77. Ganesh Prasad, *Nehru: A Study in Colonial Liberation* p. 179.
78. Michael Brecher, *Nehru: A Political Biography*, p.-230.

CHAPTER 2

NEHRU'S CONCEPT OF HISTORY

History as the recorded course of human life has been the subject-matter of study and reflection since the very dawn of civilization and human thought. While there has been a steady and progressive reconstruction of the story of man on this planet, a parallel attempt at the interpretation of the total import of the study has also engaged the enquiring spirit of man all along the course of ages, particularly in periods of reflection of the fundamentals of life.

Many know the dialectics of history, but few understand its dynamics. And fewer still having understood both the dialectics and dynamics have shaped history. To this precious few belongs Jawaharlal Nehru. While confined in a prison cell he could survey world history and wrote about it without reference-books, with clarity and in a fresh perspective. Later he was to become a determining factor in world history. Apart from being a man of politics, he was a man with a gift for history, who is not to be confused with monks intent on compiling registers and chronicles, nor with the erudites who collect stories and documents and by their industry produce reliable news, nor with scholarly compilers of historical manuals. And to be recognised as a man of mark among the equals in a concord of writers and experts on history in a highly appreciable and unique proposition for a politician, especially when the politics,he is engaged in,is not the workaday affairs of the State and nation but the abnormal revolutionary politics that leaves but few moments of rest in life. Nehru.was a politician with a difference. What sets him above and apart from the common run of popular leaders was the fact that in India, he brought thought to bear on politics; in other words he saturated politics with thought. His dominion of ideas added colour to his politics; he literally lived on the light emanated from them.

Subject-Matter of History

The question arises as to why did Nehru, a politician write history; what were the urges that led him to study history; what according to him was the purpose of studying history? Ordinarily politicians who are men of action care little for thought and knowledge, they go about fretting for power, gains and fortune only, on the other hand the historians are after truth and the idea behind every fact or truth. What distinguished him from others was his historical mindedness, a deep sense of unfoldment of historical developments. The failure, if any, of him as a politician can be traced to his selfish attachment to thought and knowledge, which goes against the nature and pretensions of pure men of action.

Nehru took to writing history as a way of escaping from the tyranny of the past to reach the warmth of the present with all its inner conflicts and problems. His views on the past, the present and the future in their relation to man and history are noteworthy: "There is a stillness and everlastingness about the past, it changes not and has a touch of eternity . . . unaffected by the storms and upheavals of the present, it maintains its dignity and repose and tempts the troubled spirit and the tortured mind to seek shelter in its vaulted catacombs".[1]

It was prison life that opened up the bright new world for the historian, for Nehru who was a popular leader and revolutionary engaged in the fight for freedom of India from British bondage, when action was denied to him, when the present was cut-off from him, took refuge in the past and through the process of thought and imagination made himself feel that he was preparing himself for action.

For him, history was not merely past but a link with the present. He approached history in its abstract sense of past and then invested it with flesh and blood as he believed that history is a series of significant events happened or an enquiry into the past conducted by the historian. In the latter sense it was not a collection of dry facts but a calling into being a moving procession of men and events and the thoughts and ideas that lived behind them. When the magic wand of the historian touches the dry bones of facts, an age suddenly springs up to life in vividness and vitality and presents before us a show with deeper meanings for the present. Writing to his daughter in one of the last letters, later to be compiled in his *Glimpses of World History*, he advised her, "If then, you look upon past history with the eye of sympathy, the dry bones will fill up with flesh and blood, and you will see a mighty procession of living men and women and children in every age and every clime, different from us and yet very like us. History is not a magic show but there is plenty of magic in it for those who have eyes to see".[2]

It is the problems of today, the desire to understand the present and the urge to make future brighter, that leads the historian to the problems of the past. Nehru tries to explain the relevance of the past for the present and also the dictum that all history is contemporary history. "The past becomes something that leads up to the present, the moment of action, the future, something that flows from it, and all three are inextricably intertwined and interrelated". This view he maintained as late as 1959 when he said, change was essential but continuity was also necessary. The future had to be built on the foundation laid in the past and in the present. To deny the past and break with it completely was to uproot ourselves. The fascination for history for Nehru was not in reading about odd events happened in the past but rather in its relation to the things that led up to the present, "Only then did it become alive to me. Otherwise, it would have been an odd thing unconnected with my life or the world. It must somehow be connected in a series--something of the past leading to something else and that something else leading to the present. Then alone can history live for us".[3]

Nehru thought in concrete terms, with an eye to the task of the day but simultaneously he sought to gain an insight into the future. Historical and philosophical meditation was not an end in itself but a search for an answer to the most important problems of concern to his homeland and all mankind. In the *Discovery of India*, he attempts to comprehend the past of his country so as to see the present more clearly and outline the ways of changing it. The past engages Nehru's interest primarily as a 'pointer to the future'. For him history is a school of life-experience and struggle, the source of origin of his world-view.

Nehru wrote history or made voyages into the past as in the case of *Discovery of India,* not only to assure himself of India's past glory, but to understand the nature and forces of the Indian spirit, which were unfolding continuity and change of Indian mind. The poverty, degradation and mental deterioration which had become ingrained in the body-politic of India, due to successive foreign dominations led him to seek evidences for india's greatness in the past. He was seeking inspiration from history which would provide him the moral strength to fight for the uplift and liberation of India. He had firm conviction that India would rise phoenix like from the ashes to be rejuvenated to her past greatness. "Though books and old monuments" wrote Nehru "and past cultural achievements helped to produce some understanding of India, they did not satisfy me or give me the answer I was looking for...The present for me and for many others like me, was an odd mixture of medievalism, appalling poverty and misery and a somewhat significant modernism of the middle-classes... I think that a country with a long cultural background and a common outlook on life develops a spirit that is peculiar to it and that is impressed on all its children... It was the spirit of India that I was after... I felt that it might give me some key to the understanding of my country and people and some guidance to thought and action".[4]

Similar urge underlay his endeavour when he wrote the *Glimpses of World History.* A visionary, he was unable to tolerate the idea of the world being subjected to the baser instincts of autocrats and tyrants like Hitler and Mussolini. The hypocrisy which Britain personified in the name of saving democracy even while enslaving half of the world, revolted him. He was worried to see the decline in the spirit of man, which had led to the division of the world into the exploiter and the exploited, conqueror and the conquered.[5] Nehru was a witness to the misery inflicted by the war--the loss of lives and wanton destruction, cut-throat competition among the nations for superiority, the fight for survival, the evils of industrialisation and above all the mental and physical agony of India due to subjection to alien rule. This curse of human fate appeared again and again in various shades in his speeches, letters and writings. The essential pathos of man's struggle for existence on the earth's surface, where endless infrastructures for destroying happy and comfortable living have been built by man's own talent and toil, can be heard ringing in woeful tales in almost all his writings.

Jawaharlal Nehru had a distinctive philosophy of history which prodded him into action and sustained all through the years of his premiership. Change and continuity is the essence of history. In his *Discovery of India,* he quotes a significant passage which has special relevance to us here and now: "John Stuart Mill wrote in his autobiography :"I am convinced that no great improvements in the lot of mankind are possible, until a great change takes place in the fundamental constitution of their modes of thought".[6]

Thus, change is the essence of life and the dynamics of a society that is moving towards progress. History is the story of change in its various forms, evolution and revolution. Here it would be relevant to quote Nehru at length: "The great ages have been full of conflict and unstability, of an attempt to change over from the old to something new. There is no permanent stability or security or changelessness, if there were life itself would cease...Destruction and construction go side by side and both aspects of man's nature are ever evident. Life is a principle of growth, not of standing still, a continuous becoming, which does not permit static conditions."[7] Nehru believed in the deep relevance of history, as the perennial process of ceaseless change and transcendence of the human spirit.

Vision of History

Jawaharlal Nehru was not just locating facts or events by peering into history; he was looking for a deeper meaning. He was trying to discover the spirit that moved the ages, the urges of men who made history or the forces that shaped history of millions of years. He made excursions into the past to feel those urges and identify them with the present, to construct a better future which would pick up the greatness of the past and throw off its weaknesses. For him history was a teacher, a framework, from where the present could be judged and the future ascertained. It has been said that history repeats itself. Nehru, by making researches into the past did not want humanity to repeat the mistakes, and desired that the world should learn from past mistakes and grasp the values and the truth instead.[8] The materialist conception that the nature of people's ideas, views and notions is inevitably dependent on the level of production of material benefits and of the place which they occupy in the system of social production, rejects the outstanding role of the mind in creating favourable conditions in the environment for the exploitation of nature. It maintains that man's labour not only transforms nature but also influences man himself. According to this theory, not only man's brain but also his hands are a product of labour. Accordingly, the materialists hold it a self-evident truth that the basis of social development should be looked for not in their consciousness but in the social being which is conditioned by the production relations.[9]

Nehru makes a significant departure from Marx. According to him man does everything, not because he has hands but because he has brain, mind and ideas. Events are a procession of ideas. His labours would be futile, his creativity would be zero had he not a mind, a consciousness. The work produced by a frail but civilized man would definitely be qualitatively different and superior to the work done by a well-built savage under given conditions. By stressing the overwhelming importance of the mind of man, Nehru rejects the Marxian conception of the primacy of labour over mind and comes closer to the idealist view and thereby, strikes a golden mean between the materialist and the idealist approaches to history.

History according to him reveals not only the action of the individual versus the environment but also the interaction of various aspects of culture. While assessing the better type of modern mind, which he believes, is practical and pragmatic, ethical and social, altruist and humanitarian, the ideal which moves. It represents the spirit of " the age the Zeitgist, the Yougadharma... humanity is its God and social service its religion".[10]

Thus the core of history, for him is Man endowed with mind, a burning spirit which enables him to fight against the elements, conquer nature and free himself from the oppression of the environment. It is the mind which is innovator of great revolutions in society, propounds religions and ideologies or enriches the world by great discoveries of science, art, literature, law, music, philosophy and all factors that combine to constitute culture are the creations of the mind of man. In history and politics, in war and peace, Nehru's main concern is man's mind and his ideas. [11] In short the story of man is the story of his mind, its growth, its development, its adventures in the realms of nature and soul. Historians who ignore the role of mind in their narration do at their peril considering it as unreal, changing, ungaugeable, they are apt to dismiss it as inconsequential in the march of events. Mind, being the prime mover of class-conflicts, wars, revolutions and all economic and cultural activities and scientific discoveries, Nehru gives supreme importance to it in his treatment of history and analysis of the civilization. [12]

Influence of Marx

It is instructive to note that Nehru's perspective of history was influenced by the Marxist interpretation of history. In fact, Marxism was one of the first influences which left a deep imprint on his mind during the formative years. It must be remembered that it was not merely romantic idolation that led him to appreciate the materialistic interpretation of history but a rational concrete and analytical study of history and the forces which are shaping the future course of the world. Summing up the Marxian impact upon him Nehru wrote: "A study of Marx and Lenin produced a powerful effect on my mind and helped me to see history and current affairs in a new light. The long chain of history and of social development appeared to have some meaning, some sequence and the future lost some of its obscurity".[13] At another place he wrote, "What then is this Marxism? It is a way of interpreting history and politics and human life and human desires. It is a theory as well as a call to action . . . It is an attempt at reducing history, past, present and future, to a rigid logical system with something of the inevitability of fate or *Kismet* about it. Marx surveyed past history as a scientist and drew certain conclusion from it". [14]

The Marxist analysis of history is said to the scientific, rational and logical. The rationality of Marxism appealed to him the most. It was different from the prior theories regarding history as none has given due importance to the concept of class-struggle which has been present at all times. Moreover, Marxism presented a rationale for the advent of socialism. Nehru came to perceive many principles of scientific socialism, thanks to his critical searching mind, he did not resist the process. He avidly studied the theory and practice of scientific socialism in the belief that very much of it was acceptable to India. He was one of the first leaders of national liberation movement who was not afraid to speak of the epoch-making world-wide significance of Marxism to the national revolutionaries and the national reformists. This is not surprising since Nehru himself saw in this science the ineluctable logic of historical development, the imperative demand of time--the epoch of transition to socialism. He repeatedly emphasised the favourable impact of scientific socialism on his world outlook. He wrote in this connection, "The theory and philosophy of Marxism lightened up many a dark corner of my mind. History came to have a new meaning for me. The Marxist interpretation threw a flood-light on it . . . In spite of the appalling waste and misery of the past and the present, the future was bright with hope . . . It was the essential freedom from dogma and the scientific outlook that appealed to me". [15]

Accordingly, Nehru held the view that, history would be the story of man's struggle for a living. And because, in order to live certain things like food, shelter and clothing in cold climates are necessary, "those who have controlled these necessaries have lorded over men". [16] It is a long drawn out process of progress and development of mankind passing various stages. In each stage can be found essential conflict of interests and cooperation, for satisfaction of economic and social need.

Nehru recognises class-struggle as an important feature of human race from the beginning of its recorded life to the present day. He observes, "The rulers and the bosses have had authority because they owned or controlled some essentials of livelihood. This control gave them power to enslave people into submission. And so we see the strange sight of large masses being exploited by comparatively few, some who earn without working at all, of vast numbers who work but earn very little". [17] This interpretation of historical process is not very different from what is given by Marx and Engels: "Free man and slave, patrician and plebeian, lord and serf, guildmaster and journeyman, in a word oppressor and oppressed, stood in constant opposition to one another, carried on an uninterrupted now hidden, now open fight".[18]

Departure from Marx

Nevertheless, it is remarkable to note that Nehru's conception of class antagonism as the dominant urge behind historical change, is less dogmatic than that of Marx. The similarity of ideas thus ends here. It is true that the fundamental conflict is between economic interests but, at the same time he points out that, there is an unending process of rival claims of different groups of the possessing classes.[19] That is not insignificant phase of the conflict relation. In the developments of peoples and nations this kind of rivalry for mastery can be found among owning classes. Therefore, the conclusion is that there is not only a class-struggle between the bourgeois and the proletariat but also a conflict within the bourgeois camp itself for domination. This inner struggle explains the scramble for the world market which formed the characteristic phase of development of capitalism and its last stage, imperialism.[20] Similarly there is unending conflict within the proletarian section itself. The rift in the communist camp, between Soviet Russia and China, cannot be otherwise explained. The doctrinal and organisational unity of the 'world-party' created by Lenin has been finally broken by the rival claims to leadership of the two communist great powers and the resulting schism has proved that class-antagonism is not restricted to the fight between the haves and the havenots only.

Thus, while accepting the inevitablity of class-conflict Nehru does not view history as a story of class struggle alone. Materialist dialectics fail to recognise higher human ideals of love and cooperation in human relations. In Nehru's view of history this humanistic element also looms large. He tried to impress this fact upon the young mind of his daughter, "I have tried to show you the idea of cooperation or working together has grown, and how our ideal should be to work together for common good. ... In one of our old Sanskrit books there is a verse which can be translated as follows: "For the family sacrifice the individual, for the community the family, for the country the community and for the soul whole world. What the soul is few of us know or tell, and each one of us can interpret it in a different way. But the lesson of sacrifice is for the larger good".[21]

To him, therefore, the reality of mutuality is as important and determining a factor as the reality of class conflict in the development of human society. Human institutions like family, marriage, law, speech, art and architecture, science etc. cannot be viewed apart from, and in opposition to this higher urge in human relations. Nehru goes to the extent of saying that cooperation and sacrifice for the good of society is the test of civilization. If the tendency to fight with his fellow-beings is predominant in man, the desire to build a family and society cannot be fulfilled. A civilization built on class-antagonism and inner strife can never be built by any society. Conflict and cooperation, sacrifice and service form the pillars of human society and cultural edifice. Nehru does not fail to notice these essential ingredients of progress. All the monumental structures, works of art and institution and in fact, all civilizations are the products of cooperative endeavour of the society of each age. This evolutionary growth through cooperation he traces thus, "This savage humanity alone, gradually forms a family and the whole household work together and for each other. Many households, cooperate together to form the village and workers and merchants and artisans of different villages later join together to form Guilds of craftsmen. Gradually you see the social unit growing".[22] Throughout his search into history, it has been Nehru's endeavour to establish that man has a mind which is universal cooperative and good, thereby having faith in the essential goodness of man.

This approach to history is more akin to the social determinism of Marx and Engels than that of Hegel and Spencer.The social determinism of the latter deduced from their metaphysical principles of evolution, is not based on historical experience. The Marxist doctrines, on the other hand, derives empirical material from the fount of historical knowledge and actual experience of societies. Nehru accepts from this, the dialectic necessity and historical inevitability and adds, to it something of the 'objective mind' of Hegel. While he stresses the economic factors and class-conflict in the development of societies, he also underscores the cooperative element and the role of culture which is a derivative of the super individual institution of speech, family, religion, law, art and science.

Nehru's questioning mind did not accept the Marxian economic interpretation of history. He writes in *The Discovery of India*, "Much in the Marxist philosophical outlook I could accept without difficulty its monism and non-duality of mind and matter, the dynamics of matter and the dialectic of continuous change by evolution as well as leap, through action and interaction, cause and effect, thesis, anti-thesis and synthesis. It did not satisfy me completely, nor did it answer all the questions in my mind, and almost unawares a vague idealist approach would creep into my mind something rather akin to the Vedanta approach.[23]

Nehru's World-View

The horrors of industrial civilization, the successive deterioration of the mind of humanity leading to endless strife and wars, the predominance of fear of each other and fear of survival which the nuclear age presented; worried Nehru. Bleeding from war wounds and frightened by the atomic Frankenstein's destructions, humanity was looking for a way out of the death-trap. It aspires for an order to displace disorder. It wants peace in place of war. Nehru dreamt of a better humanity, a greater wisdom of a finer cultural mantle for its body, than the bloody rags of a robot civilization. He was searching for an all comprehensive philosophy that would maintain an equilibrium between man's internal and external life and help him ascertain a purpose of life without which life becomes a ceaseless adventure.[24]

A deep historical perspective was the source of Jawaharlal Nehru's world-view which is value based, objective, progressive and humanistic. For him, history is a school of life, experience and struggle, the source of the origin of his world outlook. He approaches it as an active political leader stimulated to research by the requirements of struggle and practice in general. "My fascination for history was not in reading about odd events that happened in the world but rather in its relation to the things that led up to the present."

Of particular interest is the world-outlook of a man who was one of the acknowledged leaders of the national liberation movement, headed the independent Indian state and deeply influenced its present and future over the last quarter century more than anybody else, as also a leader of the emerging third world. Nehru had a rare insight into the forces which led him to foresee the course the future would take. In fact, he was ahead of his time and fellow-beings. An examination of his ideas will reveal a sensitive, broad-minded and ventilated mind. Having rejected abstract and fruitless quest of the meaning of history outside it as such, he gradually discovered and later recognized the internal laws of historical development and thereby made a fundamental step to a realistic almost materialistic but not yet dialectical interpretation of the historical process.[25]

Recognition of objective laws led him to a comprehension of the upward spiral direction of the historical process not without occasional regression - an understanding of it as an objective and progressive course of events, as an ascent in the final analysis from the lower to the higher. This led him to observe that in no case should the world head towards Nazi and Fascist tendencies. Nehru minced no words when he warned the nations and the great-powers that any outlook short of peace would push the world into another era of despotism.

To be able to reflect adequately the spirit of the age is no doubt a great quality of an individual. In the concluding chapters of the *Glimpses of World History* and *Discovery of India*, Nehru has not only made a critical analysis of the bewildering political and social developments, actions and reactions throughout the world particularly in the so-called civilized west in this century, he has also endeavoured constantly to dive below the surface and to bring out the cry of the suffering soul of universal man, what is in store for him, what is his destiny?

Voicing his anxiety over the deteriorating world situation, Nehru after returning from the Almora jail, for a short time wrote, "Europe in turmoil and with economic crisis always on the horizon; Abyssinia invaded and her people bombarded; various imperialist systems in conflict and threatening each other, and England, the greatest of the imperialist powers, standing up for peace and the League covenant, while it ruthlessly oppresses its subject peoples'"[26] Nehru's writings and speeches of this period reveal to a great extent the spirit of restlessness and violence developing into a phenomenal force striking at the roots of all that is noble and kindly and beautiful in human civilization, since the great war of 1914-18. The vicious forces of destruction regrouped themselves and reappeared in the early thirties of the century. The march of Japan on China, the Spanish civil war, the rise of Fascism as a new political form of aggressive imperialism, emergence of Nazism and its irresistible gobbling up and opportunism of Great Britain, futile but continuous struggle for independence in India and other Asian countries, these and similar other world events created an atmosphere supercharged with endless tension and the apprehension of an impending disaster. Nehru keenly followed the course of development of a series of such events and even took active part in some of them. Face to face with the grim tragedy which had been spreading its spectre, Nehru retained his conscientious adherence to the principles of peace and freedom and equality of all peoples of the strife-torn world.

In the years preceding the outbreak of World War II Nehru's assessment of the tragic situation in Europe and the rest of the world was transparent. In all his writings during the period, there is a dignified and uncompromising protest against the rise of powers of dictatorship and violence, and the resultant ruination of the basic human values. Thus from antagonism to the horrors of violence, subjection, the threat of war and the mental degradation of man arose Nehru's comprehensive world-outlook which held a vision of a future world devoid of misery, violence and exploitation, a vision of progressive world in which man would regain his humaneness.

Nehru approaches the history of mankind primarily as a rationalist thinker. He seeks within it an inner meaning, a logic of development and does not approach it with a priori, extra-historical category. He perceived in the Socialist remaking of society the logical result of mankind's historical development. He stressed that capitalism, "is no longer suited to the present age" [27] that the world had outgrown it. He pointed out that the scientific and technological revolution makes the need for socialism particularly obvious, and that the modern scientific approach is exactly the socialist approach. At the same time Nehru was one of the first leaders of the anticolonialist movement to indicate with striking clarity, forcefulness and farsightedness that the movement towards socialism was a specific requirement for the developing countries especially, and for the world, an objectively pre-determined path of progress for states which cast off the colonial yoke, for India in particular.

In this thesis and its argumentation Nehru had anticipated many propositions put forward later by a number of Asian and African political leaders. He posed clearly the unacceptability of capitalism for the liberated countries in view of the fact that the latter had no time at their disposal to achieve progress by the same method, at the same rate in the same cruel forms of exploitation of man by man as the Western world had done at one time. Should we follow the British, French or American way? he asked. Do we really have as much time as 100 to 150 years to achieve our goal? This was absolutely unacceptable, in such an event we would simply perish. [28]

Nehru followed with keen interest the progress of social transformation in Soviet Russia. He made his first visit to that country in 1927. What he saw there led him to conclude, "The Soviet Revolution had advanced human society by a great leap and had lit a bright flame which could not be smothered and. . . had laid the foundation for that, 'new civilization' toward which the world would advance".[29] It was a brilliant forecast for decades.

In his speech at a session of the Indian National Congress Party in Lucknow in 1936 Nehru said, "I am convinced that the only key to the solution of the world's problems and of India's problems lies in Socialism, and . . .I see no way of ending the poverty, the vast unemployment, the degradation, and the subjection of the Indian people except through socialism. That involves vast and revolutionary changes in our political and social structure, the ending of vested interests in land and industry...That means the ending of Private Property, except in a restricted sense, and the replacement of the present profit system by a higher co-operative service...In short, it means a new civilization, radically different from the present capitalist order".[30]

Analysis of Imperialism

By analysing the phenomenon of capitalism, fascism and imperialism,Nehru explained the advent of socialism. He declared that whether we wish it or not socialism was bound to come, it was apparent in the changing conditions of the world.[31] We can discern a consistent attack on capitalism imperialism, throughout his speeches and writings. In fact, at times, his tone was so acrimonious that he was often branded a communist. His condemnation of imperialism may have originated not necessarily from an adherence to any particular ideology like Marxism or Communism, but the sheer vulgarity of capitalism.

Nehru, believed that capitalism-imperialism were the root cause of poverty in the world, dividing it into two antagonistic classes - the exploiter and the exploited. Explaining this phenomenon Nehru opined, "Thus we see the world divided into two vast groups today - the imperialist and fascist on one side, the socialist and nationalist on the other. There is some overlapping of the two and the line between them is difficult to draw, for there is mutual conflict between the fascist and imperialist powers, and the nationalism of the subject countries has sometimes a tendency to fascism. But the main division holds and if we keep it in mind, it will be easier for us to understand world conditions and our own place in them''.[32] Nehru saw no difference between the three, they had the same goal - to subjugate entire humanity. The form is different but the content same. Elaborating the analysis of this phenomenon Nehru explains, ''Capitalism in its difficulties took to fascism with all its brutal suppression of what western civilization had apparently stood for; it became even in some of its homeland, what its imperialist counterpart had long been in the subject colonial countries. Fascism and imperialism thus stood out as the two faces of the now decaying capitalism, and though they varied in different countries according to national characteristics and economic and political conditions, they represented each other and at the same time came into conflict with each other for such conflict was inherent in their very nature.''[33]

'Socialism in the West and the rising nationalism of the Eastern and other dependent countries opposed this combination of Fascism and Imperialism. Nationalism in the East, it must be remembered, was essentially different from the new and terribly narrow nationalism of fascist countries. The former was the historical urge to freedom, the latter the last refuge of reaction''.[34] He categorically states that it was not Hitler and Mussolini who had created the crisis in Europe rather it was the policy of the British government supported by the French Government that could be held responsible for it. There was a great deal of talk of the democracies defending freedom against the so-called democracies of West Europe that had helped and encouraged Fascism and Nazism and done to death the Spanish Republic and Czechoslovakia. In a letter to the *Manchester Guardian* dated September 8, 1938, Nehru wrote, ''As an Indian, intensely interested in India's independence and world peace, I have followed recent development in Czechoslovakia and Spain with anxious interest. For some years past the Indian National Congress has criticized and dissociated itself from the British foreign policy which has seemed to be consistently reactionary and anti-democratic, and an encouragement to Fascist and Nazi aggression''.[35] He saw in Fascism a development of a more dangerous form of imperialism and condemned it. He looked upon the two as twin brothers which crushed freedom and prevented peace and progress.[36] How had Fascism grown so rapidly so that it threatened to dominate Europe and the world, Nehru asked. Explaining it he said that all the blame lay in British foreign policy. This policy in spite of its outward variations and frequent hesitation, had been one of consistent support of Nazi Germany. The Anglo-German Naval Treaty threw France into the arms of Italy and led to the rape of Abyssinia. Behind the threat of all sanctions against Italy, Britain actually refused to put effective sanction. Even when the United States of America offered to cooperate in imposing the oil sanction Britain refused and was content to see the bombing of Ethiopians and the breaking up of the League of Nations system of collective security. All talks of collective security by Britain was a sham for its actions belied its wounds and was ready to leave the field open to Fascist aggression.[37]

Nehru left no stone unturned in his effort to warn India and the world of the menace of Fascism and the impending disaster if it were not contained. He analysed that the whole ideology of Fascism was built upon the Herrenvolk and the master race and the structure of Government was based on it; indeed the idea of a master race is inherent in Imperialism, there was no subterfuge about it, it was proclaimed in unambiguous language by those in authority. More powerful than words was the practice that acompanied them, and generation after generation, year after year, India as a nation and Indians as individuals were subjected to insult, humiliation and contemptuous treatment and always reminded of the 'tiger qualities of an imperial race."[38] Nehru's democratic mind revolted against such discriminatory theorising of racial superiority. Being aware of the great civilization of India his mind revolted against such onslaught and the humiliation which a few dictators like Mussolini, Hitler and the politicians of England had unleashed. This awareness led him to be the most outspoken of leaders. He feared no consequences when mouthing antagonism to the joint venture of Fascism and Imperialism.

Criticising the twin phenomenon of Fascism-Imperialism most vehemently Nehru wrote, "Fascism crushed all progressive elements and set up new standards in cruelty and inhumanity. It gloried in brutality and openly aimed at waging war. Imperialist powers talk in terms of democracy but aided and abetted fascism and helped it grow. International morality decayed, all ideas of collective action and peace were given up and an unabashed gangsterism among nations grew up and was tolerated. Yet it was clear that by only collective action could the aggressor be stayed and peace maintained. A surrender to violence and aggression was no basis for peace, for the aggression to be checked and peace ensured if those powers who believed in peace acted together, for their strength was greater than that of the Fascist aggressor. But many of those very powers who talked of peace and democracy were imperialist and they sympathized with Fascism and encouraged it''.[39]

In most touching words Nehru voiced his contempt for the degrading Fascist mentality, 'Brotherhood, sisterhood are bastard creeds says Signor Mussolini; only the sword counts with him, the sword that kills freedom and democracy and puts an end to the culture and civilization of ages''. Elaborating further, he says, ''The light go out in Europe and elsewhere, the shadows increase and in the darkness freedom is butchered and violence reigns. Tragedy envelopes us, heart-breaking tragedy, as we see the death of nation after nation, the vast suffering and misery of millions of peoples crushed by barbarian feet...Spain of the Republic and her freedom is no more, only the bright and imperishable memory of her glorious struggle remains, Czechoslovakia used to be on the map of Europe, it is no more, and Her Hitler's minions trample on her brave children, betrayed so shamefully by England and France''. From day to day we await in suspense what this dictator or that says; anxiously we wonder what the next aggression will be''. How did all that affect India? Nehru asked, dare we ignore these tremendous happening in Europe? India's freedom would not be worth many days purchase if Fascism and Nazism dominate the world. Only a union of freedom - loving peoples and their mutual cooperation could avert the common peril. For that union India must stand.[40]

From this time (1933) dates the intense dislike of Fascism, which was never to leave Nehru, and the conviction that while communism would have to adapt itself to changing condition and different countries, its basic ideology, general outlook and scientific interpretation of history were sound. The affinity to the left, born of the visit to Europe in the twenties and nourished by reading, was confirmed by the rival philosophies that had spawned in Italy and Germany. Extensive study while in of international affairs led him to recognise India as a part of the pattern of world-forces. There was, as Jawaharlal Nehru saw in it an inevitable universal swing not necessarily to the Soviet model but towards the general lines of the Soviet conception. Fundamentally, the choice before the world was between some form of communism and some form of Fascism, and he was all for the former. There was no middle road; one had to choose between the two, and Nehru unhesitatingly, preferred the communist ideal.[41]

Nehru analysed in great detail the phenomenon of imperialism. He looked for the forces which governed it and accordingly based his world view. In an article, "The future of the colonies", he wrote, "The future of the colonies"? The obvious answer is that there is no future for them as colonies and that the whole system known as colonialism has to go. It has to go for variety of reasons. It is evident that the dependent peoples of the colonial empires are in a rebellious mood and cannot be suppressed for long, and every attempt to suppress them is a drain on the ruling country which weakens it. It is even more evident that the old style empires are decadent as empires and show signs of cracking up. In some instances indeed they have cracked up, and the attempts that are being made to join together broken pieces show a lack of wisdom and statesmanship which is amazing... All these are signs of an inevitable change and transition from one era of colonialism to another era which was yet to be given shape and form and a name".[42] This era according to Nehru would be of socialism, a world federation based on Socialist lines with cooperation as the marking ideology.

The *Glimpses of World History* is a scholastic effort on Nehru's part to unravel, the laws that governed capitalism-imperialism and trace out its systematic development. The whole endeavour is an effort to establish laws that Socialism is the only remedy for the strife-ridden world.

Where does India stand? Summing up his entire view in an article "Whither India?" he unhesitatingly answers, "Whither India?" "Surely to the great human goal of social and economic equality, to the ending of an exploitation of nation by nation and class by class, to national freedom within the framework of an international cooperative Socialist world federation".[43]

Nehru, broadly believed that what mattered were not individual or national peculiarities but impersonal world forces. One could only understand the past and face the future with confidence if class-conflict and social struggles were taken into account.[44] An appreciation of the interplay of economic interests, social relations and hegemonic ideas could alone pave the way for effective action. Instead of merely condemning British imperialism as alien domination as he could have done, he gave new emphasis to the interlinking of economics and politics, of capitalism and imperialism; and his quarrel was not just with the foreign ruler but with the system.

Historical Nationalism

This approach was aided by Nehru's capacity to see beyond India and to place the national problem in the world context.[45] His patriotism was poised on the broader platform of internationalism. Nationalism and internationalism are generally considered to be mutually hostile and exclusive. But Nehru's internationalism did not question the basis of nationalism. It actually presupposed it. His internationalism did not deny the validity or existence of national self-consciousness. He was an internationalist par-excellence, a world citizen in the truest sense of the term and not a sentimental nationalist, though he fought with all his strength to support worthy national causes. His internationalism was not utopian in conception, but the product of hard thinking and grounded on the harsh realities of life, "Nationalism has a place in each country and should be fostered, but it must not be allowed to become aggressive and come in the way of international development".[46]

Jawaharlal Nehru's world-view rests on the pillars of internationalism which has its roots in nationalism in which both are supplementary to each other. It is instructive to note that Nehru's conception on nationalism differs from the traditional definition of nationalism hitherto put forward. By nationalism he means not the narrow and fanatical nationalism propounded by the Fascists or conservative nationalism of the Chinese or the West, but a "Constructive nationalism". He has written in his *Autobiography* that he worked for independence because the nationalist in him could not tolerate alien domination, but that he worked for it, even more because for him it was the inevitable step to social and economic change.[47] It is clear that by nationalism Nehru meant, that passion and the urge which motivates an individual to work towards progress and betterment of his homeland. He vehemently opposes hegemonic aspirations which wear the garb of nationalism and eventually assume the form of imperialism.

Nehru visualised a family of nations wherein every nation whether small or big will be an important unit. His faith in man is equalled by his faith in the ability of every nation to make its own worthy contribution to the progress of mankind, "Faith in progress in a cause in ideals, in human goodness and human destiny". Intensely proud as he was of India, Nehru would have perhaps felt it a greater honour to be called a citizen of the world , for his ideal is one world, his fight is for human freedom everywhere, his deification is of the dignity of man.[48]

Nehru aspired to build the superstructure of internationalism on the infrastructure of nationalism. The goal would be towards formation of a socialist world federation, wherein every nation while retaining its independence and sovereignty would contribute to strengthening the world federation. For him nationalism would be the stepping stone to internationalism and universalism.

Nehru visualised a 'universal man' whose allegience would be not only to his country but to the whole world. He also shared in some way the collective consciousness of the Indian people which accepts diversity in the cosmic scheme of things and particularly in human society, almost as a law of nature and refuses to think in terms of polarization of ideas and forces, "Our whole culture testifies to our understanding of the variety of humanity laying stress always on the unity, but also on the variety and diversity... whatever we may do in our limit and our failings, we have had a type of philosophy which is live and let live philosophy of life. We have no particular desire to convert other people to any view or thought."[49] What better philosophical foundation there could be for a world-view ?

The method of history is to acquire knowledge through the perception of the particular but historians who concentrate on the particular lose sight of the unity of mankind and make history an immense aggregate of particular facts related to a man or group of men, religion or a nation, without reference to the larger context of human kind, family of nations and transcendent ideas. There is a universal aspect to every idea, every institution. A historian who fixes his eye on the particular aspect of an event cannot possibly know the whole significance of it, if he fails to see the universal aspect also. While dealing with the particular, he must be able to reflect on the development of the world in general. Regional history is important in as much as it leads to the understanding of the national history, regional history unrelated to national history is crude and meaningless, for no country can function in isolation. Right from the ancient times until the present, there has been a large degree of interdependence, the destiny of all nations is interlinked. The whole universe is like an organism with nations as its body parts, segregating a nation would be like mutilating a part of the body, so also, with history, there is an organic connection. Much in the same way, national history if it is linked with the universal events of the past it becomes meaningful and significant. Historians must, therefore, be endowed with the ability to transform the particular into the universal. As Ranke put it, "The final goal - not yet attained - always remains the conception and composition of a history of mankind."[50]

Nehru's view of history was not limited by a preoccupation with the particular. History had a wider meaning for him. Endowed with an ecumenical view, he treated India as just a part of the world. One's own country is greatly loved by everyone and it is great in everybody's estimation but one's country's history should not be taken as such; it is only a part of world history. "Nearly all of us", Nehru admits, "Think that the history of our own country whichever that might be, as more glorious and more worthy of study than the histories of other countries,"[51] and warned against the danger involved in this highly parochial approach to history.

Even while writing about India and about himself, he tries to keep up the spirit of this integrated world-view. India to him, is not an isolated island, in the realm of history it is a part of the whole. Despite his pride in the rich and immemorial past and heritage of India, he was not given to propounding a singularly nationalist view of history. The possibility was greater for him to adopt a purely narrow nationalist impression about India, he was in the thick of political struggle against British domination. It was in the oppressive solitude of the British prison that he completed his works on history and yet his idea of history was least influenced by anti-British, narrow, pro-nationalist outlook.

A nationalist to the core Nehru was an internationalist in his approach even in dealing with national problems. He said, "This wider international aspect of the problem grew upon me as I realised more and more how isolation was both undesirable and impossible".[52] The future that took shape in his mind was one of intimate cooperation, politically, economically and culturally, between India and the other countries of the world. Elaborating the point of necessity of an integrated history of the world Nehru writes, "Our incursions into history have shown us how the world was grown more and more compact, how different parts have come together and become interdependent. The world has indeed become one single inseparable whole, each part influencing and being influenced by the other. It is quite impossible now to have a separate history of nations. We have outgrown that stage, and only a single world history, connecting the different threads of all nations and seeking to find the real forces that move them, can now be written with any useful purpose''.[53]

Nehru was like the conscience keeper of the world who passionately and boldly reiterated that the, ''alternative to world cooperation is world disaster''. He forecast ''The end of colonialism and imperialism will not mean the splitting up of the world into a host of additional national States intent on their isolated independence. It will lead to a new grouping together of all nations, a new outlook, to cooperation gradually replacing competition andconflict, to the utilization of the wonders of modern technique an the vast sources of energy at the disposal of man for the advancement of the human race as a whole. It will lead to that one world of which wise statesmen have dreamed and which seems to be the inevitable and only outcome of our present troubles, if we survive disaster''.[54]

Speaking at a Press Conference at Vigyan Bhawan on October 21, 1960, Nehru elaborately discussed the erstwhile state of affairs and said that a world-confrontation and a nuclear holocaust could be restricted and peace established if commonness of purpose was emphasised rather than the differences. Commonness, indeed there were many. The world was undergoing a tremendous revolutionary period of change, revolutionary in the sense of Science and Technology. He said that, ''Science and Technology cannot be labelled under particular ideology-communist, capitalist, socialist etc. They are common factors, just like mathematics is not capitalist or communist or anything else. It is mathematics''.[55] A certain commonness was spreading all over the world with advance of science and technology and he foresaw that nations would have to cooperate with each other in this sphere, sinking their differences, thus bringing them closer. Has not Nehru been proved right when in present times we find that despite great differences America and Russia do come up and cooperate with each other in the technological field ? Nehru was emphasising on this commonness of purpose. ''Basically the fact that by modern technology and science you can produce the good things of life for every human being in the world instead of having them only for a limited number, does change the whole face of the world in theory and practice progressively..The world has ceased to be in theory a world governed by the laws of scarcity, although in practice it is to some large extent. So all this has made innumerable changes in the world, based not on this ideology and that, but on technology and the progress of technology and science''.[56] We see that here is an individual who rose much higher than the contemporary statesmen of the world when he transcended the difference of ideology and system to propagate a 'new world order' based on peace, justice and equality.

Perhaps the best summing up of Jawaharlal Nehru's place in the world today and the noblest tribute paid to him was contained in the citation on the occasion of the conferment of the honorary degree of Doctor of Laws on him at Columbia University, by its then President, General Eisenhower.

''Pandit Nehru, foremost disciple of the great apostle of Indian freedom, indomitable leader of his people along the thorny path of liberation, wise counsellor and moulder of policies of a reborn nation, renowned interpreter of the aspirations of a great race, his intellectual leadership has combined the profound knowledge of the West with the great heritage and enduring traditions of the East, a champion of under-previleged people, his devotion to the noble ideals of universal peace and understanding have won for him the respect and acclaim of all mankind''.[57]

It seems that through his revolutionary outlook Nehru had developed in himself some idea regarding an intimate objective of all revolution.This objective may be described as a state of perfection en-compassing the freedom of India, he developed the thought that the great aim before him was the 'human freedom' which included the freedom of his own people as well as other peoples. For long he thought that countries or continents were but geographical expansion, and that the problems which faced men were really world problems and of humanity.

''And unless we solve them for the whole world, there will continue to be trouble. Such a solution can only mean the ending of poverty and misery everywhere. This may take a long time but we must aim at this and at nothing less than this. Only then can we have real culture and civilization based on equality, where there is no exploitation of any country or class. Such a society will be a creative and a progressive society, adapting itself to changing circumstances, and basing itself on the cooperation of its members. And ultimately it must spread all over the world. [58] In short a Socialist world federation.

Socialist World Federation

After an examination of Nehru's views on history we come to the conclusion that his entire social and political thinking is deeply influenced by his idea of history which seeks discernible design of growth in the synthesis of factors inherent both in the nature of mind and in the nature of things. Even though there is no set pattern or a law of development for all time, he believed, by a proper arrangement and analysis of historical events or facts we can arrive at an understanding of the orderly evolution of law and institutions and thought. The law of synthesis of - 'Scientific Humanism' provides us a correct view of the past and certain flexible principles for objective criticism. By adapting this synthetic approach to the past, it is easy to understand the present and distinguish the real from the apparent and the true from the false. It is with this philosophical apparatus of Scientific Humanism that Nehru measures all national and international events, problems, and developments and explains the working of all institutions and ideologies. This is to say, his conceptions of nationalism, capitalism, democracy and socialism, internationalism and all other national and supernational institutions and ideas are based on his view of history. The rationale for the justification of advent of Socialism was provided by History. In fact he identified family with history.

Thus, there converged in Nehru the materialist dialectic of Marx, the objective methods of science and the idealist philosophy of the Vedanta and evolved a synthesis which made as its upshot a world-view, that is neither Marxist, not purely scentific nor absolutely Vedantic. This integrated historical view was always in search of humanity, which was forward looking, progressive and free. Freedom of all people not only of India, was the goal he had set before himself.

References

1. J. Nehru, *Discovery of India*, Bombay, Asia Publishing House, 1961, p. 20.
2. J. Nehru, *Glimpses of World History*, Bombay, Asia Publishing House, 1962, p. 986.
3. *Jawaharlal Nehru's Speeches*, 1949-53, 383.

4. J. Nehru, *Discovery of India*, pp. 57-59.
5. Address to the UNESCO Symposium, Dec. 20, 1951,*Jawaharlal Nehru's Speeches*, 1949-53, p.-391.
6. J. Nehru, *Discovery of India*, p.-560.
7. *Ibid* p.560.
8. J. Nehru, *Glimpses of World History*, p. 987.
9. Quoted in Melvin Rader, *Marx's Interpretation of History*, New York, Oxford University Press, 1979, p. 11.
10. J. Nehru, *Discovery of India*, p-557.
11. "How amazing is the spirit of man...plaything of nature's mighty forces, less than a speck of dust in this vast universe, he has hurled defiance at the elemental powers, and with his mind, cradle of revolution, sought to master them".
J. Nehru, *Discovery of India*, p-33.
12. *Ibid* p.-33.
13. *Ibid* p-15.
14. J. Nehru, *Glimpses of World History* p 563.
15. J. Nehru, *An Autobiography*, pp. 362-63.
16. J. Nehru, *Glimpses of World History*, p.-60.
17. *Ibid* p.-60.
18. Marx & Engels, *A Manifesto of the Communist Party*, Moscow, Progress Publishers, 1952 p.-41.
19. Dorothy Norman, *Jawaharlal Nehru : The First Sixty Years*, vol I, p. 307.
20. *Ibid.*, p. 304.
21. J. Nehru, *Glimpses of World History*, pp-6-7.
22. *Ibid.*, p-60.
23. J. Nehru, *Discovery of India*, P-29-30.
24. *Ibid* P-82.
25. Rostislav Ulyanovysky, *National Liberation : Essays on Therory and Practice*, Moscow, Progeess Publishers, 1978, p. 242.
26. J. Nehru, *An Autobiography*, p.-598.
27. J. Nehru, *India Today and Tomorrow*, p 28.
28. J. Nehru, *Towards a Socialist Order*, p 4.
29. J. Nehru, *Discovery of India*, p-29.
30. S.Gopal, *Selected Works of Jawaharlal Nehru*, Vol. 7, pp. 180-81.
31. *Ibid.*, p. 271.
32. Dorothy Norman, *Jawaharlal Nehru : The First Sixty Years*, Vol., 1, p. 427.
33. S. Gopal, *Selected Works*, Vol.,7, p. 173.
34. *Ibid* p-173.
35. Chakraborty, *Jawaharlal Nehru's Writings*, Calcutta, Minerva Associates, 1981 p-134.
36. J. Nehru, *The Unity of India*, pp 294-5
37. S. Gopal, *Selected Works*, Vol.7, p 101.
38. J. Nehru, *The Unity of India*, pp. 294-5.
39. *Ibid* p-295.
40. *Ibid* pp. 148-49.

41. S. Gopal, *Jawaharlal Nehru : A Biography,* Vol., 1, p-178.
42. J. Nehru, "The Future of Colonies", written in a railway train, Lucknow to Moradabad, Feb. 8, 1946, *JN. Papers,* S. No. 18, NMML.
43. J, Nehru, "Whither India" in Dorothy Norman, *Nehru: The First Sixty Years,* vol. 1, p. 378.
44. "Whither India," *Selected Works,* vol.6, p.4.
45. *Ibid.* pp-22-33.
46. J. Nehru, *Independence and After,* Delhi, Publication Division, 1949, P.300.
47. J. Nehru, *An Autobiography,* p.73.
48. K.J. Narsimha Chari, *The Quintessence of Nehru,* London, George Allen . Unwin, 1961 P.16.
49. From Speech, ICWA, New Delhi, March 22, 1949, Dorothy Norman, *Jawaharlal Nehru : The First Sixty Years,* Vol. 11, p.470.
50. T. K. Ravindran. *Nehru's Idea of History,* p-35.
51. J. Nehru, *Glimpses of World History,* p-441.
52. *Ibid* p.982.
53. *Ibid.,* p.982.
54. J. Nehru, "The Future of Colonies", Feb. 8, 1946, *J. N. Papers,* S.No. - 18 (NMML).
55. Transcript of the Press Conference held by the Prime Minister at Vigyan Bhawan, New Delhi, Oct. 21, 1960, *P. M's. Secretariat,* Vol. 16 (P.I.B.)
56. *Ibid,.*
57. K. J. Narsimha Chari, *The Quintessence of Nehru,* p-24.
58. J. Nehru, *Glimpses of World History,* Vol. 1, 1932 Nehru to Indira, June 12, 1931, p-284.

CHAPTER 3

NEHRU'S VIEWS ON CLASS-STRUGGLE

The concept of class-struggle is the most effective instrument employed by all scientific Socialists to prophesy the ultimate triumph of Socialism. The doctrine of the class-struggle lies at the core of Marx's elaboration of class-doctrine. He never denied that some bourgeois historians and social philosophers before had perceived history as the story of class antagonisms, nor did he give socialist theory sole credit for having discovered the class-struggle. He saw in his own scholarly contribution to be that of having shown "that the class struggle necessarily leads to the 'dictatorship of the proletariat' and that this dictatorship itself only constitutes the transition to the abolition of all classes and to classless society."[1]

The nature of class-conflict naturally depends on the nature of society in question. Even in the present day world it is not the same in the semi-colonial, semi-feudal societies such as those which still exist in some parts of Africa and Asia, as in industrially developed societies of Western Europe or North America. Nevertheless, the conflict of class interests exists in all class-ridden societies, even in the most affluent and developed societies. It is with this pragmatic view that the concept of class struggle should be examined.

In the study of underdeveloped countries class analysis is still being successfully employed, although rarely using a two-class pattern. Uniform application of the class concept can no longer be found even in the empirical sociology of Marxist countries. Whenever the class concept is still used, it deviates in most cases from the dichotomic Marxist conception and its use must be examined individually in the case of every branch of sociology, every sociological school, indeed every individual author, before statements about class phenomenon can be generalized.

The beginning of the19th century witnessed phenomenal changes in world social, economic and political developments and intellectual endeavours. Past concepts were breaking down to give birth to new ideas, systems and ideology. Imperialism was at its peak, but at the same time on the verge of collapse, thereby, indicating dawn of a new civilization. These new situations demanded a fresh reorganisation of forces and ideas. The question was not of class-war or class-conflict but imperialism confronted with a similar and worst kind of imperialism of the Nazis and the Fascists. At this time India was in the thick of its National Liberation Movement and Jawaharlal Nehru was one of the most revolutionary leaders involved intensely in the fight against the dual imperialism of the British as well as Germany and Italy.

Nehru was quick to grasp the changing conditions and the turn that the historical forces was taking. With his keen intellect and capacity for sharp analysis, he built his own ideas regarding the world-view, imperialism, the class-struggle and the future. Therefore, it is instructive to examine the views of class-struggle of Nehru, second only to Gandhi, who led the national movement to independence and quite naturally became the leader of the largest Democracy. A study of his views on class-struggle assumes all the more importance because his analysis of class-struggle is indigenous and keeping in view the perspective of India. This itself imparts to his socialism a different content and meaning.

Nehru admits that as early as 1920 his political outlook was entirely bourgeois, "I know, of course that there was terrible poverty and misery, and I felt that the first aim of a politically free India must be to tackle this problem of poverty. But political freedom with the inevitable dominance of the middle class seemed to me the obvious step".[2] Uptil then he was merely a keen observer of happenings and had not given much thought to the phenomenon of poverty and exploitation which was institutionalised by the British. He was not conscious enough to look for the reasons underlying the economic backwardness of his country. At this stage he was too wrapped up with Gandhi and his Civil-Disobedience to give thought to other matters. Just then, accidentally he came in contact with the Indian peasantry. He was at once aware of the poverty, misery and humiliation to which the millions in India were subjected "I was filled with shame and sorrow, shame at my own easy going and comfortable life and our petty politics of the city which ignore this vast multitude of semi-naked sons and daughters of India, sorrow at the degradation and overwhelming poverty in India. A new picture of India seemed to rise before me, naked, starving, crushed and utterly miserable ... This process was an old one and the progressive pauperisation of the peasantry had been going on for a long time. What happened to bring matters to a head and rouse the countryside?Economic condition of course."[3] The state of the peasantry made him aware of the economic side of imperialism and aroused his interest in socialism as the alternative to British capitalism and imperialism.

Influence of Marx

In his formative years the influence of Marx was quite potent. The materialistic interpretation of history stirred his intellect and for the first time he could get an insight into the forces of history. Marx's interpretation of history was different from what was prevalent till then. It was scientific, logical and rational and explained history in a much more realistic way, holding material forces as the catalyst of history rather than vague utopian ideas. Utopian socialism criticised capitalist society, condemned it, cursed it, dreamt of its abolition and the establishment of a better system and attempted to convince the rich of the immorality of exploitation. But utopian socialism could find no solution, was unable to explain the essence of the slavery of hired labour under capitalism or discover the laws of its development, could not identify that social force which was capable of being the creator of a new society. This was achieved by scientific socialism. Appreciating the scientific socialism of Marx, wrote Nehru, "the theory and philosophy of Marxism lightened up many a dark corner of my mind. History came to have a new meaning for me. The Marxist interpretation threw a flood light on it, and it became an unfolding drama with some order and purpose.The great world crisis and slump seemed to justify the Marxist analysis.While other theories were groping in the dark, Marxism alone explained it more or less satisfactorily and offered a real solution".[4]

The words "new ideology"-- found so often in his letters, essays and speeches of the period--stood in reality for Marxism, for he explicitly accepted the general validity of Marxism as "the scientific interpretation of history and politics and economics" and as representing "scientific socialism" in contrast to "a vague and idealistic socialism."[5] On May 5, 1936, he told the Indian Progressive Group of Bombay that "scientific socialism, or Marxism, was the only remedy for the ills of the world. On May 17, he told a meeting of Congress Socialists that history as well as the contemporary state of affairs "could not be explained except by socialism and Marxism." Nehru accepted the entire Marxist analysis of the economic crisis of monopoly capitalism and of imperialism and the need for its overthrow. The crisis of capitalism, he wrote in 1933, was essentially "due to the ill distribution of the world's wealth to its concentration in a few hands". The heart of the matter was that the capitalist system was no longer suited to the present methods of production." The answer, therefore, lay in "a new system in keeping with the new technique"; in other words, "the way of socialism".[6]

Existence of Class-Struggle

Nehru recognised the existence in capitalist societies not only of the conflict of class-interest but also of class-consciousness as a determining factor in attitudes of different classes. Further evidence even more categorical was provided in his address to the All India Trade Union Congress 30th November, 1928, when he said, "we are often accused of preaching class war and of widening the distance between the classes. The distance is wide enough, thanks to capitalism and nothing can beat the record of capitalism in that respect... it is not that socialist or the communist who separates the classes and preaches discontent but the capitalist and imperialist who by his policy and methods has reduced the great majority of mankind into wage slaves who are worse even in many ways than the slaves of old. The class war is none of our creation. It is the creation of capitalism and as long as capitalism endures it will endure . . . The class war has existed and exists today. By our trying ostrich like to ignore it, we do not get rid of it. Only by removing the causes are we likely to bring peace.''[7]

His stay in Europe had confirmed him in the resolve that India should look for no favours from Britain. Relatively and potentially Indian nationalism was not weak, while England was daily losing ground despite her apparent strength. His first hand contact with British Labour leaders had filled him with particular contempt for them. Nehru, therefore, was eager for wholehearted combat, with no quarter sought or given. His new radical ideas affirmed rather than diverted his enthusiasm for political action. Even the arrest of capitalist exploitation and a heightening of India's poverty required the termination of imperialist rule.

It was for this purpose that he organized the Independence for India League, as in the first instance a pressure group within the Congress. For the League was intended to keep alive not only the objective of political independence but also the concomitant ideals of republicanism and socialism. Independence, to Nehru, was not purely a political issue. Severance of British connection implied also an attack on the vested interests supported by the British in India; indeed the basis of the struggle was economic. The future republican government of India would be based not on the exploitation of the masses but on social equality.[8] The object of the Independence of India League was therefore, both to achieve independence to reconstruct Indian society by changing its capitalist and feudal basis, ''It means that the League aims at the socialist democratic state in which every person has the fullest opportunity of development and the state control of the means of production and distribution''.[9] The League should be both an active element within the parent party and a general catalyst in the nation. The Congress might lead the political campaign and take the lead in drafting the constitution, but economic and social changes could be effected only by the sanction provided by the exploited classes. For this a revolutionary fervour had to be generated in the country and the people organized on a large scale. But this required an economic programme. Nehru went ahead and formulated a precise programme.

Though he had a grand design of socialism, he wanted a modest beginning. In the U.P., in particular, there seemed to be no alternative to the abolition of landlordism, but this could be done with the payment of partial compensation and replaced by small holdings owned by peasant proprietors with no right of alienation. There would be no nationalisation but socialisation of land, agricultural debt would be written off. The state would gradually acquire key industries, ensure a minimum living wage and impose sharply graduated direct taxes.

Nehru was aware that such a programme would inevitably at some stage or other, raise issues of the class-struggle and bring about clash of interest between landlords and tenants but this could not be shirked. It was no wisdom to refuse to recognise on face conflict where it existed. Such conflicts would have to be fought and overcome. Pushed to it, Nehru was willing to concede both, that violence was not objectionable in itself and that the final goal, the resolution of the struggle, might well be communism. If India were convinced that she could become free through violence, she would undoubtedly have the right to indulge in it as other countries had done. He stood for intensive non-violent, non-cooperation only because in India's condition mass violence was impracticable, while individual acts of terrorism was a tactic of defeat. [10]

Speaking from the Presidential rostrum of the Congress he declared, "I am a socialist and a republican and I am no believer in kings and princes, or in the order which produces the modern kings of industry, who have greater powers over the lives and fortunes of men than even the kings of old, whose methods are as predatory as those of the old feudal aristocracy".

Referring to the peasantry and labour, Nehru repudiated the theory of trusteeship though it was held by no less a person than Mahatma Gandhi. In the course of his project of ideologically preparing the youth, Nehru repeatedly rejected and of criticised Gandhi's antipathy to class struggle and his notion of trusteeship.Certainly he never attacked him by name or slandered him as a reactionary, as the communists often did. For Nehru considered Gandhi's views as representative of an ideological current in the anti-imperialist struggle, not meeting individual attack. Nevertheless, he took upon himself the task to build a critique of such ideas and educate the people towards their limitations. Expressing the total disagreement with Gandhi's statement that there was no necessary conflict between capital and labour, he wrote to him of his own conviction that, "under the capitalist system this conflict is inevitable." [11] It was in the control of exactly this "fundamental difference" that Nehru addressed his audience of youth : "We are sometimes told that we must do justice between landlord and tenant and capitalist and worker", but "justice" here only meant "the maintenance of status quo. It is this kind of justice the League of Nations gives when it maintains the present status-quo with the imperialist powers dominating and exploiting half the earth. When the status-quo itself is rank injustice those who desire to maintain it must be considered as upholders of that injustice". [12] Pointing out the limitations of Gandhi's advocating "eloquently" the claims of the poor in India without, "saying a word against the semi-feudal Zamindari system which prevails in a great part of India or against the capitalist exploitation of both the workers and the consumers", Nehru set out to elaborate on these themes publically as "fundamental causes of Indian poverty".[13]

At another place he was more forthright when he said, "Paternalism in industry or in land is but a form of capitalism, with all its strings and its utter incapacity to root out the evil, the new theory of trusteeship is equally barren. The sole trusteeship that can be fair is the trusteeship of the nation and not of one individual or group". He continued, "We have to decide for whose benefit industry must be run and the land produce food. Today the abundance that the land produces is not for the peasant or the labourer who works on it; and the industry's chief function is supposed to be to produce millionaires". He ended by urging his countrymen to "forge sanctions to enforce the nations will".[14]

The Congress was, Nehru argued, an organisation of the tenants and workers, and they could not leave the peasants alone when they needed their help. The peasants struggle would be economic and not political in nature. Gandhiji accepted this position and made no serious attempt to restrain Nehru, though he did not accept the class implication of the struggle. On the other hand, the Government were apprehensive of the class implication of the movement, the more so because Nehru had been freely expressing his socialist views and his opposition to landlordism as an institution. In the report to the India Office on 25 April, 1931, they wrote : "There is no doubt that they (Jawaharlal and his school) have for a long time been bitten with the idea of making a kind of Soviet Organisation of peasants and workers which will first of all abolish the landlord and then possibly Sovietize Government."[15]

Nehru continued to lead the movement till his arrest at the end of December, 1931. Some of his pronouncements were indeed radical, for he talked of war with government and made no secret of his personal views that Zamindari as a system should go. "We should also try to have Swaraj in our country--not of the capitalist but the poor and the peasants", he had declared at the Kisan conference at Allahabad in 1921 that, "If Swaraj means that the British should leave India," he added, "and the capitalists, the rajas and the maharajas should come in their place, the lot of the peasantry cannot be improved. You should therefore, take up to campaign for Swaraj in your hands".[16]

The greatest manifestation of such class-struggle could be found in India where the peasants and workers were systematically crushed on the point of force and violence. This was not due to individual capitalists but the roots lay in the entire system which was based on exploitation of the weaker sections of society. He was convinced of the fact that British India represented a classic example of capitalism--imperialism and that only constant struggle would lead to economic betterment of the masses, "It seems to me that if we are to improve the condition of the masses, to raise them economically and give them freedom", he wrote to Gandhiji on 13 September, 1933. "It is inevitable that vested interests in India will have to give up their special position and many of their privileges". Referring to the need therefore, to divest the vested interests in favour of the masses he added, "We do no want to injure any class or groups and the divesting should be done gently as possible and with every effort to avoid injury. But it is obvious that the divesting is bound to cause loss to the classes or groups which enjoy special privileges at the expense of the masses. It is also obvious that the process of divesting must be as speedy as possible to bring relief to the masses ..."[17]

Appreciating Marx's hypothesis of the class-struggle Nehru further wrote: "Marx did not preach class conflict. He showed that in fact it existed, and had always existed in some form or other. His object in writing *Capital* was to "lay bare the economic laws of motion of modern society ... are inherent in society and they actually increase with better understanding of the conflict of interests".[18]

A clear statement of his views is contained in an essay he wrote, "Whither India?Here he accepted the Marxist analysis of the historical process, but did not give up the liberal value of freedom, "Let us give the benefit of freedom to as many groups and classes as possible; he questioned, "but essentially who do we stand for, and when conflict arises whose side must we take? To say that we shall not answer that question now, it is itself an answer and taking of side, for it means that we stand by the existing order, the status quo". Typical of the Marxian analysis of the thirties, he not only regarded the recurring crisis and depression as a feature of capitalism, but the great depression of the thirties and the rise of Fascism as marking the evening of capitalism. The difference between the East and West, he thought, indicated the different stages of economic growth. As regards nationalism he felt it was, "still the strongest force in Asia ... But the powerful economic forces working for change in the world today have influenced this nationalism to an ever increasing extent and everywhere it is appearing in Socialist garb. Gradually the nationalist struggle for political freedom is becoming a social struggle also for economic freedom".[19]

The essay attracted wide interest and naturally enough considerable criticism too. To the rising socialist group in the Congress, Jayaprakash Narayan, Acharya Narendra Dev and others it marked Nehru out as the leader of socialist thought. The conservatives, on the other hand, shrank back in "moral indignation" at the concept of class-struggle, and pointed to the "coercion" that the establishment of socialist order involved. Nehru was unapologetic. In a rejoinder entitled, "Some criticism considered", he stated, "I have no doubt that coercion or pressure is necessary to bring about political and social changes in India. Indeed our non-violent mass movements of the past thirteen years have been powerful weapons to exercise the pressure". He added, "... It seems to me a fact that cannot be disputed or challenged that non-violent mass-struggle coerces and is meant to coerce the other party. The boycott of goods is an obvious instance". He lashed out, "It is well to realise that those who belong to the favoured and possessing classes alone, and it does not lie in their mouth to talk of conversion. The principal moral argument against the present system and in favour of socialism is that the latter reduces the element of coercion and will, it is hoped ultimately do away with it, altogether".[20]

A categorical statement of his faith appeared in a letter he wrote which appeared in *the Manchester Guardian* on 15th December, 1933, "I am strongly attracted to communism, and I feel that the only reasonable and scientific explanation of history is the communist one. I do not approve of many things that have taken place in Russia, nor am I a communist in the accepted sense of the word. But taking everything together I have been greatly impressed by the Russian experiment".[21]

Referring to socialism Nehru was categorical. "I am convinced that the only key to the solution of the world problems and India's problems lies in socialism, and when I use this word I do so not in a vague humanitarian way but in the scientific, economic sense".[22]

The Lucknow Congress adopted an Agrarian Resolution declaring "that the most important and urgent problem of the country is the appalling poverty, unemployment and indebtedness of the peasantry, fundamentally due to the antiquated and repressive land revenue system and intensified in recent years by the great slump in the prices of agricultural produce". "A final solution to this problem", the Resolution added, "involves the removal of British imperialism and exploitation, a thorough change of the land tenure and revenue systems and recognition by the state of its duty to provide work for the rural and unemployed masses".[23] The Congress also called upon the Provincial Congress Committee in regard to such matters as freedom of organisation of agricultural labourers and peasants, just and fair relief of agricultural indebtedness, emancipation of peasants from feudal and semi-feudal bonds, substantial reduction for rent and revenue demands, and fostering industries for relieving rural unemployment.

An examination of Jawaharlal Nehru's ideas during this period reveal that his tone was basically anti-imperialistic, based on the framework of Marxist ideology of class-struggle. Every speech that he delivered and article he wrote, contained an attack on the vested interests and the exploitation perpetrated by the British. It was due to the impact of Marxism that he associated the political struggle with the national struggle and linked the national movement to the entire working class movements taking place all over the world. The historian Bipan Chandra has aptly described this period in Nehru's life as 'The Indian Summer of his Leftism'.[25] He was direct, uncompromising and scathing in his remark and activities and left no stone unturned to educate his countrymen about scientific socialism. He was the first leader of the national movement to attack the system and propagate socialism in so unhesitating a manner. We may agree with Prof. S. Gopal, his most recent biographer that, Nehru at this time was basically a 'Marxist - anti - imperialist'.

Class alignment--according to Nehru

The first theoretical premise embedded in Nehru's paradigm was the premise of anti-imperialism being the primary contradiction in the colonial countries. Thus it was only through the prism of the anti-imperialist national movement that Nehru viewed and discussed the role of various classes in society.

As for the classes who would be the main basis for the struggle against imperialism, Nehru felt that the peasants and industrial workers have a great deal to gain and very little to lose if the alien rule is abolished. "These are are the people who must form the armies or forces to fight the battle of India's freedom primarily the struggle will rest on them and it is bound to rest on them. The intellectuals must join along with the tenants and the individual workers. Other classes may possibly extend support to them--but without the industrial and agricultural workers it is inconceivable that India can achieve her true freedom. So you come back to the fundamental basis of socialism".[26]

Nehru held that the working class nationally as well as internationally had necessarily to fight imperialism and help the nationalist movements of oppressed countries, the role of the national working class was its logical extension. The working class in the oppressed countries was, therefore, duty bound to fight this most essential and immediate battle. Nevertheless, Nehru fully grasped the fact that the colonial working classes' conditions of life by no means automatically instilled nationalism into this section of society. "Ground down by poverty and by forces which seem to be unconquerable, the fear born that possesses (them) and makes it difficult to organise (them) with the daily struggle for wages and bread is ever before us, how can we think of larger issues ?"[27] He even saw the possibility of the national movement successfully overthrowing imperialism without the full and effective participation of the working class becoming a reality not to speak of working class leading the movement, as the communists constantly asserted. "It is possible", he said "that the nationalist movement in a country under foreign domination may succeed in gaining independence without the support of labour. That may happen, as it has happened in the past, but it will result in creating a new capitalist state, normally independent, but with little freedom for the worker. That will not bring peace any nearer or solve any of our problems".[28]

These were prophetic words in sharp contrast to the Indian communists who asserted that the working class would because of its class nature, be at the head of the national movement. For Nehru the involvement of working class in the national movement was the conscious act of the revolutionary and ideas of nationalism had to be injected into the working class. This did not mean that no worker was capable of grasping this link between nationalism and his own trade union struggle, it simply meant that the mass of backward workers "ground down by poverty" would find it very difficult in themselves to grasp this basic link.

The role of the middle class in carrying national consciousness to the workers and peasants had to be emphasised; "It is only from the middle class intellectuals that revolutionary leadership comes".[29] However, it had to be a two way process - the working class would become the backbone of the movement only to the extent that "The masses realise what Swaraj means for them. Therefore, it is essential that we must clearly lay down an economic programme, must have an ultimate ideal in view and must also provide for the immediate steps to be taken to bring them relief''.[30] The inevitable middle class leadership must look more and more towards the working and peasant masses and draw sustenance from them. Of course, only the bravest and stoutest comrades could act as a link with the mass of working people, as he was suspicious of most of their class-character the middle class act, ''as every class conscious of its interests acts... and seldom paid heed to the needs of the masses. Whenever vital questions affecting the masses have arisen they have been shelved, they have been asked to stand over till Swaraj has been attained''.[31] This could not be the way of the future. ''We must, therefore, cultivate a revolutionary outlook, one that devises a radical and far reaching change ...''[32] Nehru's intense concentration on the youth movement and middle class intelligentsia during the years 1927-1933 was precisely this attempt to cultivate a revolutionary outlook. For ''What shall it profit the masses of this country - the peasantry, the landless labourers, the workers, the shopkeepers, the artisans- if everyone of the offices held by Englishmen in India is held by Indians ?''[33]

The social content of the national movement, therefore, had to be filled in by the working masses. ''The peasants and the industrial workers'' were undoubtedly, the people who must form the armies or forces to fight the battle of India's freedom''.[34] And, ''the intellectual workers'',[35] ''the unemployed intellectual class'' was in fact a natural ally of the workers and peasants for in common with them they had little to lose and a great deal to gain from the overthrow of alien rule.[36]

Correspondingly, the struggle had to transcend narrow nationalism and gradually transform itself into anti-capitalism. Within this framework he consistently brought before them the need to link up with the peasantry and working class, initiating an ideological process in which social and economic awareness would be created. A system which produced poverty and misery had to be changed. The Public Safety Bill, the Trades Disputes Act, and the Meerut Conspiracy Case were constantly brought before the youth as examples of how the fate of the imperialist government was closely linked to capitalist exploitation.[37] ''The real danger to government comes from the peasantry and the workers and the industrial workers being more capable of organised action must inevitably take the lead in mass action ... therefore the attempts of the government to crush their organisation and prevent organised action. Whenever there is industrial trouble the whole strength of the big employer, and in addition to having to put up with starvation wages and miserable housing conditions, the workers have to face bullets of the government soldiers and police." He challenged the youth, "Are you going to take neutral attitude in the matter and allow the workers to be crushed".[38]

In the context of what kind of nation they were to build, time and again Nehru emphasised that youth must appreciate that anti-imperialism as mere hatred of foreign rule was not a sufficient end. The youth must learn that imperialism was a world system and its roots lay in the development of capitalism. And this brought one to an analysis of the role of capitalists.

"The Indian capitalists are bound hand and foot with British capitalists and Indian industries are undoubtedly run with 90 per cent of British capital and 10 per cent of Indian capital".[39] The Imperial Bank and the Exchange banks could ruin any industry if they wanted to which made it "extremely difficult" for the Indian capitalists to resist that power. They dared not offend the British capitalists. However, Nehru did not rule out the possibility of capitalists co-operating with the anti-imperialist movement, but it depended on how strong the mass movement would become.[40]

Nehru further attacked the Princes and the Zamindars, considering them to be the off-shoots of capitalism.This was amply clear when one analysed the role of various social classes in the anti-imperialist movement. The Princes and Zamindars were the embodiments of feudalism in India. Despite individual sincerity on the part of some of them, "as a class ... their interest is solely centered round the British rule in India".[41] As an institution, government feudalism depended on the British for its existence. It was based on the exploitation of the toiling peasant masses. "Without giving a death blow to feudalism one could not proceed even a step in the direction of progress".[42]

The abolition of feudalism had, therefore, to occupy a prominent place in the new economic and social programme that was necessary to change the system.[43] To speak of fundamental rights guaranteeing a living wage was meaningless in the given economic and social structure. The benefits, in such circumstances, would accrue only to the landlords and capitalists. Only socialism offered a possible solution. It followed that there could be no big Zamindars and big factories had to be owned by the state.[44]

Dynamics of Class-struggle

It is remarkable to note that though Nehru had admiration for Marxism as an intellectual concept he did not repose his full faith in its basic tenets but presented his own theory of the class-struggle. He recognised the existence of class-struggle, but particularly in the later years, proceeded from the thesis that the class contradictions could be solved through class-cooperation, by trying to win over people in a cooperative way, rather than threatening them, or through the concept of war. Recognising the presence and inevitability of class-struggle Nehru wrote that the dominant and imperialist nations and dominant classes do not leave their privileged positions by considerations of justice, and least of all in response to a beggar's bowl. They hold on to what they have and exiploit their subject nations or classes for their own selfish ends. These subject nations or classes, not unnaturally, object to this process and want a dignified place in the world for themselves. There is conflict and in the past this conflict has always been a bloody one.[45] History provides evidences that if a country or class wants to attain freedom, it must resist the dominant power and seek to dispossess it. In order to do this effectively and successfully it must develop the strength and the organisation for it. In the past this resistance has been of the violent and armed variety and it has been generally recognised as justified. At the same time he hastened to warn his countrymen and inform the world in general that India would never go the violent way, "In India we are under alien imperialist rule and we seek to be independent. We must therefore, develop the strength and organisation so that the will of the Indian people shall prevail as against foreign authority. But we had deliberately set our forces against armed revolt for a number of reasons, and tried to develop a peaceful technique to struggle. The whole basis of our struggle is thus a peaceful one, but nevertheless, it is a dynamic struggle which relies on the organised struggle of the masses... They are the peaceful equivalent of armed rebellion. In any country desiring to be free from foreign rule the choice lies between these two methods. We have chosen the peaceful and more civilised course while all the highly cultured nations of Europe arm to teeth and prepare to murder each other."[46]

His tone regarding the solution of class-struggle had considerably changed as early as 1937. It is from this period that Nehru had started taking a milder stance over the class-struggle and spoke more in favour of cooperation and persuasion than violence and coercion. After the second world war, Nehru thought that it was a changed world. Like the Revisionists of Germany, France and Britain, he viewed that in a democratic framework, Marx's violent solution had become redundant. He felt that inner contradictions of capitalism, the accumulation on the one hand, and poverty on the other, had been significantly resolved by the scientific and technological revolution in industry and the economy. Due to the extension of franchise, growth of working class movements, extension of the power of the Trade Union and comprehensive social security measures, prosperity has come within the reach of all. Instead of the growing concentration of wealth and economic power there has been considerable diffusion of the same through spread of education and technical knowledge, etc. Besides the problem posed by the advent of nuclear weapons had made the concept of class-struggle an out-moded philosophy. Thus he said, "Hence from any point of view the concept of class-struggle or wars has been, outdated". [47]

Although Nehru subscribed to the concept of class-struggle, he did not adhere to it in the Marxian sense of armed and violent struggle. Conflict of interest is there but it shall be resolved peacefully. The Gandhian technique of recourse to the method of conversion makes the dictatorship of the proletariat superfluous. Here Nehru clearly differs from Marx, for the dictatorship of the proletariat is one of the basic tenet of Marxian philosophy.

Since the Marxian theory contemplates mechanically welding the human materials into a socialist society, instead of achieving the same by appealing to their ethical and aesthetic sense and enlisting their allegiance to the system by their voluntary adherence to it, it is but natural to expect that force will be necessary to strengthen the socialist forces and forge a socialist society. Hence dictatorship of the proletariat becomes inevitable. But if the class conflict and clash of interests could be resolved by peaceful methods of persuasion, the possibility of opposition to such a step should be ruled out. That will not necessitate armed resistance from the side of dispossessed class and in turn dictatorship to suppress the rise of such reactionary elements. The very technique of change of heart shall be at the root of automatic consolidation of hearts and strengthen the forces of socialism. Hence, violence in any form shall be simply superfluous and thus the dictatorship of the proletariat.[48] Jawaharlal Nehru is very close to the Revisionist on this score.

The Bernsteinians accepted, and accept, Marxism minus its direct revolutionary content. They do not regard the parliamentary struggle as merely one of the weapons particularly suitable for definite historical period, but as the main and almost the sole form of struggle, making 'force', 'seizure', 'dictatorship' unnecessary''.[49]

Again, while Nehru accepted the Marxist analysis of the past, he was not convinced by the Marxist diagnosis of the future. Because of his commitment to civil liberties, he rejected the concept of dictatorship of the proletariat. Marx had written that in the early days of industrialisation in Western Europe, revolutionary violence, which was in the tradition of Europe, appeared to offer the only way to change. But the world and capitalism had changed, and Marxism would have to be modified to suit new conditions.

Nehru was not being unrealistic in this. A development for example, such as Eurocommunism, with its acceptance of political pluralism and its rejection of revolutionary dictatorship, is on parallel lines to Nehru's efforts. Whether such an adaptation can still be regarded as Marxism or has changed it beyond recognition is arguable for Marx thought that a drastic, forcible reorganisation of society was necessary for socialist transformations. The working class or its leader, the communist party, could not simply take hold of the readymade state machinery and wield it for its own advantage. Between capitalist and communist societies there, had, according to

Marx, to be a period of revolutionary shift: there could not be a peaceful transition, yet it should be added that Marx himself provided no complete political theory or programme: all his writings were in response to specific episodes and under pressure to immediate events and he did not rule out the occasional transformation by peaceful methods.[50]

Moreover, Nehru believed that if in some countries dictatorship of the proletariat had been adopted with success it did not imply that India would blindly follow them. He was opposed to the idea of any theory being practised as dogma rather every country would have to adopt an ideology according to its native genius. He also opposed the grafting of any ideology, if only for the sake of imitation judged on the basis of success of others. Conversing with Tibor Mende he said, "Now so far as India is concerned and I speak for India chiefly, though to some extent that might apply also to some other Asian countries. We must be judged by our own background, our background in India has been of struggling for political freedom, for economic freedom, for self-realization and for developing ourselves according to our ways of thinking".[51]

Thus, from this point of view also Nehru felt dictatorship of the proletariat was wholly unsuited to India. The large scale violence and coercion which such a step would entail, was wholly anachronistic. If a problem could be solved in a peaceful way why go breaking heads ? Nehru asked. He reiterated that socialism was not just breaking of heads and depriving forcefully people of their pockets, rather it was something else and much more, "It is perfectly true, that real socialism involves a profound transformation of the deeper habits of opinion and of character and this inevitably takes time. Under favourable circumstances and with goodwill of a large number of people concerned, these changes may be brought about within a generation".[52]

Nehru's perception of the Indian society, the forces--economic, social and political working behind it, its traditions, culture and legacy of a great civilization led him to view the class-struggle and in turn the necessity of a dictatorship of the proletariat in a different perspective. He did not mean to apply a readymade solution of the class-conflict but believed in accommodating a theory or hypothesis with the particular problems of the country.

The traditional Marxist analysis was based mainly on the industrial proletariat and it would be the proletariat who would establish a dictatorship in the period of transition to socialism. But Nehru was aware that this theory could not be applied to India because, there was an absence of industrial proletariat. Industry in India under the British rule was still in its infancy and only a handful of the industrial workers clustered mainly in metropolitan cities like Bombay and Calcutta could not be expected to overthrow the capitalist rule and establish a dictatorship. Nehru took into cognizance that the rest of India was predominantly agricultural and the Indian problem could not be disposed or treated in terms of industrial workers.

As early as 1936, the socialist leader, Jayaprakash Narayan posed a question, must Pandit Nehru, supposing he became the Premier or President of socialist India line up the Taluqdars of the U.P. and have them blown up to bits ? Must he seize the treasures of the Rajas and Maharajas and distribute them to the people--equally of course ? Must he turn over the Tata Iron Works, for instance, to the workers employed there, and leave them to make good or bad a business of it as they please? Must he split up all the land in the country, divide the total acreage over a little plot to each individual? Socialism was something more sensible, more scientific more civilized than all that. What then, must Pandit Nehru do ?

When Jawaharlal Nehru really became the Prime Minister of India eleven years later, and set about laying the foundation of a socialist state, he certainly did not blow up the taluqdars with cannons, yet they disappeared for ever, he did not wage war against the Rajas and Maharajas, yet the entire princely clans vanished from history, he did not turn over the Tata Iron Works to the workers to make good or bad business of it but yet inaugurated bigger iron works to be managed by the State and he did not divide the total land by the total population, but yet attempted to solve the problem of land for the benefit of the tiller ... And all this he tried to achieve in his own way, the method was democratic and socialist.

Speaking to Tibor Mende, for an interview Nehru said:

"That the problem of the Indian princes. Imagine over five hundred states in India which were more or less autonomous and were even supposed to be independent. Everybody thought that they would give us a great deal of trouble. But we solved that problem in a matter of months, even weeks - and peacefully. Why? And how? Every important aspect was our peaceful and cooperative approach to the Indian Princes. We did not approach them with military threats and all that. We could have done it. But instead, a mixture of our peaceful and friendly approach together with the pressure of circumstances, led to a solution of this tremendously difficult problem''.[53]

Though Nehru's policy on land could not be spectacular success and it left much to be desired, nevertheless his government did manage to make a breakthrough, and in an agricultural country like India where possession of land has been the dominating motivation since millennia, Nehru's mild but unhesitating step has taken the country a step forward, with the result that we have industrialization and agriculture existing side by side.

Nehru in this regard said :

''Take again our approach to the land problem . . . I confess that I am not quite satisfied with the rate of progress we have made. Nevertheless, we have made very great progress in abolishing the big landlord system and we are going ahead in many ways to distribute the land more equitably. It is a difficult problem. Again, that was carried out peacefully, with the payment of compensation. Not full compensation, that was impossible''.[55]

The Necessity and Legality of Coercion of Parliaments

History according to Nehru, shows that there is no instance of a privileged class or group or nation giving up its special privileges or interest willingly, individuals have often done so but not as a group. Always a measure of coercion has been applied, pressure has been created which makes it impossible or unprofitable for vested interests to carry on. And it is then that the enforced conversion takes place. The method of this enforcement may be brutal or civilized, to Nehru the latter was the real method.[56]

He had no doubt from the beginning that coercion or pressure was necessary to bring about political and social change in India.

Indeed according to him, the non-violent mass movements of the struggle were peaceful weapons to exercise this pressure. "It is perfectly true", he said, "that this method of coercion is the most civilized and moral method and it avoids as far as possible the unpleasant reactions and consequences of violence. I think that it does offer a moral equivalent for violent warfare and, if civilization does not collapse it will gradually adopt this peaceful method of settling its disputes".[57]

Long before he came to power, Nehru had laid faith in the legality of the coercive powers of a democratic state. Since the very idea of property was changing in the modern world, state coercion became apparent in dealing with it. At one time slaves were regarded as property, and so were women and children. Nehru wrote in 1934-35, "As the conception of property changes the state interferes more and more, public opinion demands, and the law cnforces a limitation of the anarchic rights of property-owners. All of heavy taxes, which are in the nature of confiscation swallow up individual property rights for the public good. The public good becomes the basis of public policy and man may not act contrary to this public good even to protect his property rights".[58]

Contrclled production and distribution of wealth for the public good was the aim of a socialist state. If individuals or institutions stood in the way of such change they would have to be removed. In brief, it was clear to Nehru that "the good of a nation or of mankind must not be held up because some people who profit by the existing order object to the change". It appeared quite moral to him that the state could pass laws of a coercive nature in order to take away some rights and privileges from various classes and groups. "Democracy indeed means the coercion of the minority by the majority" he said:

"If law effecting property rights or abolishing them to a large extent is passed by a majority, is that to be objected to because it is coercion? Manifestly not, because the same procedure is followed in the adoption of all democratic laws. Objection, therefore, cannot be taken on the ground of coercion".[59]

Though coercion was considered neutral and moral, yet he did not rule out the possibility of conversion. Rather at times he thought of large scale conversion. From earlier times he wanted to emphasize that world forces were moving in a new direction calling for certain absolute changes. He only wished that every group and class studied the symptoms of the times in order to adjust themselves to changing circumstances without feeling any bitterness towards each other.

Nehru rejected any mechanical view of human nature and looked forward to a socialist society which by removing economic and social obstacles and inhibitions would provide greater scope for individual freedom. But enduring, undistorted socialism could itself only be the result of voluntary and willing effort. It was not inevitable nor could it be imposed. He had no use for the argument that Democracy and Socialism are contrary and that Democratic Socialism is only a facade to cloak a disinclination to alter the status-quo. Socialism could only come to India when the country was ready for it and the great majority of the people demanded it. It was not a question of forcing the pace but of winning over opinion. The task was to educate the people so that they would be in a better position to decide when the issues came up. Then perhaps the socialist utopia would be attained with the support of the vast-majority and the least harm to anyone.

Though this was difficult with the assumption of power Nehru began to work out his theories with some coercive degree of practical success. His coercion became more and more democratic and he did not forget to attempt conversion. In any case violence was ruled out of the question of social reorganization. Before independence he was greatly apprehensive of the role which the Indian princes, who numbered more than six hundred were supposed to play.

A conflict between this class and the people seemed evident. But the problem could be solved in the different way. Nehru in power appeared less aggressive, giving greater attention to peaceful technique. He did not feel inclined to hear what happened in the French Revolution, or the Russian Revolution. To him, those revolutions had their lessons, but the conditions of France and Russia, America or China were peculiarly suitable to themselves. Conditions in India were different. Reflecting on the idea of class-war, he said in December, 1955·

"The communists tell us that the basis of society is class-struggle and therefore, the people must be trained for class-struggle and for destroying the upper classes. I also want a classless society in India and the world. I do not want any privileged classes. I do not want a great deal of inequality among people. The point is how we are to proceed about it. Even recognising the conflict between the classes, the right way of liquidating the conflict is to put an end to it by peaceful methods".[61]

Apparently, Nehru wanted to bring about a human outlook for the adjustment of social relations. He did not want to proceed hastily with regard to social legislation. He did not seek the consent of the landlords before he introduced land legislation. Nevertheless, he prided himself, "we have had legislation in a way so as not to throw the landlords to the wolves, that is we try to fit them into our future structure".[62] In industrial sphere, Nehru aimed at solving the problems of class-conflict both by legislation and a normal change in the outlook of the opposing classes. Since a few private industries had necessarily to continue for some time longer, the relationship between the producer and labour needed orientation. He warned the capitalists:

"You talk of labour troubles and many other problems of yours. I think you are justified in complaining against them more specially against the resort to violence. But how do you deal with it apart from the governmental or the law and order point of view ? You cannot deal with masses of people merely that way. You can only deal with them by the human approach, making them realize that they are not outside the pole, that they are not mere hewers of wood and drawers of water, but that they perform as essential function in his business, that in fact they are partners in a great undertaking".[63]

The employer-worker relationship thought Nehru, could be based on more judicious principles in modern times than hitherto practised. The conflict could be resolved through conciliation. He was in favour of trade unions and of labour's right to strike. With his background knowledge of the labour movement in England and Europe during the 19th and 20th century, he wanted every employer to realize the terrible times labour had endured for generations. That is why according to Nehru, labour prized the right to strike jealously.

But what moved him was the wastage involved in strike and lock-outs. He felt that as labour was required to move away from the tendency to strike, capital was required to give up the 'bullock-cart habit of mind' or even the 19th century or early 20th century habit of mind. "I am not prepared to accept", declared Nehru, "that the only way for industry to flourish is to encourage acquisitiveness. You may call it by the name of incentive of profit. I want you to have the incentive of profit undoubtedly, but within limitations. But to believe the human beings are such that without this acquisitive instinct they cannot function properly is to do mankind a great injustice".[64]

Nehru would point out that all the great things in this world had not been done through acquisitiveness but by the reverse of it. Great inventors, scientists, writers and musicians and engineers prospered and made the world advanced because of other urges. A broader consolidation of social relations and social interests was advocated by Nehru as the means toward social equality.

Nationalism and rural economy were the dominating considerations and European socialists seldom dealt with these. Pre-War conditions in Russia were a much nearer approach to India, but there again the most extraordinary and unusual occurrences took place and it was, "Absurd to expect a repetition of them anywhere else. I do believe that the philosophy of communism helps us to understand and analyse existing conditions in any country ... But it is doing violence and injustice to that philosophy to apply it blindfold and without due regard to facts and conditions."[65]

Moreover, Nehru had great faith in the efficacy of the institution of parliament and parliamentary democracy. He felt that what could not be achieved through force and violence could be got through consensus and persuasion. All his efforts were directed towards a revolution by participation and agreement. For the question before him was : how is it possible to devise a form of government which ensures domestic peace, invites popular participation in conditions of freedom, and also creates conditions for an assault on intolerable poverty. The answer to this was Democratic -Socialism.

As far back in 1956 replying to a question put by Tibor Mende Nehru reiterated emphatically, " My point is that these difficult questions, involving conflicts, class-conflicts can be approached peacefully and in a cooperative spirit. We do not deny class-conflict but we think that class-conflict need not be solved by aggravating class conflicts and by fighting over them first comes democratic public pressure; secondly, a friendly approach to win over people rather than to eliminate or to liquidate them. Now that is a basic difference for let us say, the communist view-point. So I do not see why the option should be placed before us to accept this or that ideology, well we think differently from either of these''.[66]

Attacking the notion of revolution as an act of destruction and positing it as the creation of ''the well-being of the vast majority of the people'', he said : ''And so you see in the history of the world, revolution after revolution, not because any group of person is a lover of bloodshed, anarchy and disorder, but because of the desire for greater security for larger number of persons ... So long as the world is not perfect, it must have the seeds of revolt in it. It must alter between revolution and consideration''.[67] He did not have an iota of doubt that only a youth gripped by a revolutionary spirit and ideas would be capable of building a new nation. It was the function of youth to supply this dynamic element in society; to be standard bearers of revolt against all that was evil and to prevent older people from supervising all social progress and movement by the mere weight or their inertia.[68]

''It is my desire'', he said, ''that the spirit that was infused in the youth of Europe after the great war, and especially by Russian Revolution, should be kindled in every Indian youth. I want youth to bring the older generation to the right path and revolutionise their rigid ideas ...[69] Drawing inspiration from the Russian revolution, however, did not mean expounding the 'Dictatorship of the Proletariat' as an immediate goal. As a prelude, the struggle against imperialism and for a new social order had to be accompanied by a regeneration of cultural forces which would develop legitimacy in everyday life for new and revolutionary ideas and institutions and undermine old notions and beliefs. Nehru was able to see clearly that imperialism and social reaction as a so-called ideology, based itself on the firm foundation of feudal authoritarianism and paternalism. Inculcating the spirit of revolt by youth would pave the way of revolt against both imperialists and socially reactionary 'ideas'.

Nehru's great emphasis on this cultural and ideological transformation differentiated him from the communists who largely concentrated on delineating the economic interests of capital and labour. He saw the movement against imperialism and for social revolution equally as a cultural movement. He did not believe that the magic of economic interest would automatically dissolve the dead-weight of antiquated and reactionary ideologies and customs even within the working class.

We find that Nehru adhered to the theory of "constructive gradualism". This is a theory which characterises his approach to the problem and the manner in which it has to be solved. The question was whether the required changes should be brought about suddenly, sweeping out the entire order by one stroke or gradually with as little strain and destruction as possible ? It is essentially a question of choice between these two methods which is very important for underdeveloped countries and tradition bound societies. In this connection it is interesting to note that Prof. Gunnar Myrdal holds the view that the required changes in under developed countries must be brought about suddenly and with as much rapidity as possible, for according to him, it is easier to carry out a big rapid change than a series of small gradual changes, "just as a plunge into cold water is less painful than slow submersion".[70]

But Nehru, evidently did not subscribe to the above mentioned idea of sudden changes as a feasible and pragmatic method to achieve the ideal. It is quite possible that absence of resistance to changes and their silent acceptance by the people whenever such changes were effected suddenly may be due to their stunned perplexity at the suddenness of the changes, in which case, acceptance of changes by people cannot be considered real. Besides such sudden and sweeping changes may destroy all existing values without replacing them by worthy ones.[71] In fact, Nehru was very much concerned about such meaningless destruction of values taking place due to sudden changes. This concern of Nehru is very much evident in his statement regarding the destruction wrought by the rapid and sudden changes brought by industrial revolution. According to him, though industrial revolution brought benefits to human beings in great many ways, the enormous and rapid changes brought by it destroyed certain basic and essential values without replacing them effectively by new and equally valuable ones, and the modern world was consequently getting out of tune with what he calls, "Life of the Mind".[72] Naturally, therefore, Nehru put forward the theory of "constructive Gradualism" as a correct solution of the problems. It is always better and prudent to move towards the goal slowly and with a certain measure of understanding with and consent of the people than brusquely and by creating stunned perplexity and sense of helplessness in them by the suddenness of such changes and approaches.

A Synthetic Approach

A study of Jawaharlal Nehru will reveal two streaks - Idealism and Pragmatism running parallel in his mind. Different people have interpreted his personality in different ways. Some regard him a staunch idealist, a dreamer who lived in a romantic make--believe world divorced from realities, while others hold that, "His was a principled, rational and emotional rather than an ideological mind".[73] But the fact is that Jawaharlal Nehru was an amalgamation of idealism and pragmatism. Mahatma Gandhi assessed him most aptly.

"A confirmed socialist, he wants for his country what only the country can manage. He is a practical statesman tempering his ideas to suit his surroundings. But for himself, he is an idealist who would ever strive to live up to his ideal..."[74] No assessment of Nehru could be more apt. He was an idealist as for as thought was concerned. He always set for himself high ideals and consequently oriented his actions towards achieving them, never forgetting that he was not alone but had to carry millions along with him. He never lost sight of reality and always saw to it that the goals which he was setting were practicable enough to be followed by others. Therein lies his greatness. It was due to a proper balancing of these qualities that he was able to steer India clear in the halcyon period after the onslaught of partition, war with China and the myriad difficulties which a newly independent nation presented.

In the fifties and sixties, Nehru tried to reconcile his recognition of class - struggle with the Gandhian concept of class harmony, "So while not denying or repudiating class - contradiction, we want to deal with the problem in a peaceful and cooperative way by lessening rather than increasing these conflicts and trying to win over people instead of threatening to fight them or destroy them .. The concept of class-struggle or wars has been outdated as too dangerous''.[75]

Analysing this quote of Nehru, the Soviet political scientist Rostislave Ulyanovysky says that, ''Leaving aside the confusion of class-struggle and the war, and the absolute opposition of non-violence and violence, of peaceful and non-peaceful ways of resolving class contradictions, it would appear that these words reflect not so much the evolution of Nehru's convictions towards the end of his life, but as a pragmatic requirement resulting from a political course largely determined by the conservative forces in the leadership of the multiclass and extremely heterogeneous ruling party--the Indian National Congress, forces that were consolidating their influence at that time, which subsequently led to the division of the Congress.[76]

Though Nehru had a grand design of socialism, he wanted a very modest beginning which would upset no one much. The Congress with its predominantly middle-class composition could not be expected to adopt a revolutionary propaganda but it could be pushed to take its first step in the proper direction. ''What Nehru was seeking was a programme for India not from the purely Socialistic standpoint which would be a fruitless paper exercise, but from a Congress viewpoint with leaning towards socialism''.[77]

In 1928, he suggested that the state should gradually acquire key industries, ensure a minimum living wage and increase taxation, but the abolition of landlordism should be brought about with the payment of partial compensation and replaced by small holding owned by individual peasant proprietors with no right of alienation. There would not be nationalisation but socialisation of land, and the most the state would do was manage model farms. Agriculture debts should be written off but after part payment. In May, 1929, Nehru persuaded the Congress finally to recognise that the poverty and misery of the Indian people was due not only to foreign exploitation but also to the economic structure of society which required, "revolutionary changes''. These revolutionary changes were not spelt out and probably those who passed the resolution thought that with Nehru in charge they did not have to worry much. His mild tactics on behalf of socialist strategy were committing the Congress to positions which no amount of pressure within or outside could have secured. In 1930, he drafted a slightly more radical plan for the U.P. : The replacement of Zamindari by peasant proprietorship and large state farms, a ceiling on rent, wide tenancy rights and sharply graduated taxation. If these raised issues of class-struggle, led to clashes between landlord and tenants or capitalist and labour, they could not be shirked. It was no wisdom to refuse to recognise or face conflict where it existed.[78] The Congress was wise to avoid precipitation of class-conflict, but this could not be wished away, while there was no point in needlessly irritating the landlords and the capitalists and adding to one's enemies in the middle of a great fight where a choice had to be made between two positions, the Congress would without fear back the Kisans, the workers and the landless, for they were the vital groups.[79]

But the facts of the political struggle and the country's socio-economic development constantly affected his views. These facts belied the concept of class-collaborations and the possibility of re-educating Indian land-owners and capitalists, indeed they abounded in social conflict in which privileged classes, the landowners, money-lenders and monopolists, resorted to every means of quelling the protest of the working people, including open violence to protect their own interests.

In the heat of the class-struggle, Nehru's sincere sympathy with the oppressed, his desire to improve their lot and constant subjective devotion to socialist ideals forced him once again to take a sober look at the depth and objective character of the class contradictions in Indian society.

Finally, Nehru recognised the existence in India of privileged groups and classes who opposed any change. He indicated that to protect their own selfish interests these social strata (and Nehru had in mind not only the semi-feudal landowners but above all the monopoly bosses) might go against the country's social progress. He admitted:

"My experience of political power has perhaps made me realize that the ideal is not so easy of achievement. There are delays, difficulties, complexities and all type of obstacles from vested and reactionary interests''.[80]

The Indian National Congresses louding of socialist slogans did not bring him to a superficial idealisation of Indian society. Always a realist, he said that the Indian economic system could be defined as a capitalist economy with considerable state control or a capitalist economy plus a social sector directly run by the state. But in essence it was a capitalist economy.

Nehru saw that the country's socialist course, its progress and democracy, was threatened not only by the traditional forces of feudal landowners and religious disparities, but also by the growing monopolies. Shortly before his death, in the autumn of 1964, he declared, ''Monopoly has grown during the last few years, we have drifted away from the goal of socialism''.[81]

A brief account of the circumstances leading to these events, particularly to the partition of the country is important for it had deep impact on his views on class-struggle. The communal passion which the partition aroused and the holocaust that preceded and followed partition was a direct blow not only to him personally, but to his ideals which accorded a high priority to the economic powers of history, and only subsidiary positions to such other motivation as religious conflicts and casteism, if not conservatism in his mental make up, and it made him less eager to carry out his economic programme without regard to other factors. In particular the communal conflict and all that it involved made him wary of class-conflict and of everything that had an element of destruction rather than construction in view. Speaking frankly, he indeed stated in Parliament on 7th April, 1948, during the debate on the Industrial Policy Resolution of 1948, ''May be I have been affected by recent events, but more and more I have felt that it was wrong to destroy something that is producing or doing good. It takes a long time to build and it does not take very long to destroy''.[82]

Thus, it was due to these considerations that Nehru did not opt for the use of force and coercion for implementation of economic programmes and certainly not because he was too soft to adopt a hard course as has been alleged by many of his critics. It is a fact that he did not engineer a revolution like Mao or Lenin on lines of class-struggle, this cannot be attributed to lack of courage on his part to launch revolutions. Nehru rather felt that such bloody revolutions were wholly anachronistic for India. Freedom as well as reconstruction could be achieved through peaceful ways, in a gradual manner.

Nehru believed that in today's world and in India in particular, any attempt to start with what might be called a clean slate in that sweeping away of all that we had, would certainly not bring progress any nearer, but might delay it tremendously. Moreover, far from bringing economic progress, it might put the country so far back politically that the economic aspect itself might be lost sight of. "Therefore, the alternative to having a clean slate is to try to rub out here and there in order to write on it again, gradually to replace the writing on the whole slate - not too gradually, I hope, yet not with a great measure of destruction and strain".[83]

Conclusion

A piecemeal constructive approach was the right approach, according to Nehru, to industrial and economic policy. An absolute and forceful eradication of the acquisitive nature of a traditional society under a democratic set-up, could not be obtained. By 1955, he had tempered his views, sufficiently on the ideas of class-struggle. At this time admitted that, it was not denial or non-recognition of conflicting interests, but merely that he did not want to encourage and intensify these conflicts. The best method of solving them would be through a peaceful and friendly approach. Nehru asserted that not only the socialist state could be attained through the democratic process, but that this was the only way to build it on firm foundation. Democratic functioning necessitated a more complicated procedure and took a longer time but justified itself, in that it gave due consideration to the individual.

We come to the conclusion that Nehru's views on class-struggle are very different from the dogmatic definition of class-conflict of the communists. He viewed it purely in the Indian context keeping in view the objective conditions pertaining to India. In this sense his courage to deviate from the traditional definition and impart to it an indigenous meaning is a remarkable contribution of Nehru to Socialist movement and thinking in India.

References

1. C. D. Kering, *Marxism, Communism and Western Society A Comparative Encyclopaedia,* Vol. II, New York, Harper and Harper, 1972, p.12.
2. J. Nehru, *An Autobiography*, p-49.
3. *Ibid.*, pp. 52-53.
4. *Ibid.*, pp.362-63.
5. J. Nehru *Glimpses of World History*, II, p.853.
6. J. Nehru, *Recent Essays and Writings*, pp.10-16.
7. *Selected Works*, vol.4, p.80.
8. Presidential address at the first session of the Republican Congress, *The Hindu*, 29 December, 1927.
9. Address to Punjab Provincial Conference, 11 April, in S. Gopal, *Jawaharlal Nehru: A Biography*, vol.1, p.-114-15.
10. *Ibid.*
11. *Ibid.*, vol. 3, pp.-10-15.
12. Address [illegible] All Bengal Student's Conference, *Selected Works*, vol 3, p.-206.
13. Address at Champaran District, Political Conference, November, 1928, *Selected Works*, vol. 3 P-263.
14. Lohore Address, Selected Works, vol. p.193.
15. S. Gopal, *Jawaharlal Nehru : A Biography*, vol. 1, p.156.
16. *Selected Works*, vol. 5, P.179.
17. Selected works, vol.5, P 527.
18. 2. J. Nehru, *Glimpses of World History*, 1962 edition, pp-566-67.
19. *Selected Works*, vol.4, P-12.
20. J. Nehru, *Recent Essays and Writings*, pp-34-35.
21. Quoted in R.C. Dutt, *Socialism of Jawaharlal Nehru*, pp. 85-86.
22. Presidential Address, Lucknow Congress, Selected Works Vol.7, p.180.
23. R.C. Dutt, *Socialism of Jawaharlal Nehru* pp.99-100.
24. "Bipan Chandra, *Jawaharlal Nehru and the Capitalist Class, 1936*", In *Nationalism and Colonialism in Modern India*, New Delhi, 1979, p.144.
26. Reply to Address of All Bengal Students Association, Sept. 1928, *Selected Works*, vol.3, pp.-198-99.
27. *Selected Works*, vol. 3, p. 153.
28. *Ibid.*
29. Presidential Address at Lucknow Congress, S.W., vol-7-170-95 *Selected Works*, vol.7 pp.170-195.
30 Presidential Address of Punjab Congress, April, 1928, *Selected Works*, vol. 3, P. 225.
31. *Ibid.*, P. 224.
32. *Ibid.*
33. Presidential Address at Lucknow Congress, *Selected Works*, vol.7, pp. 170-195.
34. *Selected Works*, vol. 3, p-198.
35. *Ibid.*
36. *Ibia.*
37. Presidential Address to All Bengal Students Conference, *Selected Works*, vol.3, p-206..

38. Presidential Address at U.P. Provincial Conference, Jhansi, Oct., 1928, *Selected Works,* vol.3, pp.255-63.
39. "On Political Situation in India", Speech at Cabinet, May, 1928, *Selected Works,* vol. 3, p.-42.
40. *Selected Works,* vol. 4, p 3.
41. *Selected Works,* vol. 3, p. 198.
42. Speech at Kathiawar Youth Conference, 31 August, 1929, *Selected Works,* vol. 4, pp. 18-19.
43. *Selected Works,* vol. 3, pp.258-9 also pp.246-50
44. *Ibid,* pp.252 258.
45. J. Nehru, *An Autobiography,* p-544.
46. To, The Editor, *The Times of Malaya,* Malaya, Allahabad, July 25, 1937, J.N. Papers, vol. - XIX (NMML).
47. R. K. Karanjia *The Mind of Mr. Nehru,* London, 1960, p 77.
48. Benudhar Pradhan, *The Socialist Thought of Jawaharlal Nehru.* Hariyana, The Academic Press pp.108-9.
49. Quoted in George Thompson, *From Marx to Mao-tse-Tung, A Study in Revolutionary Dialectics,* p.14.
50. S. Gopal, *The Mind of Jawaharlal Nehru,* pp.16-17.
51. Tibor Mende, *Conversations with Nehru,* p-74.
52. Second Letter to Lord Lothian, January 17,1936 in Dorothy Norman, *Nehru: The First Sixty Years,* vol.1. p-387.
53. Tibor Mende, *Conversations with Nehru,* pp. 77-78
54. *Ibid.*
56. J. Nehru, *An Autobiography,* p-551-2.
57. J. Nehru, *Some criticisms considered,* Essay 1, p 35.
58. J. Nehru, *An Autobiography,* p.-521.
59. *Ibid.,* P-543.
60. Dorothy Norman, *Nehru : The First Sixty Years,* Vol.1,P 34.
61. *J. Nehru's Speeches,* vol. III, p.13.
62. *Ibid.,* p.13.
63. *J. Nehru's Speeches,* vol. III, P-64.
64. *Speeches of Jawaharlal Nehru,* vol. III, p-67.
65. Dorothy Norman, *Nehru: The First Sixty Years,* vol.1,P300.
66. Tibor Mende, *Conversations with Nehru,* p-76.
67. Presidential Address At the Bombay Presidency Youth Conference, 12 Dec., 1988 in *Selected works,* vol. 3,P-203.
68. *Ibid.*
69. "Advice to Youth", Speech at Delhi, 5 Feb., 1929, *Selected Works,* vol. 4, P 2.
70. Gunnar Myrdal, *The Challenges of World Poverty,* Penguin International, 1970, p.-396.
71. *Jawaharlal Nehru's Speeches,* vol. 11, pp-380-83.
72. "There in such a thing as a national culture with its deep roots in the nations soil and its history. To uproot a nation is to destroy the soul of that nation which made it a living entity through the ages", *J. Nehru's Speeches,* vol IV, 1957-63.
73. S. Gopal, *The Mind of Jawaharlal Nehru,* (Sangam Books, 1980) p.28.
74. Young India, 9 Jan. 1930 in S. Gopal, *Jawaharlal Nehru: A Biography,* Vol. 1, P 157.
75. R. K. Karanjia, *The Mind of Mr. Nehru,* pp.-76-77.

76. Rostislav Ulyanovysky, *Present Dey Problems in Asia*, Moscow, Progress Publisher, 1978, p. 205.
77. S. Gopal, "His Formative Ideology" in *Jawaharlal Nehru : India's Man of Destiny* (ed.) B.K. Alhuwalia New Delhi, Newman Group, 1978, p. 143.
78. Presidential Address at Nagpur, in Dorothy Norman, *Jawaharlal Nehru : The First Sixty Years* vol, 1 p.179.
79. *Ibid.*, Presidential Address, 1929, p. 205.
80. R. K. Karanjia, *The Philosophy of Nehru*, p 41.
81. Congress Bulletin, Nos. 9-11, New Delhi, September-November, 1963, p. 55 in Rostilav Ulyanovysky, *Present Day Problems in Asia And Africa*, p-206.
82. Quoted in R.C. Dutt. *Socialism of Nehru*, New Delhi, Abhinav Publications, 1981, p. 185.
83. Quoted in T.K. Ravindran, *Nehru's Idea of History*, p. 113.

CHAPTER 4

NEHRU'S CONCEPT OF SOCIETY AND SOCIAL JUSTICE

The concept of society has been debated by scholars and thinkers since the time of Aristotle. From time to time, different Eastern and Western philosophers have interpreted society and its relationship with the individual and the state in their own way. However, an imbalanced society cannot last long and cannot provide vitality to the body-politic. As such if the society has to last long it must have a value system and the most important value to our mind is social justice on which a society should build its empire. As a concept, 'Social Justice' is relatively a new terminology, may be an outcome of British liberal philosophy. However, with the emergence of the concept of the welfare state it came into vogue in the 20th century. But if we look into the history, its roots may be found from ancient days. This may be termed as a concept in vocabulary of Political Science, and that too is due to the fact that, the ideological development of liberal democracy failed to solve the knotty problems of class-ridden society, viz., the problem of bridging the gap between the rich and the poor, the haves and the havenots, the privileged and the deprived etc. The guarantee of freedom to all visualised by western liberal democrats did not clinch the issue as the benefits of freedom could not be easily available to the people who were economically unprivileged and those who suffered under different forms of social discrimination. To put it differently the liberal democratic philosophers failed to establish a social order which could be fair to all the members of society. To remove this weakness of Liberal Democracy the concept of 'Social Justice' calls for a social order which provides equal opportunity to everyone with a fair amount of justice and equality.

In the broader theoretical framework of society and social justice we have to examine as to how Nehru viewed society, what were his ideas of social justice. As regards Nehru's views on society, it can be said that he had a clear vision of his own for a future society of India. He was of the opinion that the traditional values of Indian society which hold good for ever, should be preserved at all costs. However, he was convinced that there were certain weaknesses of our traditional social order which, if pursued may not lead India towards an egalitarian society and as such should not be given any protection. In short, he was of the opinion that the traditional values must be supplemented by western and scientific values. In other words, Nehru visualised a future society for India which should have a mixture of modernity and tradition. Old social values like fraternity, community feeling, respect for personality, brotherhood, kindness and eternal virtues should be preserved at all costs but conservatism, strict adherence to ritual, untouchability, exploitation of all sorts, disrespect for women, these were some of the evils of our traditional society which must be discarded. Nehru found the root of disparity and discontent in poverty and social injustice. He was convinced that unless we do not remove poverty and social injustice we cannot progress and a new India cannot be built.

Nehru's Views of Present Society

Jawaharlal Nehru has been rightly described by Dr. S. Radhakrishnan as a great emancipator of the human race, as one who has given his life and energy to the freeing of man's minds from political bondage, economic slavery, social oppression and cultural stagnation.[2] Nehru, who fought for political freedom along with the great statesmen of freedom movement, fervently felt that release of people from political bondage, would mean little to them if their economic shackles were not broken. A society is truly free if it consists of free people, and the people can be said to be free if they achieve both political and economic freedom. Whenever there is oppression whether it be of political, economic or social nature, the society can hardly be described as just society. Nehru like great thinkers, pondered deeply over the poverty of the people, exploitation of man by man, vulgar display of wealth and other deep rooted malaise in the society, and attributed this phenomenon to the present social structure. In his speech at Allahabad in 1928 he said : "Today we are a society in which there are tremendous differences between man and man. Great riches are on one side and great poverty on the other. Some people live in luxury without doing any work, whilst others work from morning to night with no rest or leisure and yet have barest necessaries of life. This cannot be right. It is the negation of justice". But he said that "it is not the fault of our individuals who happen to be rich. It is the fault of the system, which permits of exploitation of man by man and produces so much misery".[3] Explaining this further he said that it was the system which was wrong, was the "natural outcome of capitalism and imperialism".

It may be noted that while capitalism was a phenomenon found within a national society, imperialism was a feature found in the international community. According to Nehru, the system or social structure supported by them in their respective fields of operation were inherently bad and manifestly unjust.

The innate characteristic of the capitalist structure has been exposed by him on several occasions. In his speech to A.I.C.C. at Nagpur in 1930 he has pointed out that "the whole of capitalist structure is based on some kind of an acquisitive society".[4] In fact he was aware of the fact that the tendency to acquisitiveness is inherent in human being. But what he meant by the above statement, obviously, is that the acquisitive tendency is manifest in a more ugly and abominable form in the capitalist society. On another occasion he remarked that, "the acquisitive society whose chief aim is profit making, not only brings conflicts in its train but is opposed to the basic urge of modern man for social justice." [5]

Besides, "class-strugles", he says," are inherent in the present system and the attempt to change it and bring it in line with modern requirements meets with the fierce opposition of the ruling or owning classes. That is the logic of the conflicts today".[6] What is more, the entire system, according to Nehru, is based on violence in as much as it is based on exploitation of man by man and is devoid of human consideration.[7] It has not only deprived a large section of the people of their bare necessaries of life but also treated the labourers who constitue an essential part of production as "mere hewers of wood and drawers of water".[8]

But, one question that loomed large was whether industrialisation solved the basic problems of the people and redeemed the capitalist society from the stigma attached to it that it has shown scant respect for human consideration. As to this point Nehru says that, "Industrialisation has resulted in greater production, greater wealth, in the concentration of wealth in a few countries and few individuals, and a more unequal distribution of wealth".[9] Explaining this point further he said on another occasion that though industrialism solved the problem of production of wealth, it consequently failed to solve the basic problems of our country, viz., the problem of food, clothing, housing and so on.[10] Instead of solving this problem, industrialism according to him has produced, "the modern kings of industry, who have Greater Power over the lives and fortunes of men than even kings of old feudal aristocracy".[11]

From the above mentioned statements of Nehru a new idea of Nehru regarding the present social structure emerges. First according to him, the present social system is a capitalist system and it is clearly unjust because it is essentially an acquisitive society based on exploitation of man by man breeding class conflict. Secondly, in as much as the system kept perpetually increasing the yawning gap between the incredible richness of the few and the appalling poverty of the many, it is evidently based on violence and is devoid of human considerations. Thirdly, the system has by forcing many people to live a life of penuary and to struggle for sustenance destroyed man's creative spirit, his creative energy and made him a non-entity, an inarticulate and servile creature in the society. In short, capitalistic system was a negation of social justice.

Nehru's Reaction to Poverty and Social Injustice

During a conversation, Andre Malraux asked him as to what was the most difficult task before him after independence. Nehru had no hesitation in admitting to Malraux that the hardest moral problems he had to confront with was to build up a just state or a state established on principles of justice by just means.[12] In the context of his own country, where injustice of every kind abounded, where many suffer and had suffered all kinds of social, political and legal disabilities, he thought that the pursuit of justice was the foremost task of every Indian patriot.

His fight for obtaining social justice was all the more unique because never and nowhere in the world had any statesman laid so much emphasis on the purity of means in order to bring social justice, legal justice and also economic justice. But why did he think so and why did he conceive this strategy in spite of the fact that History shows that no country has succeeded in achieving a revolution be it American or French or the Russian revolution without doing injustices to some for the purpose of achieving justice for others? Where did he get this inspiration to fight for an ideal which appeared so unreal to so many of his colleagues and to some others who opposed him ? Nehru himself has given us an answer, for in his autobiography he has described almost poignantly the great emotion which surged through him when he saw the sombre, sad eyes of the harmless and helpless peasants of our country. He writes, "Yet there were people (who came to Anand Bhavan as pilgrims) looking up with shining eyes and full of affection, with generation of poverty and suffering behind them, and still pouring out their gratitude and love and asking for little in return, except fellow-feeling and sympathy. It was impossible not to feel humbled and awed by this abundance of affection and devotion".[13] In his spontaneous love and sincerity for the poor and the lonely, and in its master survey of a magnificent imagery, this passage equals the famous poem of Tagore in which he also spoke of the dumb and melancholy image of thedisabled and the disinherited.

Nehru's whole approach to human misery was not intellectual but emotional, probably of the same variety which moved the Buddha to rescue the world and made the Great Ashoka go about the country preaching the doctrine of Ahimsa. He was made of the same stuff as these two great Indians and while Nehru thought and pondered over the doctrines of Marx and Hegel, what stirred and inspired him to leave no stone unturned to secure a fair deal for his countrymen, was the compassion and this tender emotion to which he has given expression so beautifully in the passage quoted above. That is why he wanted the achievement of "a just state by just means" or social justice by not merely "justifiable means but just means." [14]

Nehru's *Discovery of India* was in a way, his final identification with the country. Though his "Discovery" was written in the thirties, Nehru was discovering India, physically and intellectually ever since his return from England after his studies. No politician in India, except Gandhi, ever achieved such total involvement with the country and its people.

Nehru's readings of socialism, his realization of the horrors of the Industiral Revolutions in England and its adverse impact on India's economy, especially the pauperisation of the peasantry had already aroused his conscience. His close association with Indian affairs also gave him a better perception of the life of the Indian people, particularly on the causes of India's degrading poverty. So, when he came face to face with millions of poor peasants and the wretched workers of the cities, who were being ruthlessly exploited, the effect on him was tremendous, henceforward he was to view every problem in the context of the deprived humanity. Perhaps it was because of his socialistic inclination, but there is no doubt that Nehru's personal discovery of the poverty of India was yet another milestone in his conversion to socialism. Nehru's concern for the masses, his resolution to try eradicate poverty is reflected in his statements which he made while making a trust for Anand Bhawan. "I am desirous of carrying out my father's wishes and of transferring the property to trustees for the benefit of the Indian people in the advancement of knowledge, health, social and economic well-being, and especially with the object of promoting unity among all classes and creeds of the Indian people, raising the status of Indian women and the elevation and betterment in all respects of the suppressed classes in India and Indian workers and peasants and classes of India, I do hereby make this declaration of trust and transfer the said property, known as Swaraj Bhawan".[15] His declaration in fact mirrors his aspirations and ideals which he sought to achieve throughout the freedom struggle, and later as Prime Minister.

Nehru made this his life-long mission and promised himself that he would not rest until 'every tear from every eye' was wiped as Gandhi had pledged. He took on himself the responsiblity of providing a decent living to every Indian as could be possible. The mighty poverty and destitution of India burdened his conscience, more so often his ascendency to power and he felt responsible towards amelioration of this curse. Writing to Chief Ministers on 6 November, 1953, he voiced his feelings, "I travel about a great deal in India and see vast crowds of people. They are friendly crowds and they give me a feeling of basic strength. And yet the sight of a child or a boy or a girl without adequate food or clothing or house to live in always produces a sense of shock as well as a sense of shame. I compare my own comfort and well- being with the lot of the child of India who is our responsibility''.[16]

Nehru's Vision of a New Social Order

Nehru had a particular vision of a just society based on, cooperation, taking the place of competition instead of profit.[17] Since he felt that the present system was based on violence, he earnestly sought, a massive, enduring and peaceful system from which the roots of violence have been removed, and where ''hatred shrivels up and yields place to nobler feelings''. [18] This view was reiterated by him in his Broadcast from All India Radio in December, 1952, wherein he spoke, *inter alia* about the necessity of fundamental transformation of the power structure and of creating a just society based on cooperative efforts.[19]

Besides, while explaining the social pattern of society he laid stress on ''to activate and dynamise the base of the Indian social structure''.[20] According to him the base of the Indian society meant millions and millions of villages, workers, peasants and unemployed people, and in short the people of the land.[21] He felt that this rapid progress of India depended on the activeness of this base and that could be done only by taking rigorous social steps which included among others, reorganization of the production distribution and other activities of society in such a way as to distribute equally the benefits of the economic activity in society, adoption of human outlook, in all economic programmes and for all economic sections, removal of unemployment, guarantee of wages, social security, provision of the minimum needs of life and assurance of equal opportunities to individuals to develop their creative abilities. All these social steps contemplated by Nehru constitute the issue of scientific contents of his socialism and socialist state which is invariably associated with his concept of social justice, the classic expression of which is found in *Autobiography* wherein, he said, ''Our final aim can only be classless society with equal economic guarantee and opportunity for all, a society organised on a planned basis for the raising of mankind to higher material and cultural levels, to a cultivation of spiritual values, of cooperation, unselfishness, the spirit of service the desire to do right, . . . ultimately a moral order.''

Having rejected the present social structure, Nehru envisaged a new social order which would be capable not only of solving the present day problems but creating a new set of values in society. Concerning such a social order he was clear about the problems to be solved, structural and institutional changes to be effected, the type of policies to be promoted and the position of individual in it.

Identifying the problems to be solved, Nehru said that the ever present realities of our society are poverty and unemployment of our millions, and the latter has taken even the middle class into grip and grows like a creeping paralysis."[22] Needless to say that these are the stark realities present in all the underdeveloped countries. Nehru, was obviously not content with mere solving of the problems. He was deeply concerned with the welfare of the people and the position of individual in the society. So, the more comprehensive task he set before himself was to raise the standard of the masses, to supply them with their needs, give them the wherewithal to lead a decent life, and help them to progress and advance in life not only in regard to material things but in regard to cultural and spiritual things also. [23] He opined that, "every man and woman must have the opportunity to develop to the best of his or her ability".[24] Furthermore he said "however merit must come from ability and hard work and not because of caste, or health or riches". The entire gamut of his thinking on this point can be discerned in his statement, which succintly presents his desire and goal "that all individuals in India should have equal opportunities of growth, from health upwards and equal opportunities for work according to their capability". [25]

If this is the objective, how could it be achieved ? According to Nehru, this can be achieved, if we put an end to all differences between class and class, and bring about, "more equality and more unitary society".In other words,"We must strive for economic democracy".[26] For this purpose, economic democracy and classless society cannot be achieved under the existing system. This saner and healthier order of his conception would be brought only in a "socialist state" and the philosophy behind it is "socialism". He stated unequivocally that if our ideal is social equality, "than perforce, we must strive for a socialist state".[27]

The foregoing analysis would show that the society or the new social order of Nehru's conception is the socialist, unitary or classless society, wherein (1) the law of life becomes one of cooperation and not of competition or acquisitiveness, and all activities social, economic and others, are carried on accordingly; (2) the distributive justice taking such shape and forms as equitable distribution of wealth, grant of basic necessities of life to all etc. . . becomes the cardinal principles; (3) the equality of opportunity is assured to all, (4) the humanistic approach or attitude to all problems and in all spheres of activities becomes the way of life; (5) wherein one enjoys the freedom coming from his release from economic and cultural bondage.

Dynamics and Methods to Achieve Social Justice

Nehru had a set vision of future society based on social justice and equality. He thought that the existence of social rigidity, caste barriers, untouchability, economic disparity were such evils which may not allow the nation to proceed in a particular direction.[28] Based on his vast experience, which he gathered by travelling extensively foreign countries, by reading the works of philosophers and scholars of the world and by directly associating himself with the freedom movement, he had a set framework for the all-round development of independent India. He was methodical and scientific in his approach and did not appreciate a lopsided development of the nation. His basic approach to development was a planned one.

Planning

Nehru was a great advocate of planning and guided approach to development. He was a keen student of history which provided him a clear cut perception of the developed western world. Taking inspiration from the planning of the Soviet Union, he formulated a frame of scheme of planning in India as, in his opinion, this was the only way of leading the country on the path of rapid development.

This was the reason that immediately after the promulgation of Republican Constitution, he went on experimenting with planning in India. The importance of planning, which Nehru had in mind and the framework he used for the planned development of the nation cannot be overemphasised.

Nehru will be remembered in History as a Planner, for the country owes to him the progress it is making towards self-reliance and self-growth in industry and in the activities associated with industries like power, fuel, transport and technical skill, with the result that today India has the third largest scientific and technical manpower in the world. Nehru concentrated on formulating five-year plans as chairman of the planning commission, trying to get them implemented as Head of the Government, and popularising them with the people and seeking cooperation in the development process by explanation and exhortation. No wonder that he is called the architect of economic planning in India.

Nehru's ideas on planning were formulated long before he got the power and authority to introduce them in independent India. His greatest contribution to economic strategy was committing the country to a policy of planned economic development. He came to this conclusion in his thinking because of the realisation that social and economic consolidation had to go hand in hand with political freedom. Political freedom without social freedom would be meaningless. Thus at Nehru's prodding the Congress passed a resolution in 1929 which emphasised the necessity for a revolutionary change in the social and economic structure, to remove the glaring inequality of income and wealth. The worldwide impression of the thinkers made regulation and control of the economic system, in the interest of general masses a fundamental principle of public policy in many countries. Roosevelt's 'New Deal' and his talk of weeding out the over privileged and effectively lifting up the under-privileged impressed Nehru and struck a chord in his heart, premises were building up in favour of socialism. The Karachi Congress Resolution of 1931 on Fundamental Rights, *inter alia* affirmed that the 'state shall own or control key industries and services, national resources, railways, waterways, shipping and other means of public transport.[29] Nehru was convinced from the beginning that the problem of Indian poverty could not be solved except by a massive increase in production and this could be possible only through the application of science to industry and through large-scale planning in industrialization.

The concept of a planned economy was, even in Europe in the late thirties, still vague and ambiguous. And it was felt that only in Soviet Russia was there national planning in the real sense, with the whole economy geared to the production of plenty for human welfare and not driven by profit motive or intended for efficacy in war. In other words, planning was a part of socialism.[30] Nehru agreed with this. However critical he might have been with the political aspects of Stalin regime, he was deeply impressed by the economic progress achieved by the Soviet Union. "The argument about the success or otherwise of the Five Year Plan was rather a pointless one. The answer to it is really the present state of the Soviet Union. And a further answer is the fact that this plan has impressed itself on the imagination of the world. Everybody talks of planning now, and of Five Year and Ten Year and Three Year Plans. The Soviets have put magic into the world."[31] He believed that India too had much to learn from the Soviet example. But to apply these lessons in a colonial economy and to consider planning in a country which was not yet free showed a bold and pioneering mind. This was the kind of work, long term, adventurous and leading to socialism, which excited him, even much later he called it an 'exciting pilgrimage.'[32]

The National Planning Committee was set up in 1938, with Nehru as its Chairman. Nehru took up his work seriously and prepared the blueprint for the future which would mirror the hopes and aspirations of a backward, struggling country. He took up the work with enthusiasm and constituted a committee with not only congressmen but socialists, economists, businessmen and industrialists as well. The Congress ministries were represented. In addition, Punjab, Baroda and Mysore agreed to send representations, and contacts were established with departments of the Government of India. A long question was drafted and widely distributed and nearly thirty sub-committees were constituted to make detailed recommendations on specific subjects.

Nehru's own contribution, apart from holding the assorted crowd of planners together, was a clear statement of the general objectives of planning in India. To him planning was inevitably connected with a socialist economy. Effective coordination was possible only through planning by the state. Nehru's concept of planning was an integrated approach to all-round development. Through planning he hoped to spread industrialisation and to develop a self-generating economy. The most important goal was removal of mass poverty. Mere increase in national income or per capita income was not enough, it was more important to ensure a standard of living which provided the minimum amenities of food, shelter and clothing for his people. For effecting this objective, Nehru sought to ensure full employment.[33] He described his participation in the National Planning Committee with enthusiasm. 'As we proceeded with this work it grew till it enhanced almost every phase of national activity. We appointed 29 sub-committees for various groups - agricultural, industrial, social, economical, financial and tried to coordinate their activities so as to produce a scheme of planned economy for India. For me this has been fascinating work and I have learnt much from it. It is clear that any scheme that we may produce can be given effect to in a free India. It is also clear that any effective planning must involve socialisation for the economic structure.[34]

Nehru made the people and the Congress planning conscious. Through planning he sought to give an economic content to freedom. To Nehru political freedom without economic and social freedom was a mere shadow without substance. Nehru had found his mooring. He clearly saw what had to be done in a free India. The doctrine of socialism now ceased to be a subject of barren ideological polemics or a bone of academic contention, for it was through the apparatus of planning that Nehru endeavoured to render flesh and blood to his socialist ideas. Submitting a memorandum to National Planning Committee, on 4th June, 1939, he pointed out, ''The ideal of the Congress is establishment of a free and democratic state in India. Such a free democratic state generates an egalitarian society in which equal opportunities are provided for every member for self-expression and self-fulfilment and an adequate minimum of a civilised standard of life is assured to each member so as to make the attainment of their equal opportunity a reality. This should be the background or foundation of our plans''.[35] A year later he acknowledged that the over-all objective was to socialize national life in all sectors.[36]

As the fascination of this work grew on him, he came to realize the basic realities which faced planning in a country like India, with diverse interest and social diversities. Broadly he faced two problems, the socialist one aiming at the elimination of the profit motive as far as possible, and laying greater stress on production. There were other approaches as well. National self-sufficiency was taken, however, to be the objective for the country, and planning had to be thought with that end in view.[37] It is to the credit of Nehru that in that first attempt of comprehensive planning for India he could lead the committee to think that the future of India lay in democratic socialism, ''constituted as we were, not only in our committee but in the larger field of India, we would not then plan for socialism as such, yet it became clear to me that our plan, as it developed was inveitably leading toward establishing some of the fundamentals of the socialist structure. It was limiting the *acquisitive* factor in society, removing many of the barriers to growth and thus leading to a rapidly expanding social structure. It was based on planning for the benefit of the common man raising his standard greatly, giving him opportunities of growth and releasing an enormous amount of talent and capacity. And all this was to be attempted in the context of democratic freedom and with a large measure of cooperation of some at least of the groups who were normally opposed to socialistic doctrine''.[38]

The concept of planning is one of the greatest contributions made by Nehru to a non-socialist, non-communist society - like the Indian society with all its deviation and with all its hesitancies about the narrow aspects of economic development. The capitalist system also accepts planning as a methodology of development but the context in which the capitalist society has accepted it is different from the purpose and the connotation that Nehru had given to the concept of planning in Indian economic development. As far the methodology of planning is concerned it can be neutral between capitalism and socialism but it depends upon the person, the society, the purposes and values for which the society fights for, as to how this concept of planning can be used; Nehru said that in every phase of economic development, planning must generate such comulative social forces that would take the country forward on the road to social transformation. That should be the type of social force that will come out as a result of planning. Speaking at the Indian Merchants Chamber, February 3, 1958, he said, ''Planning is essentially a process whereby we stop those cumulative forces at work which make the poor poorer, and start a new series of cumulative forces which enable the poor to get over the barrier of poverty."[39]

To Jawaharlal Nehru, planning was not merely an apparatus for allocation of resources towards economic progress, it was much more. "At one hand of the scale, planning was "Science in Action"[40] and at the other, it was the forward movement of a whole people building their own future. ''A plan of this type does not merely mean establishing a number of problems or increasing it but something with a deeper significance..., the gradual development of a particular structure of society was to be achieved''.[41] A British journalist described this basic attempt in India as `Nehruism: India's Revolution without Fear'[42] though Nehru disliked the word Nehruism, the outlook as a whole seemed to him a fair assessment, for it pointed out that a socialist revolution by consent was under way in India. To Nehru, planning would be the weapon of such a revolution, and it was a revolution without class war, heretics or victims as its essence was a series of tedious legal acts based on the active participation of the people. Describing the essence of planning Nehru explained, "I mention these broad features because I feel that our minds must have the dynamic quality which even our experts lack, not to speak of the layman. For instance, our economists and planners have become very static in their approach. We talk of revolutions, believing all the time that revolution is merely a process in which you can break one another's head. That is not a revolution good or bad, a revolution is something that fundamentally changes the political and economic structure of the existing society. It is with this kind of background that we must consider this first attempt at planning".[43]

Nehru visualised planning as the vehicle of transformation of society. In India, it would be a catalytic agent towards the moral and physical integration of the country. "This is the first attempt in India to integrate the agricultural, industrial, social, economic and other aspects of the country into a single framework of thinking. It is a very important step and even if the thinking is partly faulty it does not deflect from the magnitude of what has been attempted and accomplished. It has made people think of this country as a whole. I think it is most essential that India, which is united politically and in many other ways, should, to the same extent, be united mentally and emotionally also. We often go off at a tangent on grounds of provincial issues, communalism, religious or caste, we have no emotional awareness of the unity of the country. Planning will help us in having an emotional awareness of problems as a whole. It will help us to see the isolated problems in villages or districts or even provinces in their larger context. Therefore, the more act of planning, the more act of having approached the question of progress in this way and of producing a rapport of this type is something on which we might I think, congratulate ourselves."[44]

Nehru always emphasised on the 'human factor' involved in planning. He never conceived the plan in isolation for purely material gains. He categorically reiterated to the people involved with planning that "Planning is not merely a question of drawing up a list of projects and finding resources to execute them. These two tasks no doubt form the base of planning. The financial aspect is important but is far less important than the human aspect. The process of planning involves the changing of the human beings, their thinking and their ways of work. The technical aspect of planning is very important. But I think the human aspect is much more important than the technical. The two have to fit into each other''.[45] The real change which has to be brought about in the future is a change in the mind of the human being to make him self-reliant and stand on his own feet and do the job. At another place, while moving the third plan in the Lok Sabha Nehru read out the objectives of planned development: 'As this process develops, there is a certain rhythm of expansion in the development of the people, and a sense of enterprise and achievement comes to them. They are conscious of a purpose in life and have a feeling of being participants in the making of history. Ultimately, it is the development of the human being and the human personality that counts. Although planning involves material investment, even more important is the investment in man.[46] The people of India today, with all their burdens and problems live on the frontiers of a new world which they are helping to build. In order to cross this frontier they have to possess courage and enterprise, the spirit of endurance and capacity for hard work and the vision of future.[47] Thus, we can assess the importance which Nehru attached to the human side of planning and the place which it would have to occupy in the socio-economic transformation of Indian society. This is a unique contribution.

Community Development

Community Development programme started to operate on 2nd October, 1952. Nehru's optimism towards bettering society derived additional support from it. It was a programme to rejuvenate the long-dormant peasantry of India, who constituted eighty-two per cent of the population and lived in India's 600,000 villages; to teach them self-help; and to mobilise their energy in changing the centuries old face of rural India. This was to be achieved by persuasion. Speaking to the Development Commissioners at the Community Projects Conference, in May 1952 Nehru advised, "I want this neither to be explained, not in this business like way but in a more human way, so that somehow it may catch the imagination of the people concerned''. . . Cautioning them he said, "Scc that you get to invite them to work with you: not under your command but with you so that you gradually form some kind of brotherhood, a fraternity of workers.''[48]

Village India was to be organised in blocks, each block consisting of a hundred villages. Government officers and agrarian specialists were made available at all levels within each block to guide and coach the villagers in the formulation of their needs (health clinics, schools, new roads, new methods of cultivation, new seeds) and in pooling their efforts and resources in cooperatives.[49] By the end of the second plan period the programme was to cover the whole of the rural India.

All specific schemes for improving living conditions in the countryside and providing the ordinary peasant with interest in the future were soon included in Nehru's mind in the need for integrated development of the village communities, with the active assistance of the local inhabitants. This would encourage growth from the bottom, and enable the ordinary villager to a certain extent to govern his own destiny. The initiative had to be given to the people and they had to be vested with a sense of partnership and purpose. Backwardness was not an attribute of a few sections of Indian society; basically ninety-six per cent of the Indian people were backward but they had all to be involved in the building of a new India, and a measure of equality in opportunity and fulfilment progressively produced.[50] The inauguration on 2nd October, 1952 of fifty five community projects, covering about 17,000 villages, offered to him the promise of the small beginning of something big. "That idea is to change the whole face of rural India and to raise the level of the vast majority of our population".[51]

In 1953, as a development of the community project programme, the national extension service, whose purpose was to provide trained workers, was formulated. This service was intended to lay the broad foundation over the whole country for the community project. Nehru saw in this twin programmes the possiblity of a great revolutionary change carried out peacefully and without conflict. As the two schemes materialised, almost every part of India came within their reach, and by 1955 there was no gap of more than fifty miles between any two areas touched by either one or other of them.[52]

The community development programme was involved to activize the base of Indian social structure--the village. Nehru visualised an industrially advanced India but he never neglected the villages and believed that it was more important to dynamise the village than the role of industrialisation. It was intended to lift the backward and unprivileged, "What we are committed to is not a few community centres but to working for the biggest community of all and that is the community of the people of India, more specially those who are more backward... We must aim at progressively producing a measure of equality in opportunity and other things... so that this tremendous problem of backwardness may be tackled in the best and quickest way possible".[53]

The community development programme was a welcome step towards developing rural India. It was dedicated to raising the standard of living fo the rural people, with their consent, participation and initiative. It was a new hope and vision for the masses living in villages. The targets were fixed to reach every village in India within stipulated time. Finances were in abundance and the administrative set up was converted into a full- fledged ministry at the centre.

Panchayati Raj

The review of the working of the community development and national extension service movement revealed that its attempt to evoke popular initiative was one of its best successful aspects.[54] In line with the committee's recommendations, Nehru decided to reactivate the Panchayat system, "It was seven years ago that we started this great movement with the community projects and the national extension service. These have by now covered more than three lakh villages... But we have not been able to do as much as we expected.., It became imperative that a bold step be taken whereby more and more responsibility could be transferred to the people. Therefore, we decided that in every village there should be a village panchayat with more power, as also a cooperative society which well help its economic effort. [55]

The proposal of the Planning Commission for the Second Five year Plan stressed the need for creating within the district a well organised democratic structure of administration in which village panchayats would be organically linked with popular organisations at a higher level. The National Development Council constituted this committee with a view to securing economy and efficiency in development administration. The study team which was presided over by Balwantrai Mehta submitted its report in 1957.

The adults of the village would elect the members of a panchayat, with added representation given to women and scheduled tribes as these groups were unlikely to secure it through elections. Beyond the village panchayats would be the panchayat samitis, each covering about forty to fifty villages, consisting largely of indirectly elected members and with jurisdiction coextensive with the development block; and the Zila Parishad, comprising mostly the chairman of the samitis, would deal normally with an administrative district.[56]

The three bodies, fully elected and non-official, could give farmers a sense of responsibility and help to unleash the latent energies in the rural areas, and according to Nehru now that the community development programme had lost its flavour, glamour and colour and had become a hackneyed part of the bureaucratic machinery, he looked to the cooperative and panchayats for accelerated rural development and fresh springs of rural life. He believed that these panchayats had enabled India to turn the corner in agriculture by stepping up production; and he expected them to do even more and help create better men and women. It was the building of right type of men and women which underlay all planning and made possible industrial and agricultural progress; and Panchayati Raj, to Nehru the most important thing in India''.[57] It would above all change the quality of the human being. Panchayati Raj was the most revolutionary development in India because behind it were hidden all forces which, when released, would change the structure of the country. Most significantly through Panchayats democracy would reach grassroots and enable popular participation in the democratic functioning of the country.

Land Reforms

Since India is predominantly an agricultural country, the problem of land reform has been one of the most important issues before political and administrative leadership since British days. Even during freedom movement the Indian National Congress attached great value to the question of achieving far reaching land reforms by removing feudal intermediaries, by providing security of tenure and economic stability of peasantry. Immediately after independence under the able stewardship of Jawaharlal Nehru abolition of Zamindari became more or less a symbol of socio-economic revolution through peaceful democratic and non-violent means. Nehru reiterated ''Land reforms have a peculiar significance because without them, more especially in a highly congested country like India, there can be no radical improvement in productivity in agriculture. But the main object of land reforms is a deeper one. They are meant to break up old class structure of a society that is stagnant.''[58] It may not be out of place to point out that the unitary efforts of Acharya Vinoba Bhave and his 'Bhoodan Yajna' proved extremely helpful in creating healthy and congenial atmosphere for the introduction of radical reforms in our country.

Nehru regarded the land problem as India's, or Asia's basic problem. In his view, until a satisfctory approach was evolved in regard to this problem and until proper programmes were evolved to solve these problems, it would be difficult even to tackle other problems fully.[59] In other words, Nehru regarded the land problem as the key to India's basic economic, social, political and cultural problems, he was perhaps the first national leader in the history of the Indian National movement who put the land problem in the centre of deliberations on the Indian economic problems before and after independence. He also made an enduring contribution in terms of evolving an approach to this problem, a programme for tackling it and in terms of using state power for implementing the programme.

Central to this agrarian programme of the Indian National Congress adopted under Nehru's leadership was concept of land to the tiller, land to the working peasant, who was the backbone of Indian agriculture and of India's economy and society.[60] While Nehru conceded that the Congress should utilise the resources and talents of all other productive and patriotic classes in the task of national reconstruction, he regarded the involvement of the actual tiller or of the working peasants in the development processes as the basic objective of national planning.[61] In his view this involvement would not be assured if the actual tillers did not enjoy control over the land resources of the country. The basic direction of Nehru's agrarian policy, therefore, was to restructure the land system in a manner that control over land gravitated more and more towards the peasant, who is the actual tiller of the soil from time immemorial.

The first dimension of land reform in Nehru's conception, therefore, involved a restructuring of property relations relating to land, bringing about transfer of land from parasitic landlords to toiling peasants. All compromises with parasitic or enterprising landlords were to be subordinated to the basic goal of land to the tiller, the elimination of such wasteful feudal relations was essential for rehabilitating the nation's economy and for effective radical improvement in the conditions of the peasant masses. Nehru argued that the peasantry had to be assured that the end of foreign rule was not just to be a change of masters but also a fundamental change in their daily life. He further stated that it had to be realised that agriculture in India had ceased to be a profitable occupation and continuance of feudal economy with its burden of rent, debt and illegal exactions was impossible if an economic collapse had to be avoided.[62]

In his presidential address, in March 1936, at the 49th session of the Congress at Lucknow Nehru drew attention to the land question. In view of the fact, however, that land tenures and revenue system differed not only from province to province but were different in the same province, the Lucknow Congress decided to invite different provincial Congress Committees to submit detailed reports on agrarian condition in their areas under their jurisdiction.

On the basis of the recommendations of the provincial reports, and in the light of the discussions that had taken place in the country, the 30th session of the Congress at Faizpur, again presided over by Nehru, adopted the famous Agrarian Programme. The resolution adopted by the Congress said that the congress was convinced that the final solution of the problem involved the removal of British imperialistic exploitation and a radical change in the antiquated and repressive land tenure and revenue systems. [63] The necessary steps towards realisation of this goal were as follows:

(1) Rent and Revenue should be readjusted having regard to present conditions and there should be substantial reduction in both.

(2) Uneconomic holding should be exempted from rent and land tax.

(3) Agricultural incomes should be assessed to income tax like all other incomes, on a progressive scale, subject to a prescribed minimum.

(4) Canal and other irrigation rates be substantially lowered.

(5) All feudal dues and levies and forced labour should be abolished and demands other than rent should be made illegal.

(6) Fixity of tenure with heritable rights along with right to build houses and plant trees should be provided for all tenants.

(7) An effort should be made to introduce cooperative farming.

(8) The crushing burden of rural debt should be removed. Special tribunals should be appointed to enquire into this and all debts, which were unconcessionable or beyond the capacity of peasants to pay, should be liquidated. Meanwhile a moratorium should be declared and steps should be taken to provide cheap credit facilities.

(9) Arrears of rent for previous year should generally be wiped out.

(10) Common pasture lands should be provided and the rights of the people in tanks, wells, ponds, forests and the like recognised, and no encroachment on these rights should be permitted.

(11) Arrears of rents should be recoverable in same manner as civil debts and not by ejectment.

(12) There should be statutory provision for securing a living wage and suitable working condition for agricultural labourers.

(13) Peasant's Unions should be recognised.

The policies pursued by Jawaharlal Nehru, regarding land reforms after independence were in fact a continuation of the policies which were formulated before by the Congress. A broad outline of the land policy to be followed in the states was set out in the first Five Year Plan. Following the recommendations in the First Five Year Plan the Government of India set up the Central Committee of Land Reforms which included members of Planning Commission and the principal Central Ministers concerned to review from time to time the progress of land reform in diffrerent parts of the country and to advise the states on their land reform proposals. Before formulating the proposals for the second plan, the Planning Commission constituted the Panel on Land Reform with the object of reviewing the progress in the implementation of land policy proposed in the first plan and studying further steps in connection with the second plan. Following the deliberations in the Panel detailed proposals on land reforms were set out in the second Five Year Plan. These proposals were essentially in the nature of a broad common approach which had to be adopted and pursued in each state with due regard to local conditions and in response to local needs. [64]

The proposals for land reform in the Second Five Year Plan related to:

(1) Abolition of intermediaries

(2) Tenancy reforms i.e. regulation of rent, security of tenure for tenants and conferment of ownership on them;

(3) Ceilings on land holdings; and

(4) Agrarian reorganisation, including consolidation of holdings and prevention of sub-division and fragmentation.

Intermediary tenures like Zamindari,, Jagirs, etc. which covered more than 40% of the area of the country, have almost been entirely abolished. Legislation had been enacted in all States and the Union Territories but for a few minor tenures and *inams* as in Assam, Gujarat, Madras and Maharashtra. In most States the legislation was implemented. In others, it was in the process of implementation.

On abolition of intermediaries, the vestiges of feudalism had been removed and a large body of tenants estimated at 20 million had been brought into direct relationship with the State. As a result the social and economic position of the tenants had considerably improved. In some cases tenants had acquired full ownership rights including a right of transfer without any payment. In some cases peasants acquired full ownership rights including a right of transfer without any payment. It may be mentioned that the rents payable by tenants to the ex-intermediaries, had been regulated over the past many decades by legislation.[65]

Nehru regarded this a remarkable achievement.The A.I.C.C. met at Bangalore on July 13, 14, and 15, 1951 to which Nehru submitted a report as "A Prime Minister drawing his mandate from the Congress".He said : "From a social point of view, the biggest achievement has been the legislation in many States for the abolition of the Zamindari system. Unfortunately, this was held up by an interpretation of the constitution in the courts and it became necessary to amend the constitution to get over these difficulties. I trust that progress in this respect will now be rapid and there will be no further impediments". [66]

It was in this view of speedy reforms that emphasis was placed on Land Ceilings. It was proposed in the second Five Year Plan that steps should be taken in each state during the plan period to impose ceiling on existing agricultural holdings. The Standing Committee of the National Development Council which reviewed the progress of land reforms in September, 1957 decided that States which have not enacted Legislation for ceiling, should complete the legislative measures needed by the end of 1958-59 and State which had enacted the necessary legislation should ensure that the programme was administratively implemented within a given period of three years. The committee also suggested the adequate safeguards should be provided for preventing evasion. [67]

The 58th session of the Congress, which met at Hyderabad on January 17 and 18, 1953, under the Presidentship of Jawaharlal Nehru, generally approved of the progress made and welcomed the land policy as formulated in the final report of the First Five Year Plan. The All India Congress Committee met at Agra on July 6 and 7, 1953. Among the resolutions it adopted, one was on "Social and Economic Programme". This resolution is of more than usual importance in so far as it emphasised the need of fixing a ceiling on existing holdings with a view to effecting a redistribution of land. it said, : "The pace of progress, must, however, be more quickened especially in regard to land reform and industrial growth. The committee attaches the greatest importance to the introduction of far-reaching land reforms in India. While progress has been made in this direction by several State Governments, much yet remains to be done in order to make the actual tillers of the soil the owners of land. The State Government should take immediate steps in regard to the collection of the requisite land data and the fixation of ceilings of land holdings, with a view to redistributing the land, as possible, among landless workers". [68] This statement reflects the urgency and the importance that Nehru attached to land reforms and their speedy implementation towards a restructurisation of the entire rural infrastructure, in order to provide maximum benefit to the people in the villages.

Cooperative Farming

The second dimension of land reform which concerned Nehru was that of very low productivity of land. He was clear in his mind that while a restructuring of the land's rights in favour of the tiller of soil would redistribute the fruits of production in favour of the tiller and would psychologically motivate the tiller for greater production, it was necessary and not a sufficient condition for achieving higher levels of productivity. Land reform therefore, should involve not only restructuring of the land ownership pattern but also such redesigning of the land operation pattern as was by the necessity of modernising the production techniques. Nehru was led towards consolidation of holdings and cooperative farming as indispensable for agricultural modernisation as in his view small land holders could not absorb modern technology because of the smallness of their holdings and the paucity of resources at their disposal.

Especially in comparison with achievement in industry, there was in agriculture a sense of stagnation. The trends indicated by the fall in the annual production of foodgrains by 6.7 million tonnes and the rise in population by about five million every year had clearly to be reversed. Scientific as well as mechanized, agriculture had to be promoted and attention given to providing better ploughs, seeds and manure rather than tractors and to extending credit and market facilities. "If I have to say in one word what is wrong with agriculture in India, I would say it is the complete lack of anything that might be called scientific agriculture."[69] Despite official decisions at every level the average cultivator with a small holding seemed to have become less self-reliant than ever before.

Nehru's mind reverted repeatedly to cooperative farming, with the peasant owning his small holding but working with his neighbours for purposes of production. Indeed, given that both the other alternatives, of large estates in the hands of landlords and collectivization by the state were ruled out by him on principle, the only solution, midway between individualism and expropriation, was cooperative farming. Small cooperatives run by the villagers themselves, would increase production and help in securing reasonable prices for the produce, strengthen the self-reliance of the peasantry and provide the momentum for development. Nehru even suggested that, to encourage farmers to step out of the rut of old thinking, Ministers and officials might provide evidence of their own earnestness by working in the fields for a while. Nehru suggested, 'If we have to shake up the millions of agriculturists, we have first to shake up ourselves'.[70] Nehru was obviously influenced by the Chinese example of awakening the latent powers of the people, although he did not contemplate farm labour for urban folk as a punishment and rejected the element of compulsion involved at that time in Chinese communes. To discipline the whole country as a military camp would never be to him the right way for India. [71]

The Congress, which had been committed to cooperative farming on principle for many years, resolved, at its session at Nagpur in January, 1959, at Nehru's bidding, to foster, over the next three years, cooperatives for servicing agriculture in every village as a prelude to joint farming. There should be about 400,000 such cooperatives for the 550,000 villages in the country. These service cooperatives, as far as possible are non-official and administred by the Panchayats, would provide, as of old, credit to the cultivators and in addition, assist them with seeds, fertilizers, and even if need lies, small tractors and help them to sell their produce. [72]

The resolution sounded unambitious and business like, but its implementation would obviously require courage, hard work and a revolutionary mind. [73] Cooperation was at once economic doctrine, a higher form of social organization, a democratic process and an attitude to life. There would be no uniform pattern for these cooperatives and the State should do more than train personnel in cooperative management. Conversion of cooperatives into official organization was a waste of time and went against the very idea of cooperation. Our cooperatives must be run by villagers, no matter if they were foolish and ignorant. Membership would be voluntary in the cooperative village farms where they come into existence; and, even after joining, members would continue to retain their individual property rights. There would be no rigid rules, and service cooperatives would decide many points for themselves; but generally they would be expected to work closely with the village panchayats. In the joint farms, peasants should be discouraged from selling land to outsiders and, except in the cases of minors and widows, would be expected to till their own lands. Members would be paid in accordance with their share of land and their labour. [74]

The entire idea behind cooperation and cooperative farming was genuine participation of agriculturists in the production process, leading to their political participation as well. Decentralization, diminution of bureaucratic control, lack of compulsion and voluntary collaboration would be the distinctive mark of the Indian model of socialism in the countryside. An agrarian economy of small farms organized cooperatively on a village basis seemed the ideal solution. He believed that it would change gradually, the whole fabric of the countryside, strengthen democratic tendencies, raise the yield, provide a 'glimpse of socialism improve the quality of the individual and lift the peasantry as a whole to a higher level of life and closer contact, social cohesion and mutual obligation would be the essential characteristics. If one of the basic problems of the modern world was to balance the inevitable tendency to centralization with individual freedom and initiative which came from decentralization, the cooperative method offered a proper combination of the two.

The progress of the cooperative movement before independence was rather slow. On the eve of independence i.e. on 30th January, 1947, the number of primary agricultural societies was 1.17 lakh, their membership 55.38 lakh and the working capital Rs.30.56 crores, the loans advanced by them were of the order of Rs.19.60 crore. From the moment, India won independence, till his death, Jawaharlal Nehru led the nation in its endeavour to petrify poverty. During the first 17 years of post independence era, the number of agricultural credit societies increased to 2.09 lakh with membership of 2.42 lakh covering 40 per cent of the agricultural population and 83 per cent of the villages. Short and medium term credit to the cultivators increased to Rs. 291crores during 1963-64. A network of 25,000 primary cooperatives covered most of the important secondary markets in the country. The value of agricultural produce marketed by cooperatives increased to Rs. 225 crores during the year. Forty-eight co-operative sugar factories were in production during 1963-64 season and accounted for 23.3 per cent of the total production of sugar in the country, 5 modern rice mills were in different stages of installation, 222 wholesale consumer stores and 3,937 retail units were set up under the centrally sponsored scheme. 1,300 new cooperative farming societies were organised in pilot and non-pilot areas during 1964. Special cooperative programme for backward classes and for the benefit of the weaker sections were launched.[75] This record of performance is really remarkable.

Development of cooperatives during Nehru era may be characterised as self-introspection, vertical and horizontal expansion of cooperative institutions, diversification and decentralisation of various activities and authorities, acceptance of the cooperative ideology as an integral part of planned development of the country and promotion of genuine federal structure of the movement at the various levels. Above all, it was an important step towards imparting social justice to the deprived humanity, that is *kisans* of India. It was fulfilment of a long cherished dream of Nehru.

The third dimension of the land problem that concerned him was the social and cultural backwardness of the man behind the plough, the small peasant burdened by the customs, habits and social institutions of a semifeudal social structure. He was of the view that all the gains of land reforms would be nullified if the peasants' social outlook and the social framework surrounding him were not reformed and reconstituted. Even the opportunities given would not be perceived, or gains from opportunities utilised would be dissipated through conspicuous consumption, if the tiller of the land was not reformed as part of the programme of agricultural development, or rural development.[76]

Nehru's position was thus different from that of the romanticists who taught that the mere provision of property in land to the peasant would turn the land into gold. The social reform of the peasant was essential part of Nehru's conception of agrarian reorganisation. Spread of literacy, education and skills and continuous movements for social reform were to contribute to social change in the desired direction.

The fourth dimension of the problems which concerned him was the tremendous and growing population pressure on land, a burning index of India's backwardness. The fourth dimension of land reform in his view therefore, encompassed the gradual transfer of population from agriculture to non-agriculture occupations. Though Nehru did not view with optimism the prospect of transfer of population from agriculture to modern forms of industrial production, he emphasised the importance of non-agriculture occupations comprising village-based cottage industries and small-scale and medium-scale industries as an outlet to relieve excessive pressure on land. [77]

In this background land reforms were basic to Nehru's perspective of economic development with social-justice within the framework of political democracy for India. He was of the view that what happens in the field of solving the land problem would decide whether India was moving towards this fundamental perspective or not. In other words, the strategy to solve the land problem would determine to a large extent whether the goal of development based on justice, socialism and democracy would be reached or not.

Social Legislation

It was Nehru's aim to establish a just society through just means. He endeavoured to achieve this within the framework of parliamentary democracy, through a series of tedious legal, and social legislation. Though this meant a lot of delay, nevertheless, Nehru's belief in the efficacy of parliament did not allow him to introduce drastic measures which would upset the smooth continuity of Indian life. He moved slowly but steadily and was, to quite an extent able to give India the breakthrough which she needed. The eighteen years of his premiership was an era of building and construction, keeping in view the Indian mind and scientific temper.

Nationalisation

The question as to how to effect the much needed change, and what would be the dynamics of the new social order, it may be noted that Nehru has rejected decisively Gandhiji's theory of trusteeship. He says that the lot of the worker cannot be improved much by charity or goodwill of the employer, and the theory of trusteeship is equally barren "for trusteeship means that the power for good or evil remains with the self-appointed trustee and he may exercise it as he wishes". [78] According to him, "since even the best of men are not so perfect as to be trusted in this way, it is hardly reasonable to believe in the theory of trusteeship and to give unchecked power and wealth to an individual and to expect him to use it entirely for the public good." Even Plato's philosopher-king, he says could hardly have borne this burden worthily. [79] So he tersely remarked, 'that the sole trusteeship that can be fair is the trusteeship of the nation and not of any individual or a group''.[80] Therefore, Nehru's opposition to trusteeship theory stems from the fact, that though the theory might help to alleviate to certain extent the miserable conditions of the people, it would be incapable of effecting the structural changes in the system contemplated by him.

Naturally, therefore, Nehru has contemplated pragmatic methods. He says that equality, which is essential for meaningful liberty and democracy, ''cannot be established so long as the principal instruments of production are privately owned''.[81] One fact to be noted here is that he has carefully used the expression ''principal instruments of production'', which connotes that he contemplated nationalisation only of major means of production which are of national and social consequences. This point has been amplified by him when he said: ''the state would acquire and control key industries which are of vital importance and other industries only if they obstruct the progress''.[82] Besides, he is of opinion that state must become more and more the organiser of constructive industry.[83]

Again here the use of the expression ''organiser of constructive industry'' indicates that he had been thinking more in terms of bringing the major industries of vital importance under the state control leaving a narrow field in terms of embarking on reckless acquisition of enterprises, big and small. Because, his views for national ownership of, and control on, industries and other major undertakings were obviously conditioned by the consideration that such ownership and control must lead to the transformation of the present system and induce social justice.

Change in Property Relations

Nehru's views regarding property, in the context of social justice is quite revolutionary. He was convinced that property relations had to be altered to suit the needs of the country. Excess of property to some and total absence of even the barest necessaries for the masses, created an unequal and unjust society. Fundamental changes had to be brought about to remove the inequality and disparity accruing from the accumulation of property in few hands. He refused to conform to the views of some of his colleagues that, ''Men will sooner forget the death of their relatives than the confiscation of their property''. He made a bold departure and declared, ''We would rather not encourage such men in this country. It is a monstrous thing that property should be made a God, above human beings. To say that whatever a man may do, he may even murder - is nothing, but property is a God and must be worshipped, is a view of property which Government is not prepared to accept at all''.[84] Thus according to him, property relation is the fundamental issue in society, for it, ''ultimately governs our institutions and our social fabric and the transformation of the existing property relation is essential to remove the inherent defects of the present system''. [85]

The amendment to change property relations, proposed by Nehru and accomplished by his government is fundamental step towards the socio-economic emancipation of the country. At that time Nehru's effort-aroused a lot of controversy. It is worthwhile to examine his views regarding this matter.

On the 19th of September, 1949, Jawaharlal Nehru opened the debate in the Constituent Assembly on the provisions of Art. 31 of the Constitution, which he introduced for incorporation in Part III of the Constitution. The Article he moved in the form of an amendment was, according to him, a compromise solution.[86] His characterisation or description of Art. 31 as a compromise solution must be understood in the context of two conflicting views on the subject mentioned earlier. Then explaining the significance of the Article, he said that there were two approaches to the property right embodied therein. One approach was from the point of view of individual right to property and the other was from the point of view of community's interest in that property or the community's right, and the Article, according to him, not only tried to remove or avoid any possible conflict between them but also tried to take into consideration fully both the rights.

Evidently, in the above statement emphasis has been laid on both the rights, namely, the individual right to property and the community's interest or right in the property. The obvious implication of the emphasis seems to be to forestall any attempt to inflate unduly the individual right to property at the cost of the community's interest in it. Individuals being part of the community, individual right to property must of necessity be exercised consistent with the community's interest or right. The compromise between the two rights, which the Article supposed to effect, therefore, connotes that what has been contemplated in the Article is not obliteration of individual right to property as such but its effective restriction or control so that de-concentration of property and wealth in the hands of a few individuals could be effected and limitation on the holding of property and wealth could be imposed to enable greater number of people to exercise the right to property and thus further the interest of the community as a whole. A natural corollary to this connotation is that if a legislation intends to bring about socio-economic and agrarian reforms and puts a ceiling on the holding of property and wealth by an individual and takes away the surplus of property and wealth concentrated in a few hands for distribution among the members of the community, there is no obliteration of the property right as such but only a compulsion that property and wealth should be shared and right therein should be exercised by as greater number of people as possible to subserve the common good. In other words, socialisation of property is not obliteration of the right to property as such but only the diffusion of the right within, and extension of the right to greater number of persons in the community. Legislation for such social purpose can hardly be expected to stipulate adequate compensation for those who have to part with excess property or wealth. On the other hand, if the state acting under its eminent domain power acquires for governmental purpose property of an individual, whose holding is within the ceiling imposed by agrarian reform laws, the acquisition amounts to obliteration of the property right conceded by the community. In such cases of obliteration of property right for governmental purposes adequate compensation must be paid to the person who is deprived of the property.

This idea has been made clear by Jawaharlal Nehru in the course of his speech in the Constituent Assembly. He said that there was no question of any expropriation without compensation so far as this Constitution was concerned and the law was clear enough regarding acquisition of property for public purpose, compensation to be paid in such cases and the method of judging that compensation. Normally speaking, he said, this principle applied only to, what might be called, petty acquisition or acquisition of small bits of property or even relatively large bits for the improvement of a town, etc. But today the community had to deal with large schemes of social reform and social engineering which could hardly be considered from the point of view of the individual acquisition of a small bit of land or structure. If the chosen representatives of the people sitting in the legislature passed such a social reform legislation which affected millions of people, it would not be possible to leave such a piece of legislation open to widespread and continuous litigation in the courts of law without damaging the future of millions of people and the foundation of the State itself. [88] "If we have to take the property, if the State so wills" he said " we have to see that fair and equitable compensation is given, because we proceed on the basis of fair and equitable compensation. But when we consider the equity of it we have always to remember that equity does not apply only to the individual but to the community. No Individual can override ultimately the rights of the community at large. No community should injure and invade the rights of the individual unless it be for the most urgent and important reasons." [89]

The above statement of Jawaharlal Nehru strikes clearly a dichotomy between acquisition of property for "governmentalpurposes", such as improvement of a town, etc., and acquisition of property for "social purposes", that is, for implementing large schemes of "social reform and social engineering". It is also clear from the statement that the question of fair compensation applies only to the former case and not to the latter, for the latter cannot be considered from the point of the individual acquisition of a small bit of land or structure. Again, his words "no individual can override ultimately the rights of the community" emphasise the fact that the right to hold property guaranteed in the Constitution is not an absolute or undiluted right to hold all the wealth and assets of the community by a few individuals for all time to come to the detriment of the community as a whole. Nor does it mean that the community could be prevented from readjusting the socio-economic structure of the society to ensure economic justice to all. Then, his words, "No community should injure and invade the rights of the individual unless it be for the most urgent and important reasons" are intended to send home the fact that once the right to property is determined in accordance with the interests of the community, the minimal right cannot be invaded or obliterated by the community unless it be for the important and urgent reasons necessitated by the governmental schemes and functions.

It was in this context that Jawaharlal Nehru dealt with the payment and determination of compensation. He said that it was left to Parliament to determine various aspects of it and "there is no reference in this to any judiciary coming into the picture. Much thought has been given to it and there has been much debate as to where the judiciary comes in. Eminent lawyers have told us that on a proper construction of this clause, normally speaking, the judiciary should not and does not come in. Parliament fixes either the compensation itself or the principles governing that compensation and they should not be challenged except for one reason where it is thought that there has been a gross abuse of the law, where in fact there has been a fraud on the Constitution. Naturally the judiciary comes in to see if there has been a fraud on the Constitution or not. But normally speaking, one presumes that any Parliament representing the entire community of the nation will certainly not commit a fraud on its own Constitution and will be very much concerned with doing justice to the individual as well as the community.[90]

Digressing a little Jawaharlal Nehru spoke on the changing concept of property and attendant problems. He said that it changed from the earlier conception of "property in human beings", which reflected in the institution of slavery in olden days, to the modern conception of "property in a bundle of papers" which consisted of securities, promissory notes, etc. In addition to this, there was another change in modern times and that was according to him, the "property in shares" in a joint company. This, in an industrialised country, led to concentration of wealth more and more in a limited number of hands. The result was that a few persons with a monopoly over capital could crush small shopkeepers out of existence by their method of business and, in fact, they could do so without giving the slightest compensation. In such a state of affairs to-day the question of protecting individual right to property, he said, was by no means simple and no legal argument of extreme subtlety would solve it unless the solution took into consideration the human aspect of the problem and also the changes that were taking place in the world.[91] Obviously, what has been contemplated in the Article is the protection of limited individual right to poverty consistent with interest of the community and not the absolute right which leads to concentration of assets of the community in a limited number of hands to the detriment of the exercise of the same right by others.

Finally, in conclusion he stated that the National Congress had laid down years ago that the Zamindari institution and big estate system in India must be abolished, a pledge which would undoubtedly be honoured. No judiciary could stand in judgement over the sovereign will of Parliament representing the will of the entire community. The duty of the judiciary was only to see "in such matters that the representatives of the people did not go wrong."[92] In a detached atmosphere of the courts, he said, 'they should see to it that nothing is done that may be against the Constitution, that may be against the good of the country, that may be against community in the larger sense of the term. Therefore, if such a thing occurs, they should draw attention to that fact, but it is obvious that no court, no system of judiciary can function in the nature of a Third House, as a kind of Third House of correction. So, it is important that with this limitation the judiciary should function.''[93] It may be noted that Nehru, while defining the role of the judiciary with respect to Art. 31, said that the duty of the court was to see that ''nothing is done that may be against the Constitution''. In this expression the use of the word Constitution instead of the phrase 'right to property' is significant in that the court is not expected to view the right to property in a narrow perspective or from the point of view of the interest of a few individuals but to view it in a broader perspective of the Constitution and of the good of the country and community as a whole. So the duty of the court, as visualised by Nehru, is to see whether a particular measure taken by the State under Art. 31 is 'against the Constitution' or against the good of the country and the community, but not merely against the property right. That is to say, a legislative measure taken under Art. 31 effecting the right to property is not tantamount to unconstitutional act if the measure is intended to implement paramount socio-economic policies laid down in the Constitution. Therefore, the constitutionality or unconstitutionality of the State act must be judged not from the extent of dents it makes on the right to property alone, but from over-all consideration of the Constitution and the extent to which it succeeds or fails to implement the socio-economic policies and ideals embodied in the Constitution.

Changes in property relations, was intended by Nehru to be fundamental, peaceful and legitimate means toward socio-economic transformation of society, a revolution without fear and minus violence, a democratic step towards achievement of social justice by just means.

Education

Jawaharlal Nehru held education as a prime factor in the building up of a good society. Most of the ills of Indian society were due to mass-scale illiteracy. The villages of India were unaware of the importance of education and were as a result steeped in superstition, tradition and ignorance. In the absence of education the entire rural India as well as many in the cities were cut off from the mainstream of development -

scientific and technological, taking place around the world. In fact, Nehru felt that, it was the reason for poverty and backwardness with which India had come to be associated.[94]

Thus, it was very natural that, one of the first tasks which he undertook, after becoming the Prime Minister was to plan for mass-scale education, especially in the rural areas. Mass education, was important for industrialisation, which was not a matter merely of putting up steel plants at odd places but of building up from below a nation used to thinking in terms of technical change and advance. It would be an instrument of mental change, leading to a change in attitude, habit and orientation.

Though the government had not been able to fulfil the directives in the Constitution that, by 1961 every child up to the age of fourteen should have free and compulsory education, it set out to do so by 1966 and to reduce the age to eleven. The Third Plan aimed to have in schools about twenty million children comprising 60 per cent of those aged six to fourteen years. But it was also proposed to provide in merely 30 per cent of schools the type of education which was suited to the developmental activities of the local community. The object was the schooling of the Indian peasant, the promotion of his ability to adapt himself to the changing environment, teaching him to modernize without losing his roots in the cultural past.

Some people seemed to believe that one of the fundamental human rights was that to be stupid. "Are we to encourage stupidity in this country? Is it a fundamental right to stand on one leg in the river Yamuna when the eclipse is taking place?" [95] Education was the foundation of social and economic progress and a major step towards the equalising of opportunity; and Nehru was prepared, despite his keenness on industrialization to reduce expenditure on engineering projects rather than education. "I have come to feel that it is the basis of all and, on no account unless actually our heads are cut off and we cannot function, must we allow education to suffer". [96]

In the final analysis, a modern nation was not the product of heavy industry and scientific agriculture but of educated and trained human beings. Nehru also revived his old ideas of a year's compulsory training for students in social work. The number of urban schools and colleges were increasing fast and many were attaining proficiency in engineering and technology; but they had little knowledge of rural conditions. A stretch of work outside the towns would provide a rounded view as well as strengthen the sense of discipline. [97]

Nehru also had the imaginative idea of setting up panchayats in the schools. He wanted pupils of each village school to elect a small body for dealing with such matters as discipline, recreation and sanitation and even to run a cooperative. In short he had images of maintaining and coordinating the rhythm of life between the individual and society and the past and the present and getting the Indian peasant in line with the rhythm of the modern world, all by means of the cooperatives, the panchayats and the schools.

Nehru looked to education in itself, rather than as a prelude to the proper working of panchayats, for giving confidence to the peasants. Education took in his view the first community development, and then Panchayati Raj, had occupied as the most revolutionary factor which would change the face of the country. The spread of education would make the people conscious of their conditions and surroundings, and awaken them from the depths of inertia and lethargy towards progress and prosperity.

Welfare of Women

Nehru was especially sensitive towards the position of women in India. His concern for their emancipation and uplift to bring them at par with their male counter-parts found an important place in his writings and speeches. Whenever he spoke about women, he made an effort to arouse their consciousness and to shake them off from a state of mental slumber. Social justice to him meant the betterment of the condition of the women in India. The importance that Nehru laid on the position of women, raises him to level of great reformers like Raja Ram Mohan Roy and Mahatma Gandhi who understood the indispensable place of women in society. Speaking at the Mahila Vidyapith, Allahabad, in a historic assessment of women's role Nehru said, "A great French idealist Charles Fourer once said "Onecould judge the degree of civilization of a country by the social and political position of its women."And if we are to judge India today, we shall have to judge her by her women. The future that we built up will also be judged by the position of Indian women." [98]

The moral and physical subjugation of the womenfolk revolted him and he was very much aware of the precarious position of the Indian women, " I must confess to you that I am intensely dissatisfied with the lot of the Indian women today''. He castigated the tendency to chant the glory of revered women like Sita and Savitri in a bid to hide the present deficiencies and to prevent us from attacking the root cause of women's degradation in India today.[99]

Nehru admonished the tendency to orient the women with the thought that their sole aim of existence was marriage, rearing children and serving their revered elders only. "May I say that I do not agree with this ideal of women's life or education. What does it signify? It means that women have one and only profession, that is the profession of marriage and it is our chief business to train her for this profession. Even in this profession her lot is to be one of secondary importance. She is always to be devoted help-mate, the follower and the obedient slave of her husband and others''. [100]

Vehemently opposed to the idea of women being in 'Purdah', enforced child marriages, their treatment like mere playthings leading to mental, physical and intellectual exploitation, he said, "The future of India cannot consist of dolls and playthings and if you made half the population of a country a mere plaything of the other half, an encumbrance on others, how will you ever make progress? Therefore, I say that you must face the problem boldly and attack the roots of the evil''.[101]

Nehru strongly supported the political participation of women and felt that if India were to progress, women would have to emerge out of seclusion and take an active part in the nation's politics. A nation could never progress with half of its population enslaved in the kitchen. [102] He visualised an active role of women in the freedom struggle and urged them to come forward and do their duty in freeing their country. In a message to the U.P. Women's Conference held in Kanpur in November, 1945, Nehru said, "I have long been of opinion that a nation's progress depends on the position of women there. The fall of India from her high status was partly at least due to the deterioration of the status and position of women in India. In a subject country men and women both suffer the indignity of subjection to foreign rule and the numerous disabilities that flow from it ... We have seen during the past quarter of a century how the participation of women in the great National struggle in India has in fact raised their status in many ways and opened out opportunities to them ... Now we are on the verge of great changes, but for this great efforts and sacrifice will be needed''. He visualised an important role of women in the attainment of freedom, ''In these I hope women will take a leading part and thus fit themselves for the responsibilities ahead. They will have the further task of getting rid of the many disabilities, legal, social and others which today attach to their sex, so that they may play an equal part with their menfolk in the building up for a free India.[103]

In this context he sincerely appreciated the role women were playing in the freedom struggle and was full of praise for their active participation and determination to assist in the achievement of freedom. During the Civil Disobedience Movement women came out of their homes in large numbers and took active parts in the picketing and boycott activities. Appreciating their role in glowing terms Nehru wrote in his *Autobiography,* ''Many strange things happened those days but undoubtedly the most striking was the part of the women in the national struggle. They came out in large number from the seclusion of their homes and, though unused to public activity, threw themselves in the heart of the struggle. The picketing of foreign clothes and liquor shops, they made their domain. Enormous processions consisting of women alone were taken out in all the cities, and, generally, the attitude of the women was more unyielding than that of the men. Often they became Congress 'dictators' in provinces and in local areas''. [104]

Nehru had definite plan for the uplift of women. One such way was education, to which he attributed supreme importance. He was specifically concerned about women education and the role it would play in moulding and forming their personalities. Since women were the actual home makers, Nehru, believed that it was important that women get proper education. In this context speaking at the International Congress on Planned Parenthood in February, 1959, he said, ''Of the spread of education the most important aspect in India today is the spirit of education among girls. That is even now changing, powerfully, effecting the home life of our people because home life is affected more by the woman than by the man. These large numbers of girls that go to high schools and colleges, naturally bring all kinds of ideas with them, the ways of living gradually bring change in their homes. I do not know if this particular aspect is appreciated fully - the change in the Indian home that is coming about through the girls who have gone through the high school or college education... It is these girls who are likely to change the living habits of our people more than we do and it is these girls who will probably succeed in carrying the message of family planning further than some of your official workers''. [105]

The proposal to codify and make uniform the various personal laws of the Hindu (laws relating to marriage, succession, inheritance, adoption, the joint family), which was first mooted in 1941, received an impetus from the Directive Principles of the Indian Constitution of 1950, which enjoined upon the state the duty to endeavour to secure for the citizens of India (Hindus, Muslims, Christians, Parsis and others) a uniform Civil Code. The modernisation and codification of Hindu Laws was considered the first step towards the modernisation of other personal laws, undividing Christians and Muslims. The draft Hindu Code Bill, prepared in 1947, was discussed in the Constituent Assembly in 1948. Nehru was in favour of the general principles embodied in the Bill. In 1955 the Hindu Marriage Act, in 1956 other Bills like Hindu Succession Act, the Hindu Minority and Guardianship Act and the Hindu Adoption and Maintenance Act were passed.

Nehru put all his weight behind the legislation and from 1952 to 1956 he tutored the members of Parliament and the general public in the principles underlying the bills. Political and economic changes, and the bills he claimed, stress to bring in a long overdue social change in India- the emancipation of women. [106] By rendering Hindu marriage monogamous, by giving the daughter an equal share along with son and widow in the intestate succession to a father's estate, and by making provisions for the dissolution of marriage in certain cases the proposed legislation was intended to restore to women their dignity and rights as human beings. Hindu orthodoxy found the introduction of divorce into Hindu marriage a peculiarly bitter pill to swallow. But Nehru insisted that by providing for divorce they were making for happier marriage. [107] He pointed out to the members of Parliament that in just one State of India, the State of Saurashtra, 'there is on average one suicide a day among women because of maladjustment, in human relationships.'[108] Though not all members of Parliament were generally converted to the ideas, they did not want to be branded as reactionaries. Besides, Nehru's personality had come to assume a force which none in his party could think of openly defying. The Bills were passed with considerable majority.

Drive Against Untouchability

The just society of Nehru's conception was one in which there would be no discrimination. India, a land with traditions and culture of millennia, nevertheless, abounded in social evils, exploitation and discrimination on the basis of caste, creed and race, "I saw around me superstitious practices, outworn ideas, and above all, our subject and poverty stricken state".[109]

One of the greatest ills eating into the vitals of India, as recognised by Nehru is untouchability--a practice which had divided her into many parts and brought in its train acute differences between its citizens. "It is a doctrine of hatred, and is a cause of spilt and division among the people. It affords an easy ground for divide and rule. It is repugnant to all true religion and humanity. It is against true social democracy and is a block in the way of one united India. It has been the cause of India's downfall and impotency of her teeming millions... This irreligious, religious: imperialism must go."[110]

Nehru got the opportunity to do away with this malicious practice in the form of constitutional amendment, which declared untouchability as a cognizable offence. In 1946 at a meeting of A.I.C.C., moving the resolution Nehru said, "In order to have and lay a firm foundation for a strong, durable, one and united grand India, it is necessary to remain and abolish untouchability that exists in the land by the Iron rod Authority. It would not be removed by mere preaching. Times demand its abolition". [111] He resolved to ameliorate this evil from its root from the body politic of India.

Elimination of factors which create inequality among the people in the society, is as essential for the realisation of equality in fact as the equilibrium creating protective discriminations. This is essentially a theory of levelling which helps to level up artificial social contours. Two provisions in the Constitution, which seek to eliminate factors of social inequality, are Arts. 17 and 18. The former prohibits "untouchability" and the latter abolishes 'titles'.

Prohibition of Untouchability

Art. 17 of the Constitution states, "Untouchability is abolished and its practice in any from is forbidden. The enforcement of any disability arising out of untouchability shall be an offence punishable in accordance with law". Art. 35 authorises Parliament to prescribe punishment for those acts which are declared offences under Part III of the Constitution.[112]

Exercising the power under the provision, Parliament enacted in 1955 the Untouchability Offence Act. The Act outlaws the enforcement of disabilities on the ground of untouchability in regard to, among others, entrance to, and worship at, temples, access to occupation and trade, use of water sources, places of public resort and accommodation, public conferences, hospitals, educational institutions, construction and occupation of residential premises, holding of religious ceremonies and procession etc. [113]

Though untouchability has not been removed from the Indian society despite constitutional enactments, still Nehru's effort to ameliorate this curse, has paid dividends. Today we find that in many metropolitan cities as well in small cities there is not much of discrimination and the idea of social equality has come to be accepted by all. It can be said with optimism that a day will arrive when all types of social discrimination shall be wiped out. Nehru, by his ceaseless efforts extricated India out of age - old dogmas and tried to lessen many discrepancies which abounded in the nation. Gandhi pioneered the social revolution against untouchability, Nehru as Prime Minister provided legal resolution for its abolishment.

Conclusion

The concept of social justice is primarily based on the idea that all men are equal in society without distinction of religion, race, caste, colour or creed. It also means the absence of privileged classes in society. The concept of social equality has been considered a *sine qua-non* for effective exercise of the rights guaranteed in the constitution to all citizens: "The more likely they are to be able to utilize their freedom in realms worthy of explanation. Certainly history of the abolition of special privileges has been, also, the history of the expansion of what in our inheritance was open to the common man. The more equality there is in a state, the more use in general, we can make of our freedom" [114] Jawaharlal Nehru channelised all his effort towards attainment of social-justice in India through just and democratic means. His premiership offered him the opportunity to translate into reality the aims and objectives that he had set up for himself and for the country. It is remarkable to note that all steps taken in that direction were in conformity with the democratic tradition of India, the temper and the need of the country.

Nehru fought hard against forces of disruption, coservatism superstition and inertia, to make India self-reliant. Planning, Community Development, National Extension Service, changes in the right to property, emphasis on education, reform in the Hindu Code Bill, drive against untouchability and poverty, are some of the steps that Nehru took to achieve his goals. He may not have succeeded fully, nevertheless he made a phenomenal breakthrough to gear up India on to the path of development and distribution of social justice to her citizens.

References

1. Dorothy Norman, *"Nehru: The First Sixty Years"* vol.1, p.319.
2. *Ibid.*, pp. 153-54.
3. *Ibid.*, pp. 153-54.
4. Presidential Address, Trade Union Congress, Nagpur, Nov. 30, 1939 in Dorothy Norman, *"Nehru The First Sixty Years"* vol.I, p-178.
5. *J.Nehru's Speeches*, vol. III, p 52.
6. Dorothy Norman, *"Nehru: The First Sixty Years"* vol.1, p-626.
7. *Ibid.*, p-451.
8. *J.Nehru's Speeches*, Vol. III, p-63-64, Address to Associated Chambers of Commerce, Calcutta, Dec. 14, 1953.
9. Dorothy Norman, *"Nehru: The First Sixty Years"* vol.1, p. 155.
10 *J. Nehru's Speeches* Vol. 1, P.140.
11 Dorothy Norman, *"Nehru: The First Sixty Years"* vol.1, p-204.
12. Andre Malraux, *Antiomemoirs* Gellimond, 1967, p. 205.
13. J. Nehru, *An Autobiography*, pp. 20-24.
14. Andre Malraux, *Antiomemoirs* p. 205.
15. Deed of Trust of Swaraj Bhavan, A.I.C.C., File-628, p.249 (NMML).
16. Dorothy Norman, *"Nehru: The First Sixty Years"* vol.1, p. 451
17. *Ibid.*
18. Dorothy Norman, *"Nehru: The First Sixty Years"* vol.1, p.451.
19. *J.Nehru's Speeches*, vol. II, p. 93.
20. *J.Nehru's Speeches* vol. III, p. 133.
21. From *Presidential* Address, Lahore, Dorothy Norman, *"Nehru: The First Sixty Years"* vol.1, p.205.
22. Nehru's Presidential Address, Faizpur Congress Dec. 1936 *"Nehru: The First Sixty Years"* vol.1, p-470.
23. *J. Nehru's Speeches*, vol.1, p-141
24. Dorothy Norman, *"Nehru: The First Sixty Years"* vol.1, p-154.

25. *J. Nehru's Speeches*, vol.III, p.85.
26. *Ibid.*
27. *Ibid.*, p. 164.
28. J. Nehru's Speech at the All India Congress Committee, 10th October, 1946, *A.I.C.C. papers* 725, 1946 (NMML).
29. Economic and Social Programme I.N.C. Resolution on Fundamental Rights and Economic Policy, passed at Karachi, 1931, in Dorothy Norman, "*Nehru: The First Sixty Years*" vol.1, p. 250.
30. S. Gopal, *Jawaharlal Nehru: A Biography*, vol.1, p.240.
31. Letter to Indira, 9 July, 1933, *Glimpses of World History*, p.857.
32. From Speech in Lok Sabha while moving the Third Five Year Plan be taken into consideration, August 21, 1961, in *J. Nehru's Speeches*, Vol. IV, p-142.
33. Dorothy Norman, "*Nehru: The First Sixty Years*" vol.1, p.690.
34. *Ibid.*
35. Memorandum to National Planning Committee, June, 1939, *Nehru's Papers*, (NMML).
36. Note to National Planning Committee, 30 August, 1940, *Ibid.*
37. Dorothy Norman, "*Nehru: The First Sixty Years*" vol.1, p.691.
38. J.Nehru, *Discovery of India*, p.371.
39. From a speech at the Golden Jubilee of the Indian Merchants Chamber, Bombay, Feb. 3, 1958. *J. Nehru's Speeches*. vol. 4, p-112.
40. *J.Nehru's Speeches*, Speech at the I.D.P.A., April 6, 1957.
41. Speech in the Lok-Sabha, Dec. 15, 1962, *J.Nehru's Speeches*, vol. II, p.86.
42. Taya Zinkin, *Pacific Affairs*, Sept. 1955.
43. Speech in Lok-Sabha, Dec. 15, 1952, *J. Nehru's Speeches* Vol. II, pp. 86-87.
44. *J. Nehru's Speeches*, Vol 1, p.96-97.
45. *J. Nehru's Speeches*, vol.4, From inagural address to Asian Economic Planners Conference, New Delhi, Sept. 21, 1961, p. 148 and 150.
46. Transcript of Prime Minister's Press Conference held in Vigyan Bhavan on June 4, 1958, P.M.'s Secretariat, vol. 8, (P.I.B.). New Delhi.
47. *J. Nehru's Speeches*, vol.4, p.-147-48.
48. Speech at the Community Project Conference, New Delhi, May 7, 1952, in *J. Nehru's Speeches*, vol. II, New Delhi, Publication Division, p-55.
49. P.Singh, *Community Development Programme in India*, New Delhi, Deep and Deep Publication, 1982, p-28-30.
50. Nehru's Speech at Conference of Development Commissioners, May, 1962, August, 1952, in *Jawaharlal Nehru on Community Development, Panchayati Raj and Cooperation* (Delhi, 1965), p-2-3 and 12.
51. Nehru to Chief Ministers, 2 Oct., 1952, in S. Gopal, *Jawaharlal Nehru: A Biography*, Vol 2, p-199.
52. S. Gopal, *Jawaharlal Nehru: A Biography*, vol.2, p 200-201.
53. *J. Nehru's speeches*, vol.1, p-89.
54. Report of the team for the study of Community Projects and National extension Service, 1957, (Balwantrai Mehta Committee Report).
55. From Speech in Hindi at Nagaur in Rajasthan on the occasion of the inauguration of Panchayati Raj in the State, Oct.2, 1959, in *J. Nehru's Speeches*, vol.4, p.93.
56. In S. Gopal, *Jawaharlal Nehru: A Biography*, Vol.3, p.167.
57. *Ibid.*, p-168.

58. *Nehru's Speeches*, vol. 4, "The Basic Approach", p. 122.
59. "When you think of the land question in India today, you are really thinking of something dynamic, moving and changing, something revolutionary. It may well change the face of India," a speech while moving an Amendment to Article 24 of the Draft Constitution *Assembly*, New Delhi, Sept. 10, 1947, *J. Nehru's Speeches*. vol. II, (Publication Division), p. - 477.
60. Presidential Address at the A.I.C.C. Session, Lahore, 29 Dec., 1929, in S. Gopal, *Jawaharlal Nehru : An Autobiography*, p-83.
61. Dorothy Norman, "*Nehru: The First Sixty Years*" vol.1, p.469-70.
62. Lahore Address, *Selected Works*, vol. 4, p-993.
63. Presidential Address, Faizpur, Dec., 1936, In Dorothy Norman, "*Nehru: The First Sixty Years*" vol.1, p-471.
64. *Progress of Land Reform*, New Delhi, Govt. of India, Planning Commission, 1963 Preface.
65. *Ibid.*
66. H.D. Malviya, *Land Reforms in India*. New Delhi, A.I.C.C., (1954), p 91.
67. *Progress on Land Reforms Planning Commission*, 1962 p. 14
68. H.D. Malviya, *Land Reforms in India*, (First Edition, New Delhi, INC, 1954) p-95.
69. Speech at a Seminar on Planning, Ootacmund 30 May, 1959, A.I.C.C. Papers, Box, 312, File G 36 of 1959, in S.Gopal, *Jawaharlal Nehru: A Biography*, vol. III, p-113-14.
70. Nehru to Chief Ministers, 6 Sept., 1958, *National Herald*, 7 Sept, 1958.
71. Speech at Bhopal, 1 Nov., *National Herald*, 2 Nov., 1958.
72. S. Gopal, *Jawaharlal Nehru: A Biography*, vol. III, p - 114.
73. Nehru at A.I.C.C., Nagpur, 9 Jan., *The Hindu*, 10 Jan., 1959.
74. S. Gopal, *Jawaharlal Nehru: A Biography*, vol. III, p - 114-15.
75. B.R. Sinha, *Cooperatives in India*, National Cooperative Union of India, New Delhi, 1969), p-54.
76. *Selected Works*, vol. 4, p.993.
77. Speech at Madurai, April 15, 1959, *Jawaharlal Nehru's Speeches*, vol. 4, Publication Division Govt of India, New Delhi, p-129-31.
78. Dorothy Norman, "*Nehru: The First Sixty Years*" vol.1, p.178.
79. J. Nehru, *An Autobiogrpahy*, p-528.
80. Dorothy Norman, "*Nehru: The First Sixty Years*" vol.1, p.205.
81. *Ibid.*, p.625.
82. *J. Nehru's Speeches*, vol.1, p-126.
83. *Ibid.*, p-124.
84. Speech in Lok Sabha on Bill to Amend Article 31 (2) of the Constitution, April 11, 1955 in *J. Nehru's Speeches*, vol. III, p-53.
85. Dorothy Norman, "*Nehru: The First Sixty Years*" vol.1, p.625-26.
86. *Constituent Assembly Debates*, vol. IX, p-1193.
87. *Ibid.*, p.1192.
88. *Ibid.*, p.1192.
89. *Ibid.*, p.1192.
90. *Ibid.*, p.1193.
91. *Ibid*, p.1194-95.
92. *Ibid.*,p.1195.
93. *Ibid.*, p.1195-96.
94. *J. Nehru's Speeches*, Vol-III, 1953-57, pp-402-406.

95. Address to Congress Parliamentary Party, 14 April 1961, in S. Gopal, Jawaharlal *Nehru: A Biography*, vol. III, p. 169.
96. Speech at the National Development Council, 31 May, 1961, P.I.B., New Delhi.
97. S. Gopal, *Jawaharlal Nehru: A Biography*, vol, III, p. 169.
98. Speech at Mahila Vidyapith, Allahabad, 31st March, 1928, in *Selected Works*, vol. 3, p-361.
99. *Ibid.*
100. *Ibid.*
101. *Ibid.*
102. J. Nehru, *Glimpses of World History*, p. 683.
103. Message to U.P. Women's Conference. 1 Nov., 1945, in *Selected Works*, vol. 14, p-224-25.
104. J. Nehru, *An Autobiography*, p. 214-15.
105. Prime Minister's speech at International Conference on Planned Parenthood, New Delhi, 14 Feb., 1949, *P.M.'s Secretariat* - 13, March - 1959, p-I 13.
106. Speech in Lok Sabha, 22 May, 1954, *J. Nehru speeches*, vol. 3, p. 440-2.
107. *Ibid.*
108. *Ibid.* Speech in Lok Sabha, 5 May, 1955, vol.3, p 446-54.
109. J. Nehru, *Discovery of India*, p-49.
110. Speech at the A.I.C.C. Feb. 25, 1946, (NMML).
111. *Ibid.*
112. K.P. Krishna Shetty, *Fundamental Rights and Socio-Economic Justice in the Indian Constitution*, p. 173.
113. *Ibid.*
114. Harola J. Laski, *Liberty in the Modern State*, 1948, p. 52.

CHAPTER 5

NEHRU AND THE INDIAN NATIONAL MOVEMENT

For several decades Jawaharlal Nehru's name has been inseparably linked with the struggle for liberation of India from colonial yoke, for its re-birth and development. He led the independent country for almost seventeen years, helping it come to life again and abolish colonialism, the legacy of feudalism and age-old backwardness.

Nehru's monumental role in the national liberation movement can be equalled only to Gandhi. He was perhaps the only leader in the liberation movement who had a vision, a concrete programme for the future and a definite ideology for the nation. While the other leaders were mostly concerned with 'Swaraj' or 'Self-Rule' or 'Dominion Status', Nehru alone declared "Complete Independence" as his goal and the goal of the national movement. He did not stop at that, but went ahead and made it categorically clear that the national liberation struggle was not merely struggle for independence, but also for social revolution leading to social reconstruction. Under the leadership of Nehru the movement became multi-dimensional. It stepped out of the national contours to step into international frontiers, thereby becoming an important part in the world-wide struggle for human emancipation.

For a proper assessment of Jawaharlal Nehru's role in the formation of the ideology of the national movement, its functioning and its programme, it is necessary that we have a look into the ideological currents of the movement, before the advent of Nehru on the political scene or his plunge into politics.

Currents of National Struggle

The achievement of freedom by India was a unique phenomenon. It was the transformation of a civilisation into a nationality. It is the fulfilment of nationality through the establishment of national sovereignty. It was throughout the course of its advance a movement directed as much against the violence of the other as against the unreason of the self. In essence it was an ethical struggle both in relation to the foreigner as well as members of its own body. And where similar struggles have been accompanied with bloodshed, the movement in India, through intense and accompanied with much suffering, was non-violent.[1]

The illusion of permanence held powerful sway over the minds of the British in india in 1885. An ideology of paternalistic benevolence, occasionally combined with talk of trusteeship and training towards self-government, thinly veiled the realities of a Raj uncompromisingly white and despotic. Political decision making and administration at higher levels were entirely the privileges of the Europeans. The inclusion in 1861 of a handful of nominated 'natives' in Provincial and Supreme Councils had been accompanied by a reduction in the powers of the latter. Even the local self-government introduced with much fanfare by Ripon was essentially no more than a measure of necessary financial decentralization. Indian collaboration were obviously indispensable for the day today running of a huge country. The post 1857 years had been the renewal and consolidation of links with princes, Zamindars and a variety of urban and ruler notables and the 662 native rulers in particular were to remain the most loyal bullworks till the very end.[2]

There was, however, another class in india, the small, growing elite of Indian educated in the English language, the middle-class. By 1885 they were not more than about 50,000. Some of them went into official service, but the majority, the lawyers, the doctors and journalists, familiar with English political literature and political thought, were eager for wider avenues for public work. They were not revolutionaries, asserted their loyality, and sought only greater opportunities of official employment, administrative reforms, facilities for trade and a measure of elections to the legislative council.[3]

The middle-class enjoyed patronage of the British and in return pledged full loyalty and support to the government. Imbued with liberal ideology--they conformed to the Rule of Law, accepted British sense of jusitice, were anti-medieval, believed in the assertion of reason, and were anti - authority as is characteristic of liberalism. Faith in reason enabled the new middle class to question and oppose tradition, superstition and authority. The concoction and authority of priest-craft were the first targets of attack. Soon administrative and political affairs came under scrutiny. Reason, made this class accept the progressive role of the British rule and western contact, imbibe and transmit the progressive elements of the west, and strive for the attainment of liberal-cum - democratic values, ideals and institutions. In the social sphere agitations for removal of archaic, inhuman and inhibitory practices, traditions and institution characterized new India. In the field of culture, the rich flowering of vernaculars was made possible. In economics, the achievements for Naoroji, Ranade, Dutt and Gokhale prepared the ground for the birth of the nationalist school. In political life, reason was employed as a weapon for justifying all sorts of causes ranging from national freedom to narrow factionalism.[4]

The history of the ideology and programme of the national movement before the advent of Mahatma Gandhi was history of the struggle of the two vitally different thought currents - Liberal patriotism and Militant nationalism. This history can be divided into four clear cut periods, namely 1885 to 1905, 1905 to 1907,1907 to 1915 and 1916 to 1919. Out of these, during the first and the third periods the Liberals dominated the movement and during the second and fourth Nationalists were in ascendancy.

The early movement under the influence of liberal patriotism was vague and indefinite. Even the Congress which was formed in 1885, like a small child was unable to recognize itself. Fathered by one I.C.S. Englishman, Sir A.O. Hume, and blessed by Viceroy Lord Dufferin - it naturally looked to the Government for encouragement and help.

During this period, unlike the Gandhian era the movement was not of the masses but only of the intelligentsia. All the problems of those days of untampered British rule with which the Indian leaders were chiefly concerned were not the grievances of the masses but of the classes. Not that there existed no cause for mass grievances but a sharp distinction was created in the Indian peasantry, the educated as against the unsophisticated and the illiterate.

The history of the movement during 1905 to 1919 was characterized by intense turmoil and civil strife, yet these were the days when the foundations of the ideology and programme of the movement were firmly laid and it tended to become truly national and revolutionary. In 1905 came into prominence a new party, the Nationalist Party, under the triple leadership of Bal Gangadhar Tilak, Bipin Chandra Pal and Lala Lajpat Rai, " The superiority of the new party", says Acharya Narendra Deva, "consisted in its realization of the basic truths of modern politics. In their hands Indian politics gave up the old shibboleths and its solid foundations were laid for the first time. The new party also succeeded in destroying many of the old illusions, to which our leaders of the moderate school still passionately cling." As against the Liberals, the policies of the nationalists were aggressive, advocated self-reliance, Home rule and Swaraj. The liberals looked towards the west, the nationalists sought inspiration and guidance in ancient India. With the advent of the nationalists the Indian National Movement got a new programme and ideology and a new orientation.

The most important change that took place was that with Tilak dawned the era of anti-imperialism hitherto unknown to Indians. More aptly, it may be called nationalist anti-imperialism. He awakened the nationalist sentiments to achieve the ouster of the British. Tilak rallied all the forces of nationalism in an endeavour to combat British imperialism. In fact he sowed the seed, of anti-imperialism which was later to become the hallmark of the national movement.

The year 1920 marks the beginning of a new era the Gandhian-era in Indian history in general and the Congress history in particular. He was able to alter the old creed of the Congress in such a way as to eliminate the declared adherence of that body to the British connection and to the constitutional methods of agitation. He infused fresh life into the national movement. Before the advent of Gandhi the movement was mainly dominated by the upper-class and the middle-class intelligentsia. Now the peasants moved in. He touched the emotions of the multitude, his message reached every nook and corner of the seven lakh villages of India and captivated the hearts of the peasants, which constitute real India. The struggle now became mass movement. His leadership gave the movement a dynamism and drive it never experienced before.

Gandhi carried forward the goal of anti-imperialism which was sowed by Tilak and made it a mission for all sections of society. Anti-imperialism now became an all-embracing ideology for the movement. Under the patronage of Gandhi even the Indian capitalists joined the national movement, thus making it a unified struggle against imperialism.

Nehru's Role in the National Movement

The years after 1925 saw the advent of Jawaharlal Nehru on the political scene. Uptil then the movement was mainly dominated and influenced by Gandhiji. The entry of Nehru changed its content and substance. Under his leadership the struggle took a qualitative leap forward. He defined anti-imperialism for the first time. It is instructive to note that the anti-imperialism of Tilak and Gandhi was based mainly on nationalist sentiments and lacked a clear-cut definition and meaning. Anti-imperialism then meant opposition to British rule leading to national independence. But for Nehru anti-imperialism was not merely opposition to British rule, but opposition to the entire system of imperialism. A sharp analysis of the imperialist phenomenon led him to comprehend the forces underlying it. His greatest contribution is that while defining and analysing imperialism he put forward the thesis that the national movement had to have a socialist orientation. Anti-imperialism had essentially to be enjoined with socialism to become the ideology of the national movement. By doing so Nehru made the movement more realistic, more concrete and rational. It was no more merely romantic as it had hitherto been, it was now imbued with a scientific ideology and a new internationalist and socially radical perspective.

Educating the Youth and People

The period from 1920 to 1938 was of crucial significance as Nehru played a leading role in shaping and pushing the national movement nearer to its goal of 'complete independence'. By his magnetic personality he created an awakening among large masses of the people. In his wanderings among the *Kisans* in the year 1925 and later in 1936-37, he was able to penetrate the mass mind and develop a sense of communion. His deep insight into the socio-economic problems of the people enabled him to discover India. It was during this period also that Nehru untiringly preached the gospel of socialism, and evoked wide support for a change in the socialist direction.

Initially, Nehru was not able to create the supporting socialist organisation because the conservatives and Rightist elements within the Congress would not allow it to proceed beyond ceremonial discussion and pious resolutions. Therefore, the response remained mainly amorphous and diffused. But later due to the ceaseless effort of Nehru, the socialist idea was transformed from a mere intellectual postulate into a mobilising force with a national appeal, when the Congress incorporated Socialism as an important part in its programme.

Nehru's priority was clearly stated--anti-imperialism.The other dimension he could foster in the movement would depend greatly on the strength and organisation of workers and peasants mobilised in the movement. The task in its turn could be fully performed only with the support and sympathy of various groups of the left-wing intelligentsia chiefly the educated youth for such a perspective, and then consequent politico-ideological activity. The logical result of this was Nehru's concentration on youth.

First of all, revolutionary temper had to be promoted. Only spirit of revolt could create a generation of youth with sensitivity to the broader issues of exploitation of man by man, nation by nation and class by class. Before one could preach with what to replace the present system it had to be preceded by the spirit of utter disgust and revolt against an antiquated system. "The world changes and progresses because of those who are dissatisfied and who are not prepared to tolerate the evils and injustice of thing as they are or have been."[6]

Nehru did not have an iota of doubt in his mind that only a youth fired by a revolutionary spirit and ideas would be capable of building a new nation. It was the function of the youth to supply this dynamic element in society; to be the standard bearers of revolt against all that was evil and to prevent older people from suppressing all social progress and movement by the mere weight of their inertia.[7] "It is my desire", he said, "that the spirit that was infused in the youth of Europe after the Great War, and especially by the Russian Revolution, should be kindled in every Indian youth. I want youth to bring the older generation to the right path and revolutionise their rigid ideas"[8]. The use of the phrase "Bring to the right path" openly expressed his own rejection of the path the Congress was following under the leadership of older men. The struggle against imperialism and for a new social order had to be accompanied by a regeneration of cultural forces. Nehru was able to see clearly that imperialism and social reaction as an ideology based itself on the firm foundation of feudal authoritarianism and paternalism, including its manifestation in family life. Inculcating the spirit of revolt by the youth would pave the way for revolt against both imperialist and socially reactionary ideas.[9]

Thus, Nehru put forward a minimum programme for building the 'New Youth' ideology and movement. The fundamental planks of a cultural revolution had to be anti-caste, anti-communal, and anti-feudal and strive for equality and an egalitarian order. These were the essential mediation which would take the youth along the road towards acceptance of a socialist ideology - "a complete whole comprising all areas of life", aware of all forms of oppression and inequality whether between classes and groups or men and women, would they be ready to march forward in the battle for socialism.[10] It was necessary to inundate the youth with rebellion of mind and spirit "against all forms of authoritarianism", with a conception of progress and forward looking action. This liberation would enable them to see why "the present system was a failure and is to be condemned" and would generate a scientific attitude towards the distressing inequalities of class and caste towards which the thinking men and women would specifically the "young, were already sensitive".[11] Once the inertia of the past was broken down, the ideology of socialism would not be the rootless and sterile abstraction it became when addressed to persons still submerged in old communal and caste-loyalties. Only a radicalised youth could stand on the threshold of absorbing our social organisation.[12]

What would be the precise programme for the socialism in India? To these and all other questions there could only be a single answer: Study, for socialism was a complex subject, it had to be thought, studied and practised seriously and thoughtfully.[13] It was for the youth of the country to think out the solution and work for it. The spirit of intellectual revolt, should be followed by intellectual inquiry, "A clash of ideas leading to clear thinking and ultimately its translation into action".[14]

The main purpose of youth organisations should be to discuss social, political and economic problems and hammer out the truth.[15] The average student knew next to nothing about communism and socialism.[16] The various Youth Leagues would have their principal object self-education by discussion, study circles and by developing contacts with the masses.[17]

Nehru left no stone unturned to educate and inform the youth, to inject into them the spirit of revolt against the entire system that was imperialism and prepare them for the harder tasks of the freedom struggle. It was mainly due to the influence and presence of Nehru that the youth were attracted to the movement in a big way. Even an Englishman like Sir Evan Scott, President of the Bengal Legislative Council 1922-25, grudgingly admitted that Nehru had "undoubtedly captured the ear of young India".[18]

International Orientation to the Movement

Another remarkable contribution of Jawaharlal Nehru to the Indian National Movement was his effort to give to the movement an international orientation. Among the prominent leaders of India, Nehru was undoubtedly the most knowledgeable and sensitive to the moving currents of world politics and their impact on the freedom struggle. His profound study and reflection found expression in his writings and speeches, mostly in the *Glimpses of World History, An Autobiography* and *The Discovery of India* and his *Presidential Adddresses to the Congress* in 1929, 1936 and 1937.

Nehru came to the conclusion that new and challenging forces were on the rise and that a future stable world order could be built only on a rational basis. He was witness to the revolution in science and technology which helped mankind to overcome vast distances, creating a broad community of interests even though nations widely differed in economic and political institutions. "The world has become internationalised; production is international, markets are international, and transport is international. Only men's ideas continue to be governed by a dogma which has no real meaning today. No nation is really independent. They are all interdependent.[19] The world had truly become interdependent and indivisible. No longer could nation-states remain mutually exclusive and isolated from the mainstream of global politics.

Nehru often declared in unmistakable terms that India's struggle for independence must also be viewed in an international context, divorce from which was unreal and harmful. Isolation meant insulation and that led to the creation of an abnormal psychology among the people of a country, as they were cut-off from the moving currents of world politics, thought and progress. Nehru viewed the national struggle in India as a part of the wider whole and always related it to the forces which were moving the twentieth century. He said, "We thus see that the world has become a delicate and complicated organism, each part depending on the other, and more wholly capable of standing apart. How then can India ignore the rest of the world, or keep herself in splendid isolation? India must understand world forces and take her proper share in shaping them. India must also get her ideas in line with facts and realities".[20]

The Indian freedom struggle was only a part of the struggle which being waged all over the world. He always made it a point to emphasise that India's liberation would hold no meaning if the remaining parts of the world were locked in conflict. Thus, " India's struggle today is part of the great struggle which is going on all over the world for the emancipation of the oppressed. Essentially, this is an economic struggle, with hunger and want as its driving forces, although it puts on nationalist and other dresses".[21]

Nehru had no use for narrow nationalism which alienated a country from another, "National isolation is rather a detestable war on possible ideal in a world which is daily becoming more of a unit. National and international activities dominate the world and a nation's ideal and objective cannot go against this historical tendency, and we must be prepared to discard a narrow nationalism in favour of world cooperation and real internationalism".[22]

A critical analysis of the functioning of imperialism led him to believe that the whole world were interwoven in that chain. Merely, liberation of one unit or link from the chain would not break it, unless the complete chain was broken, which meant liberation of all nations from the shackles of imperialism, the vicious cycle of enslavement would never end. The problem of imperialism was universal and international.

Having made a radical critique of world capitalism--imperialism, Nehru began to argue for the integration of India's anti-imperialist struggle with Asia's struggle against colonialism and with the world struggle against capitalism "for the emancipation of the oppressed." In his Lucknow address Nehru developed the linkage further. India's problem was "but a part of the world problem of capitalism - imperialism."[23] Moreover, Socialism in Europe and America and the nationalist movements in Africa and Asia formed a single camp against that of Fascism and Imperialism.[24] Thus Nehru's internationalism of the period was politically significant, and quite radical, he hoped to use it to radicalise Indian politics, and to spread Socialist consciousness and ideology among the Indian people.

Nehru's visit of Spain in 1938 gave him vivid glimpses of the civil war, while its untold misery and destruction left a permanent impression on his sensitive mind. The Spanish struggle symbolised to Nehru the overall world conflict between democracy and the forces of freedom on the one hand, and fascism and imperialism on the other. The agony of Spain and its epic struggle forcefully brought into question the highest values of western life democracy, socialism, human dignity, self-determination, freedom and justice. This saga of human courage and endurance deeply moved him. The intensity of his feeling was evident from his writings of that period. "For Spain was not Spain only, but the new world locked in a death struggle with the barbarous hordes of reaction and brutal violence... they (Spain and Czechoslovakia) represented to me precious values in life... If I deserted them, what would I cherish in India; for what kind of freedom do we struggle here"?[25]

Thus Nehru asked, "Whither India?" unhesitatingly he answered, "Surely to the great human goal of social and economic equality, to the ending of an exploitation of nation and class by class, to national freedom within the framework of an international cooperative socialist world federation".[26]

Nehru placed the Indian national movement in a broad perspective, indicating its place in the moving currents of world forces. He argued that the Indian National Congress was based on intense internationalism. Nehru was the first important leader among the Congressmen who saw India's struggle in a broad world perspective, while most Indian nationalists never rose above the limited national horizon. This link-up with other national movements continued around the world and gave strength and sustenance to the Indian national movement. The credit for imbuing a world consciousness to the national movemen also goes to Nehru.

Socialist Orientation to the Movement

Nehru's significant role in the national movement was his formulation of an economic ideology that lent substance to the struggle. A movement can succeed only when it has a strong economic ideology which can attract the support and participation of the masses. Nehru had clear vision of renascent Indian society after the attainment of independence, a land in which the ills of immemorial poverty, hunger and disease would be eradicated in the shortest possible time. In this he was alone among the Congress leaders. His specific role was to impart a socio-economic content into the meaning of 'Swaraj', and give to the movement for freedom a materialist and socialist orientation. He said, "Mass support cannot come for vague ideal of Swaraj. It can only come when the masses realise what Swaraj means for them. Therefore, it is essential that we must clearly lay down an economic programme. One must have an ultimate ideal in view, and must also provide for the immediate steps to be taken to bring them relief." [27]

This would be the consequence of further struggle and the extensive involvement of masses in the movement who would bring their specific class demand into it. As Nehru remarked, "The agricultural proletariat, the large numbers of landless labourers in rural areas... for all these classes 'nationalism' or 'Swaraj' meant fundamental changes in the land system".[28]

Time and again in the course of the national movement, Nehru argued that political freedom was the immediate goal, but it was only a prelude to social and economic freedom of the people. In preparing for such a goal he recognised the need for a radical programme even during the political struggle. In his Presidential Address to the Congress in 1929, 1936 and 1937 and 1956 and his voluminous writings and countless speeches throughout the country, this theme was taken up with earnestness and dedication.

Despite strong opposition from the conservative elements in the party, he succeeded in getting party approval for the Karachi Resolution and Fundamental Rights in 1931. This was indeed an initial step towards the intimate goal of socialistic pattern of society. Nehru's predilection for economic and social reforms also found cogent expression in the Congress election manifesto of 1936 and 1940 which were drafted by him and contained the core of his socio-economic ideology. He gave a social and economic philosophy to the national movement, thereby providing its substance and intrinsic strength. A movement lacking such specific ideology would certainly degenerate into meaningless anarchy. By emphasising the need to unite political struggle with economic emancipation, Nehru imparted to it a positive dimension.

A sharp analysis of the imperialist phenomenon led him to comprehend the forces underlying it. His greatest contribution is that while defining and analysing imperialism he put forward the thesis that the national movement had to have a socialist orientation. Anti-imperialism had to be enjoined with socialism to become the ideology of the national movement. By doing so Nehru made it more realistic, more concrete and more rational. It was not merely romantic, but was now imbued with a scientific ideology and internationalist and socially radical perspective.

Role of Nehru in Modernising the Movement

Jawaharlal Nehru came more and more to realize the urgency of a permanent and just solution to India's very many problems. Political morale was rapidly deteriorating with the resurgence of Hindu communalism, national politics was steadily degenerating into communal faction. The communal responsivists had seceded from the Swaraj Party and together with the Independents joined a National Party. What was left of Motilal Nehru's secular Swaraj Party was being torn to pieces by the Hindu Mahasabha and the Muslim League. The year 1926 ended with the assassination by a Muslim the Hindu nationalist Swami Shradhananda, who had in the days of Rowlatt Satyagrah in 1919 risked his life fostering Hindu Muslim Unity. Gandhi himself had withdrawn from the hurly-burly of active politics and advised agitated politicians to let the evil forces of communism play themselves out, and in the meantime to "wait, watch and pray".[29] Muslim politics had also became communalistic. Even the nationalist Muslims were fast losing their confidence in Congress, which seemed to be sinking under the weight of Hindu communalism.

Nehru displayed more positiveness in his thoughts on India's social and economic problems. Religion to which he had been attracted in 1920-22, now seemed to him India's deadliest enemy. It was at the root of stagnation and inertia from which the country was suffering. The very factors which made for India's strength in the past were now a heavy load on her back, preventing her from going forward, or adopting herself to present day conditions. The basis of Indian society was authority--the authority of sacred books, of old customs and of immemorial habits. Nehru admonished "No country or people who are slaves to dogma and the dogmatic mentality can progress, and unhappily our country and people have become extraordinarily dogmatic, and little-minded".[30]

Thus religion and all that which went with it must be scotched before it swamped the country and its peoples. Mass education alone would release Indian society from the clutches of religion, lessen the evils of joint family system and a host of other social evils. But large scale education must go hand in hand with industrialization. Nehru was fully committed to progressive scientific industrial civilization or there was no other alternative; Gandhi's ideal of 'Ram Rajya' meant regressing to a primitive agricultural civilization which was just not possible . "I think that western or rather industrial civilization is bound to conquer India, may be with many changes and adaptations, but nonetheless in the main based on industrialism".[31]

Nearly two years of free thinking and policy making for India had revived Nehru's zeal. He had conceived a solution for the Indian problem which he believed was more comprehensive than the Gandhian theory, which seemed to have collapsed in recent years into a dogma of inaction. Gandhi had occasionally tried to restrain Nehru from cultivating too wide a world consciousness. "On our side there is danger of people again looking to external forces and external aid for salvation instead of seeking to achieve it by evolving internal strength".[32] Nevertheless, with due respect he pointed out to the Mahatma : "Our salvation can of course come only from internal strength that we may evolve but one of the methods of evolving such strengtth should be studying other people and their ideas'.[33] He was determined to organise and lead a movement which would challenge both British imperialism and Indian conservatism.

Nehru differed from Gandhi on the latter's mixing up of religion with politics. He could not understand as to what religion had to do with politics. He resented Gandhi's stress on the religious aspect of the Civil-disobedience Movement. The frequent reference to 'Ram Rajya' was jarring to his sensitivity. The movement was strongly influenced by such an outlook, but according to Nehru the consequences were harmful to long term interest of the country. The induction of the religious element into politics took on a revivalist character, as far as the masses were concerned. It was going back to the middle agess when religion dominated the entire atmosphere and there was an astonishing throw-back for finding solutions to problems in the twentieth century.[34]

On another occasion he wrote. "Our politics must either be those of magic or science. The former of course requires no argument or logic, the latter is in theory at least entirely based on clarity of thought and reasoning, and has no room for vague idealistic or religious or sentimental processes which confuse and befog the mind". He had no faith in use of magic and religion, "I can only consider the question on scientific ground".[35]

Gandhi's espousal of the Khilafat issue, which primarily involved the protection of the Muslim's religious interests, and his attempt to link up the Muslim's with the mainstream of Indian nationalism did not bring about Hindu-Muslim unity, on the contrary, it led to the growth of religious element in national politics both on the Hindu and the Muslim side. The rise of sectarian nationalism generated a feeling of rivalry between the Hindu and Muslim. The Muslim League under Jinnah's leadership played upon the religious sentiment and roused the Muslim masses, giving way to 'Muslim nationalism. This developed primarily into a 'religious nationalism' which widened the gulf between the two communities. Gandhi set the tradition of introducing religion with politics, and the Muslim League was quick to take advantage of this practice to divide Indian nationalism and which ultimately resulted in the partition of India.[36]

Nehru believed that in a national movement of vast dimensions, precise definition of priorities and objectives were the essential conditions for its success. The religious element confused the issue and undermined the priorities and progress of the national movement. When every political issue was given a 'religious twist', it prevented clarity of thought and action. It dissipated the energy of the masses in countering the harmful influence of peripheral and inconsequential problems.

Therefore, Nehru's objection was relevant and based on clear understanding of the interaction of socio-political forces. Criticising Gandhi's blanket denunciation of western civilisation on the basis of "some newspaper cuttings" which seemed similar to Katherine Mayo's drawing conclusions from some unsavoury hospital statistics", Nehru announced that he neither thought "the so - called Ram Raj was very good in the past, nor do I want it back".[37] Counteracting such belief he exhorted the people to abandon harkening back to the mythical values of *Vedas* and the *Koran* and to learn and assimilate the best thought and ideas that were revolutionary in the western countries and thus equip India for occupying her rightful place in the modern world".[38]

In all his addresses and messages to the youths Jawaharlal Nehru focused on two majore themes. First, that India was a nation in making "a tremendous country which comprised of various provincial groups with different ideas. Hindus, Christians, Jains and Mohammedians, expressing their respective views".[39] Consequently, a cultural revolution against all divisive and fragmented consciousness had to be waged. Second, they must simultaneously raise the question : What kind of nation would they strive for ? Here he held up the necessity to grasp socialist ideas and to work out a pragmatic unity of the left on this basis. Given the nature of Indian problems as he had outlined them in the first theme, " The Socialist's fights in the country were going to be a stiff fight, but they would have to fight against a number of prejudices courageously".[40] But on the other hand they could more successfully "remove the communal spirit . . . work for the unification of different groups in the provinces" as socialists.[41]

Alarmed by Gandhi's way of springing surprises upon the people and his manner of interpreting national issues in the religious terms, Nehru was now intent on getting the socialist objectives clearly embodied in the Congress constitution. Congress must define what was meant by full independence (Swaraj) and what kind of social, economic and political system it intended to establish in an independent India. The Indian National Movement had to be at once uncompromisingly anti-capitalist, anti-feudal, anti-bourgeois and of course anti-imperialistic and secular in short. Nehru made every possible effort to use the weapon of socialism to eradicate the above evils deep rooted in Indian society, according to him Socialism was the only remedy.

Role of Nehru in Intensifying the Struggle between Nationalist India and the British *imperialism.*

As early as 1921, Nehru spoke of direct fight with the British. There could be no half-measures, no compromise on vital issues. It is instructive to note that though being a staunch disciple of Gandhi, he continued to carry on the struggle individualistically and often against Gandhi's wishes. Many a time Gandhi suspended Non-cooperation and Civil Disobedience Movements, but Nehru continued his work of organising, educating and informing the people of their plight unconcerned of the shifting policies of Gandhi. On many occasions Gandhi went to jail leaving a vacuum in the leadership, of the movement. It was on these occasions that Nehru provided leadership, never openly but indirectly and with consistency.

Throughout his tone remained defiant and uncompromising on the question of the British connection and independence. In 1922, when Gandhiji called off the Civil-Disobedience campaign due to increasing violence, Nehru, like most others was bitterly upset and he gave vent to his indignance through his speeches and writings. Gandhi's action enabled the government to relax but made Nehru's task of sustaining the morale of the Congressmen so much the harder, "I have only to say this --keep fighting, continue to work for independent India and do not stop. Do not abandon your creed. Do not accept false compromises. Continue to follow your great leader Mahatma Gandhi and remain true to Congress. Be efficient and well organised".[42] As the government recognised, 'quiet propaganda work was widespread'. Nehru addressed public meetings in the city and elsewhere and circulated pamphlets in Hindi--He declared that non-cooperation could never die, until the goal was reached--the goal of an Indian victory.[43]

Strengthening the party organisation and extension of its network, the training and discipline of volunteers and the creation in the country of a general atmosphere of resistance and of indifference to the government--these were to him the important tasks.

It was in a mood of thoughtful commitment to revolutionary change that Nehru returned to India from a trip to Europe and reached Madras in time for the Congress session in 1927. From December, 1927 to 1929 Nehru was instrumental in intensifying the struggle between the nationalists and British government and in strengthening and mobilising Congress for the Civil- Disobedience.

The controversy over 'independence' and 'dominion status' may seem academic now but in the years 1927-29 it was most significant and real. In the government view it was sedition to talk of independence for India with no ties with Britain.[44] Advocacy of independence therefore, signified an utter defiance of the Raj. This then, became one of the main reason for Nehru's setting independence as the Congress goal. Also during his stay in Europe he was regularly briefed by his father on the rapidly deteriorating political morale of the country. There had recurred a resurgence of the Hindu communal politics and national politics had steadily degenerated into communal factions. The Swaraj Party had been torn to shreds by the Hindu Mahasabha. Almost all Muslims in the Congress, expect A. K. Azad had come to distrust the Hindus. Congressmen in the Assembly and Councils were now, "trembling over each other to shake hands with officials".[45] Gandhi, who was seriously ill in 1927 had given up hopes of resolving the communal problem and advised his followers, to "wait, watch and pray". Summing up the entire political situation, Motilal Nehru wrote, " I do not think there is one man among the old or the new set of Congressmen who will not go into a fading fit on hearing the words complete independence. . . I think there can be no greater misfortune for the country than the appointment of a Royal Commission of Reforms at this juncture. Any crumb which will be thrown on us will be accepted by all the same people".[46]

Nehru took this as a challenge and was therefore, eager for a whole-hearted combat,with no quarter sought or given. His new radical ideas affirmed rather than diverted his enthusiasm for political action. Even the arrest of capitalist exploitation and a lightening of India's poverty required termination of imperialist rule. But the mirage of Dominion-status weakened resistance in India to the British and generally strengthened reformist as against revolutionary forces. It was with such determination that Nehru secured the passage of a resolution committing the Congress to independence.

However, due to Gandhi's opposition to the independence resolution Nehru realized that it was difficult to fight Gandhi in the Congress. It was for this purpose that he organised the Independence for India League as in the first instance, a pressure group within the Congress,

Severance of British connection implied also an attack on the vested interests supported by the British in India. Independence, therefore, was a composite ideal, and for its attainment Nehru looked far beyond the Congress.

Once again Nehru took up the occasion of arrival of Simon Commission to intensify the struggle against the British. To Nehru, the failure to nominate any Indian to the membership of the Commission seemed a minor incident of imperial rule. What should be boycotted was the whole conception behind it.[47] Freedom was India's fundamental right, and as all commissions sent out from England deprived that right they could receive no quarter from India. He believed that the affront to the Simon Commission could be used as an occasion for united action, to bring together members of various parties in a common cause. The boycott might not lead India on to the path of independence, but it would certainly help to create a healthy atmosphere in which work of national organisation could be expedited.[48] As General-Secretary of the Congress, he set about organizing the boycott on countrywide scale. While protesting against the Commission at Lucknow Nehru suffered multiple injuries. The news of Lathi Charges and injuries to him aroused widespread anger in India. Apart from the impact on the development of the national resistance to British rule, the police actions at Lucknow confirmed Nehru's national standing.[49]

In pursuance of a Congress directive the representatives of all parties had met, and in May 1928 they appointed a sub-committee under Motilal Nehru to draft the outline of a constitution of India, which came to be known as Nehru Report. Jawaharlal Nehru was not in favour of this document. He thought that in order to maintain the facade of all party unity the Report restricted the national goal only to Dominion-Status, which contradicted the Independence-resolution passed earlier at Madras.[50]

Nehru's opposition to Nehru Report was like his confrontation with Gandhi, based on a point of strategy. A national demand for independence would demonstrate an utter rejection of the Raj, would intensify the conflict with the imperial system and mobilise the masses behind the national movement. He was aware of the fact that even a demand for Dominion-Status was not going to be accepted by the British Government unless it had a sanction and a force behind it. The call for independence would create that mass sanction and embolden Congress to declare war against the government. The demand for Dominion-Status represented a middle-class council chamber politics and consequently would fail to arouse the revolutionary spirit among the masses.[51] The Nehru Report seemed to prevent Nehru's strategy of resistance finding its way into national policy. But he was not disheartened, nor did he abandon his hope of setting the national movement on a war path.

Nehru thus continued building up a belligerent force amongst the youth, the labourers and the peasants. There was labour unrest in the industrial cities of Bombay, Bengal and Bihar. This was to erupt into a number of major strikes early in 1929. The government suspecting that there lay behind these industrial troubles a communist conspiracy to undermine the government rounded up thirty-one labour leaders in March,1929 and put them on trials in Meerut. Nehru reached the urban labour force through the trade unions and while steering the middle course between the rightist and leftist managed to establish a rapport with both wings. By late 1928, he was elected president of All India Trade Union Congress.[52]

Jawharlal Nehru had taken upon himself the task to intensify the struggle against the British and it was in this vein that whenever he was not in prison he was engrossed in organising protests, demonstrations, breaking laws and inciting the people against the British. In October, 1930, during a brief respite from prison he succeeded in injecting new life into the Civil-Disobedience Movementat least in his own state of United Provinces. The movement was beginning to lose momentum at once he sensed the staleness of the movement and the only way he decided, that the movement could be revitalized only by involving the rural masses in a no-rent campaign.

The Great Depression of 1929 had brought about a phenomenal fall in the price of agricultural products and consequently put the cultivators of India under the severe distress of money scarcity and starvation - condition conducive to the building up of a peasant movement. Nehru took the initiative and sanctioned a no-tax campaign in the district of Allahabad; the other district were to follow suit. "It is war", Nehru was reported as having said, 'war now and ever till the end of our lives".[53] He did not however conform though half-heartedly, to the official Congress policy of not sponsoring class-war, and accordingly called upon both parties, landlords and large peasants not to pay. He addressed a number of meetings and a large peasant conference and was duly arrested, tried for sedition and sentenced two years of rigorous imprisonment. His re-arrest and conviction raised the tempo of the Civil-Disobedience Movement, not only in U.P. but throughout India.[54] The reaction was so sharp that the government observed, "Jawaharlal and his school have of course a great influence locally, and there is no doubt that they have for a long time been bitten with the idea of making a kind of Soviet organization of peasant workers which will first of all abolish the landlord and then possibly Sovietize government".[55]

Again at the time of Gandhi-Irwin Talks Nehru disagreed in the manner things were taking shape. Though he was willing to fight for years if necessary, he found the Congress leadership tired and weary and anxious to reach a compromise. He resented Sapru, Jayakar and the rest to the liberal band for their work in hiring Congress into the constitutional arena. Nehru was fiercely opposed to the principle of gradualness that lay at the foundation of liberal thinking, for he believed more in conquest than the transfer to power. It would be dishonourable, and also contrary to the stand Congress took in 1929 to accept any arrangement whereby Britain conceded only a part and not the whole of India's independence. Moreover this token power would benefit only those with vested interests in the country - the feudal lords, the princely order, the bureaucracy, the industrialist and financiers, the religious and communal leadership.[56]

The parleys between Gandhi and Irwin began on 17 Feb,1931 with an earnest desire on both sides to reach agreement. This was a joint endeavour to find a meeting point between nationalism and imperialism. To Nehru it looked like a surrender.[57] He believed that a continuous war against imperialism would give strength and success to nationalism; it was absurd to think of linking these two forces, for they were incompatible. Having overcome the initial shock at the idea of peace negotiation Nehrru set himself to the task of restraining gandhi and the right wingers from striking any compromise with the enemy.[58]

The Second Civil-Disobedience began on 4 January 1932 without leaders and without an elaborately planned strategy, except for a Congress plan to boycott foreign cloths, picket liquor shops and disregard any law deemed to be immoral. The movement was suppressed rapidly, and more ruthlessly than the first. The timing of virtual suspension of the Civil-Disobedience coincided with Nehru's third release from prison on 30th August, 1933. He was orgaged with the liberals for having cooperated with the British endorsed the 'monstrous abortion' which were the outcome of the third and final round of the Round-Table Conference.[59]

Once out of prison, he set before himself the task of rebuilding the ideological base of the national movement, which he felt had become lost in the politics of compromise and expediency. He began his ideological crusade by attacking the Round-Table Conference as merely an effort to consolidate the vested interests in India which supported the British government. He condemned each of these interests as reactionary, they 'must be and will be ended'. Both Hindu and Muslim leaders came under his heaviest attack, for he thought it was necessary to destroy the bogy of communalism which the British were using as excuse to perpetuate their rule in India.[60]

Nehru next attacked the proposed Indian constitution document worthy only of the waste paper basket. The national movement stood for full independence, there could be no winning of powers in installments. People who imagine that they can gradually get the freedom of India, either delude themselves or are thoroughly ignorant of history because such a thing never happens and will never happen in India, he warned.[51]

This verbal demolition of the existing order was followed by a theoretical reconstruction of a new order. Nehru reaffirmed his belief in socialism. The choice before the world was between some form of Communism and some form of Fascism, his preference was entirely for the former. He was all for class-war, for turning the Congress into peasants and workers union, but his theory was tempered by the realisation that a class-war might damage the national movement.[62]

From the beginning of his political career Nehru took upon himself the task to keep the momentum of the national movement accelerated and played an indispensable role in intensifying the struggle between the British and nationalist India. It was precisely for this reason that the British government preferred to have him in jail rather than let him free and risk revolt. His activities were made dangerous enough to require his speedy return to prison. All local governments were authorized to arrest him if opportunity arose not on some minor issues but on a serious charge which would involve a substantial sentence.

While out of prison, he sought to keep up the struggle, even if at a lower pitch, for the only alternative was a compromise with imperialism, and this was unacceptable not only to him personally but manifestly to the Indian people. Travelling round the country, Nehru was convinced that never, at any rate since 1857, had there been such extraordinary bitterness against the government and such passionate desire to get rid of it. So he concentrated on the sustenance of the struggle, and declined to be distracted by such side- shows as village uplift and Harijan movement. 'This kind of safe and pious activity can well be left to old ladies. It was a question not merely of time and energy but creating a psychological atmosphere. The national fight had to continue and it would be strengthened by making it a social and economic fight for the masses and purging it of Hindu and Muslim communalism.[63]

A United Front

The conception of nation -in-the-making is the central conception of the historiographical framework which Dr. Bipan Chandra has over the years, developed to understand the various aspects of the Indian national movement. A long quotation expounding this conception would not be out of place here:

"The colonisation (the Indian economy, society and polity produced many sided consequences. One was the initiation of the prolonged historical process of welding the Indian people into a nation. Another was the rise of a national, anti-imperialist movement as the central contradiction between imperialism and the interests of the Indian people. The national movement was based on the phenomenon of the nation in-the-making while it was itself a powerful factor contributing to this phenomenon. Its growing strength depended in part on the extent to which people became conscious of their being part of a nation whose essential interests required a struggle for the overthrow of imperialism. The consciousness of nation of being a people did not, however, flow automatically from the objective reality. It had to be a hard, painstaking process in self-discovery in which the anti-imperialist struggle would play a crucial role. But by its very nature, the process of nation-in-the making was, and is, highly differential process. Moreover, the formation of new social classes and stratas and the impact of imperialism on the people also occurred in a differential manner leading to the emergence of a varied relationship between imperialism and different sections of the Indian society. This resulted in the extremely uneven development, both in time and space, of national and anti-imperialist consciousness among different social classes and stratas as well as people belonging to different religions, castes, linguistic areas, etc. One of the major tasks facing the leadership of the national movement was to impart a common national consciousness to the Indian people and to unite them in the common struggle against imperialism''. [64]

This was precisely the task which Nehru took upon himself to complete. Gandhi revolutionised the national movement by bringing in the peasantry into the national mainstream, now it fell on Nehru to collect all other forces--the peasantry, labour, youth and intelligentsia and to channelise them into formation of an anti-imperialist united front. This was a difficult task.

''The real object before us is to build up a powerful joint front of all the anti-imperialist forces in the country. The Congress has indeed been in the past, and inevitably the Congress must be the basic and pivot of united action... The most urgent and vital need of India today is this united national front of all forces and elements that are ranged against imperialism''.[65]

Mobilisation of the classes in urban areas and bridging the gap between them and the rural masses as well as simultaneously bringing them into the mainstream of national movement was one of the complex problems which Nehru tirelessly tried to solve. ''The problem of today in India is the problem of peasantry''.[66] Industrial Labour was only a small part of India, although it was rapidly becoming a force that could not be ignored. However, the biggest problem in India which cried loudly for solution was that of the Peasantry.[67] Of course, ''Peasants are seldom revolutionary after their immediate objective is attained, and it is likely that some time in the future the usual problem of city versus village and industrial worker versus peasant will arise in India also''.[68] But this Nehru saw as problem of the future. He saw quite clearly that ''as yet urban India even the new industrial India has the impress of the peasant upon her''. Thus the immediate and the most urgent task for the Congress was to find ways of relating to the peasant and thus to the Congress, whose workers "have spread all over the rural areas and in the course, the Congress must develop into a vast peasant organisation".[69] Nehru emphasised that the alliance between the working-class and the peasantry was a must for the success of the national movement.

Nehru felt that the peasants and industrial workers "have a great deal to gain and very little to lose if the alien rule is abolished. These are the people who must form the armies or forces to fight them and it is bound to rest on them. The intellectuals must join along with the tenants and the individual workers. Other classes may possibly extend support to them--but without the industrial and agricultural workers it is inconceivable that India can achieve her true freedom".[70]

The role of the middle class in carrying nationalist consciousness to the workers and peasants had to be emphasised; "It is only from the middle class intellectuals that revolutionary leadership comes".[71] However, it had to be a two-way process--the working class would become the backbone of the movement only to the extent that "the masses realise that Swaraj means for them".[72] The inevitable middle class leadership must look more towards the working and peasant masses and draw sustenance from them".[73] Nehru's intense concentration on the youth movement and middle class intelligentsia during the years 1927 to 1930 was precisely this attempt to cultivate a revolutionary outlook. For, "what shall it benefit the masses of this country--the peasantry, the landless labourers, the workers the shopkeepers, the artisans--if everyone of the office held by Englishmen in India is held by Indians?"[74]

Presiding over the Republican Congress in 1927, close cooperation with peasants in the 'Workers and Peasants' parties till they were disbanded, the presidentship of the A.I.T.U.C., the consistent infecting of socialist ideas into the youth movement, and the formulation of the Independence for India League affiliated to the League against Imperialism--these were attempts to link all these sections to the national movement in an effort to establish a united front against imperialism...

Conclusion

Nehru was not born to politics as his early life suggests. There was a lack of purpose and a void in his life which gave birth to intense frustration and a feeling of uselessness. The massacre at Jallianwalan Bagh in 1919, when Nehru was thirty years of age, was the decisive, liberating moment in his life. It focused his energies and clarified his mind and made action urgent. Thereafter, he was caught up in the emotional logic of the national movement and his consuming singleness of vision gave him heroic and symbolic force. But, even as he threw himself into the vortex of freedom struggle and never shirked prison, he began after a time to worry about the future and gave unceasing thought to the policies which a free India should follow.

The period 1920-39 is important in the history of the national movement for these were the years which saw the building up of the nationalist ferment, building of its ideology, inner strife and consolidation, ultimately leading to independence. During this entire period Nehru actively participated in the movement and created an impact on every aspect of it.

Nehru was in the dead centre of Indian struggle and his role as a nationalist as a staunch champion of freedom and as an ardent socialist were of immense significance. He formulated the concepts of freedom, nationalism and socialism and provided a three-way link up with the national movement. By such a process he gave the structure of a socio-economic ideology which the national movement was lacking in. Nehru played a major role in the consolidation of various forces, as divergent and amorphous groups sought national identity. A political and socio-economic movement of vast dimensions was of no mean order and Nehru guided by Gandhi provided an able leadership.

References

1. Tarachand, *History of the Freedom Movement in India*, vol. 1, Publication Division, 1961, Preface.
2. Sumit Sarkar, *Modern India*, 1885 - 1947, Delhi, Macmillan India, 1983 p. 7.
3. S. Gopal, *Jawaharlal Nehru: A Biography*, vol.1, p. 14.
4. Ganesh Prasad, *Nehru : A Study in Colonial Liberalism*, p. 28 29.
5. P.D. Kaushik, *The Congress Ideology and Programme*, p.26.
6. Presidential Address at the Bombay Presidency Youth Conference, 12 Dec. 1925, *Selected Works*, vol.3, p. 20.
7. *Ibid.*, Vol. 3,p-203.
8. 'Advice to Youth' Speech at Delhi, 5 Feb, 1929, *Selected Works*, vol. 4,p.2.
9. *Selected Works*, vol.3,p. 185.
10. Presidential Address at the All Bengal Student Conference, Calcutta, 22 Sept. 1928, *Selected Works*, Vol.3, p. 191.

11. *Selected Works*, vol.3,pp.179-80,198,vol.4,pp.1-23.
12. *Ibid.*
13. *Ibid.*
14. *Ibid.*
15. Address to Allahabad Youth League, Dec., 1928. *Selected Works*, vol. 4, p.16.
16. Letter to Bhagwat Dayal, A.I.C.C., File G/39/1928 NMML.
17. *Ibid.*
18. In V.T. Patil, *Nehru And the Freedom Movement*, p. 55.
19. Presidential Address, Punjab Provincial Conference, 11 April, Dorothy Norman, *Nehru: The first Sixty Years*, vol. 1,p.155.
20. *Ibid.*
21. "*Whither India ?*"1933, p-315.
22. *Ibid.* p.317.
23. *Selected Works*, Vol. 7, pp. 177-90.
24. J. Nehru, *India and the World*, pp. 70-81, London, 1936.
25. Jawaharlal Nehru, *China, Spain and the War*, Allahabad, Kitabistan, 1940 pp.17 and 92.
26. Dorothy Norman *Nehru : The First Sixty Years*, vol.1, p.473.
27. Presidential address, Punjab Provincial Conference, 11 April, 1928, Dorothy Norman, *Nehru: The First Sixty Years* , vol.1,p.159.
28. J.Nehru, *An Autobiography*, p.281.
29. Motilal Nehru to J. Nehru, 11 August, 1927, *Nehru Papers*,NMML
30. Nehru to S. Mahmood, 12 September, 1926 in B.N. Pandey, *Nehru*, p-126.
31. J. Nehru to Gandhi,11 January,1928, *Nehru Papers*, NMML, New Delhi.
32. Gandhiji to J.Nehru, 11 January, 1928, *Nehru Papers*, NMML.
33. *Ibid.*
34. J. Nehru, *An Autobiography*, p-8.
35. "*Whither India ?*" In Dorothy Norman, *Nehru : The First Sixty Years*, vol.I,p.306.
36. V.T.Patil, *Nehru and the Freedom Movement*, New Delhi, Sterling, 1977, p.242.
37. *Selected Works*, vol. 3,p.15.
38. Address at the Champaran District Political Conference, November, 1928, *Selected Works*, vol.3,p 263.
39. Presidential Address at Socialist Youth Congress, *op. cit.*
40. *Ibid.*
41. *Ibid.*
42. Nehru's Message on Release from Prison, 'Aaj', 10 March, 1922, in S.Gopal, *Jawaharlal Nehru: A Biography*, vol.1,p-64.
43. *Ibid.* p-65.
44. Government of India Telegram to Government of Bombay, 29 Dec. *Home Political File, 179/29/* National Archives, New Delhi.
45. Motilal Nehru to Jawaharlal Nehru, 30th March, 1929, *Nehru Papers*, NMML.
46. *Ibid.*
47. Speech at Allahabad, 10 Jan. *The Leader*, 12 Jan. 1928.
48. *Ibid.*
49. S.Gopal, *Jawaharlal Nehru: A Biography*, vol.1,p.117.
50. Dorothy Norman, *Nehru: The First Sixty Years*, vol.1, p 170.
51. *Ibid.*
52. B.N Pandey, *Nehru*, p.133.
53. *The Tribune*, 25 October, 1931, in S.Gopal, *Jawaharlal Nehru : A Biography*, Vol.1, p-166

54. B.N.Pandey, *Nehru*, pp.154-55.
55. S.Gopal, *Jawaharlal Nehru: A Biography*,vol.1 p.156.
56. J. Nehru, *An Autobiography*, p.273.
57. J.Nehru, *An Autobiography*, p.259.
58. B.N.Pandey, *Nehru*, p.160-61.
59. Jawaharlal Nehru's Prison Diary, 22 September, 1932, *Nehru Papers*, NMML.
60. Jawaharlal Nehru, 'Reality and Myth', 4 Jan. 1934, *Nehru Papers*, NMML.
61. J. Nehru's Speech at Albert Hall, Calcutta, 18 Jan.1934, *Home Politics File*, 4 January,1934, National Archives, New Delhi.
62. S.Gopal, *Jawaharlal Nehru: A Biography*, vol.1, p.184.
63. *Ibid.*, p.184.
64. Bipan Chandra, *Nationalism, Colonialism in Modern India*, New Delhi, 1979, p.252-53.
65. Faizpur Congress, Dorothy Norman, *Nehru: The First Sixty Years* vol.2, p.470.
66. J.Nehru, *An Autobiography*, p.368.
67. Speech at Lahore Congress, *op.cit*.
68. J. Nehru, *An Autobiography*, p.368.
69. *Ibid.* p.254.
70. Reply to Address of All Bengal Student Association, Sept. 1928, *Selected Works*, vol.3, p-198-99.
71. Presidential Speech at Lucknow Congress, 1936, *Selected Works*, vol. 7, pp. 170-195.
72. Presidential Address at Punjab Provincial Congress, *Selected Works*, vol.3,p.225.
73. *Ibid.* p.224.
74. *Ibid.*, p.225.

CHAPTER 6

NEHRU'S VIEWS ON NATIONALISM SOCIALISM AND DEMOCRACY

Nationalism

The twentieth century has been a century of war and revolution, of bright dream and shattering hate, of heroic valour and wretched squalor. The wars were in part produced by nationalism and they in turn accentuated it. The revolution principally, were for socialism, and nationalism and of the two 'isms', the second proved the stronger. Regardless of political ideology, nationalism continued to be the principle sentiment of unity and diversion among peoples, and socialism, where attempted was less international than national. Jawharlal Nehru's remarks about Asia could alpply to Africa and, for that matter, the rest of the world in the twentieth century. He said ''Any other force (communism) any other activity that may seek to function, must define itself in terms of nationalism. No argument in any country of Asia is going to have weight if it goes counter to the nationalist sipirit of the country''.[1]

In the age of imperialism the emergence of patriotic sentiments in a subjugated country is historically given. It is the product of long-standing colonial oppression and results from the torturous realisation and internationalisation on the part of the insulted and the injured of their experience embodied in the self-perception of the'they being people' as excluded from their 'oppressiors"- the latter being characterised as alien rulers. At the initial stage of their unfolding of the new awareness this nebulous feeling of nationalism may articulate itself into ideological forms heavily charged with religious overtones and racial animosity, though in the case of India ,both, especially the latter, were rather muted.[2]

The emergence of anti-imperialist nationalism produces a distinct national identity which heralds the process of 'nation in-the-making'[3] committed to a separate and passionately defending its rights to independence. Such an identity is not merely a geographical category. It is rooted in the process of formation and growth of national consciousness, which alone infuses this identity with its dynamic content, implying a necessary opposition to all forms of imperialism.

Nationalism in its wider meaning referred to a psychological attitude which ascribed national identity and individuality a prominent place in the hierarchy of values. From this point of view it was natural and inevitable phenomenon of all national movements. It basically represented the tendency of subject national groups to achieve independence. Therefore, nationalism and the national movement represented the continuation of a democratic movement which after achieving the elimination of all privileges, distinction and differentiations of every form of aristocracy within its own midst, set up its own nation as against the outside world.[4]

Indian nationalism rooted in a peculiar soil was conditioned by the social fabric, the intellectual traditions and socio-cultural history of the people, and the geographical location of the society. It was traditional, social and culture-oriented, very closely connected to the religious and social attitudes of the past. Nationalism represented an effort by the people to imbibe and adopt western nationalism to their local scene without any radical departure from ancient traditions. Nationalism in

India was the product of a reaction against foreign rule and a form of rebound against external domination and oppression. In the initial phase it was essentially negative in character. In due course of time, nationalism was followed by a lessening of the dominance of religion, the gradual fading away of tribal, clannish or feudal loyalties, the spread of urbanisation and industrialisation; and the growth of communications. Modernisation of a non-western people and industrialisation of an agricultural society disrupted and displaced the intelligentsia. They were uprooted and their interest was vitally affected. It was these groups backed by excluded mass of less skilled workers and peasants, which led the movement for national independence. The emergence of a group which spurned western values but mastered organisation andmethodsgave the movement weight and depth.[5]

The awakening in India was twofold: She looked to the west and at the time, She looked at herself and her own past. This awakening was the Renaissance. Its best products were modern nationalism and the national liberation movement with Raja Ram Mohan Roy as its fountainhead of liberalnationalism,the Renaissance threw up its representatives at different times. Of all the representative of the Renaissance, Nehru is by far the best. He eptomised almost all its traits and added in it the socialist values. A typical aspect of intense nationalism symbolised by him was his legitimate pride in the nation's past as well as his love of the people and even the inanimate object of the motherland, "My reaction to India thus was often an emotional one,... It took the form of nationalism... Nationalism was and is inevitable with the India of my day; it is natural and healthy growth. For any subject country national freedom must be the first and dominant urge; for India, with her intense sense of individuality and a past heritage, it was doubly so." [6]

Nehru was aware that in spite of the growth of internationalism and proletarian movements, nationalism was still the dominating urge underlying the freedom struggles being waged all over the world, "The nationalist ideal is deep and strong; it is not a thing of the past with no future significance. . . The abiding appeal of nationalism to the spirit of man has to be recognized and provided for."[7] Even the labour and proletarian movements deliberately based on internationalism were drifting towards nationalism.[8]

Nationalism was the magnetic phenomenon which was moving the world towards a new direction, inspiring revolutions, leading to change and revolutionary transformation. In short, nationalism was the catalyst which would make new history, "We were engrossed in our national struggle and the turn it took before the powerful impression of our great leader and of our national genius... and the forces that moved us were moving millions of people all over the world and driving them into action. All Asia was astir from the mediterranean to the far East, from the Islamic West to the Buddhist East, Africa responded to the new spirit; Europe, broken up by the war, was struggling to find a new equilibrium. And right across a vast area in Europe and Asia, in the Soviet territories, a new conception of human freedom and social equality fought desperately against a host of enemies."[9]

Endowed with a deep sense of history, Nehru very aptly comprehended the cataclysmic power of nationalism and the role it could play in the liberation struggle. Only the logic and sentiment of nationalism could lift the Indian people out of state of mental subjugation and inertia and transform them into agents of change. Speaking enthusiastically from the Presidential rostrum at Lucknow he exhorted to the people." A handful of our old friends, representing an age and a class which had had its day, left us fearful of this democratic upsurge, and preferring the shelter and protection of British imperialism to joining hands with the new vital forces which convulsed the country and struggled for freedom. Historically they lapsed into the past . . . But we sensed the new spirit of mass release, of psychological escape from the cramping effects of the mental bonds that encompassed us... We represented the spirit of the age and were marching step by step with countless others in our country and outside. The exhilaration of being in tune with the masses and with world forces came upon us and the feeling that we were the agents of historic destiny."[10]

When Nehru spoke of the 'National genius', he meant precisely the specfic character of India which she had inherited from millennia, that element which made her different from all other nations in spite of occasional regressions, setbacks and vicissitudes leading to foreign rule. It was the nationalist in Nehru that inspired him and imbued him with tremendous optimism with which he viewed his country and her future. This enthusiasm and optimism for the attainment of freedom and establishment of a new India, was in turn gradually but positively permeated into the people through his numerous pronoucements and writings. *The*

Discovery of India is written in a nationalist hue and is an effort to discover the spirit of India, the element that has sustained her despite numerous onslaughts, and the message that India could give to the world. Through him were speaking Raja Ram Mohan Roy, Vivekananda, Gandhi, Tagore and above all, the true spirit of Indian nationalism.

Nehru's nationalism represented the hopes and aspirations of a subject people and it was not a thing of the past with no future significance. Yet he was not unaware of the dangers of unbridled nationalism, often referring to its revivalist nature as it drew inspiration from the past. The fundamental defeat of the cult of nationalism was its negative character. ''Nationalism is esentially an anti-feeling and it feeds and fattens on hatred and anger against other national groups, and especially against the foreign rulers of the country.''[11]

Nationalism was a narrowing creed and aggressive nationalism in direct and open conflict with colonial rule led to all sorts of complexes and frustrations. A subject nation long accustomed to domination acquired a defeatist mentality or complex. It was a state of mental torpor, inertia and despair that worked as a disintegrating, disorganising and dissipating factor on the masses. The conflict of interests created bitter memories of ceaseless struggle and suffering, which was inevitable and unavoidable, ''Nationalist struggle generates feelings of bitterness, almost of hatred. After all nationalism is something anti, anti-foreign government, may be almost racial - it is a negtive thing which has a definite positive side to it also. It is not a good thing taken by itself. Usually too much of it - too great a dose of it -stunts a race, although at the same time, at a certain stage, it is something that makes a race grow''.[12]

The pervasive influence of nationalism and its impact on the spirit of man was clearly recognised by Nehru and he led the Indian people out of their narrow grooves of thought to consider the wider issues affecting humanity as a whole. ''And it is nationalism which is the driving force today in the countries of East which suffer under foreign domination and seek freedom. To them it bring unity and vitality and a lifting of the burden of the spirit which subjection entails. There is a virtue in it up to a certain stage; till then it is a progressive force adding to human freedom. But even then it is a narrowing creed, and a nation seeking freedom, like a person who is sick, can think of little besides its own struggles and its own misery''.[13] Nehru referred to the constructive-destructive character of nationalism and how it could be unifying as well as a devisive force.

The pioneers of Indian nationalism were influenced by the nineteenth century European liberalism, particularly, by its British variant. Consequently, like the latter, the early nationalism lacked a higher rational and positive norm. It could not contain the revolutionary urges of the youth, resulting in adoption of symbols, cults, slogans or norms which were mostly irrational, obscurantist or mystical. Also, negativism in one form or other came to characterise the radical national thinking of our two decades. In fact, negativism became the hallmark of extremism. It was the dominance of this negativist phenomenon that made Nehru define nationalism as 'essentially an anti-feeling.'[14]

Besides overcoming spiritual defeat, nationalism had to tackle complicated problems and perform difficult tasks. The increasing mass consciousness had to be harnessed to the liberation movement. The new humanistic and progressive ideas, coming from other lands, had to be assimilated in the main current of national thinking. A correct stand had to be taken in the world-wide struggle between reaction and progress. The mounting reaction of narrow nationalism had to be combated ideologically and organisationally. A new direction to patriotic thinking and a new concept of nationalism were urgently called for. These came from Nehru. The nationalism of Nehru, as opposed to the traditional concept was a definite ideal a positive norm, a fraternal movement, a strong faith and a mass phenomenon. Indian nationalism became a complete ideology having definite positive ends.

Nationalism and Socialism

With this view, Nehru incorporated Socialism with nationalism, thereby making nationalism a creative urge, a natural phenomenon and a progressive movement. By joining together these two historic forces, he diverted nationalism of its negative character and saved it from becoming a degenerate and reactionary force like the nationalism of the Nazis and the Fascists.

Nehru gave to the Renaissance a new impetus, a new outlook, a new turn and onward push. In the mid-twenties contact with socialist movement, thought and experiment had resolved his nationalistic predicament. Nationalism is usually a negative phenomenon, a narrowing creed. Marxism taught him to view it in the larger perspective of world events. He felt and underlined the urgency of equipping nationalism with a rational and positive norm. In the realities of the thirties, its rationale was appreciated and its value acknowledged. The new generation agitated for its quick incorporation in the national movement. It was through Nehru that the national debate, which had so far been limited mainly to the ways and means of achieving merely the negative end of throw-away foreign yoke, was now turned into a debate on positive socio-economic objectives of independence. This phenomenal change in outlook was a great landmark in the history of colonial nationalism. The content of the norm that Nehru suggested was liberal democratic and secular and socialistic. This was in tune with the conditions of India and the age.

The years immediately following the October Revolution in Russia saw a distinct change in thc struggle of the oppressed peoples of the world for liberation. Pressure on imperialism from its colonial and semi-colonial fringe began to acquire global proportions as hundreds of millions of people awoke to the prospect of liberation. Looking back over those years, we see the rise of the liberation movement in India, gaining of independence of Afghanistan, the victory of the Peoples' Revolution in Mongolia, the revolution of Kamal Ataturk in Turkey, the overthrow of the Quazar dynasty in Iran, numerous uprisings among Arabs, increasing insurgency in Indonesia, and an anti-imperialist revolution in China, all of which took place during the first decade after the October Revolution.

Nehru viewed the rise and consolidation of the socialist forces as an alternative to the capitalist system which had its roots in exploitaion and subjugation. In socialism Nehru saw the liberation of mankind from political and economic bondage. Speaking from the Presidential rostrum at Lucknow in 1936, Nehru announced, " I am convinced that the only key to solution of world's problems and of India's problems lie in socialism."[15]

Nehru infused the fervour of socialism into indian nationalism with a view to creating a classless, equalitarian, national society. Socialism was an international system of society and its message cut across national boundaries. Not only did it stimulate the spirit of national well-being, it also fervently appealed to an international brotherhood. The integration of nationalism with socialism is a signficant contribution of Nehru to the national movement. This set the pattern, for the development of nationalism in many underdeveloped countries in their fight against foreign political intervention, ecnomic penetration and exploitation.

Nehru's greatest contribution was his constant desire and effort to unite with all the progressive forces on the world stage, thereby, linking the two in the national liberation forces and the socialist or progressive forces in a joint endeavour to combat imperialism. As early as 1927 at the Brussels Congress he wrote 'ideas of some common action between oppresed nations *inter-se* as well as between them and the labour left-wing were very much in the air. It was felt more and more that the struggle for freedom was a common one against the thing that was imperialism, and joint deliberation and where possible, joint action was desirable.[16] This was an important step towards recognising the unity between the national liberation struggle and the revolutionary worker's movement.

For Nehru the link between the two movements was to be unaerstood thus : "On the one hand, labour could hardly better its lot even in the smaller field of wages and hours of work and standards of living, so long as imperialism continued and capital had full freedom to exploit the weak and organised labour of colonial countries and pit against the worker at home. Apart from this the viewpoint of self-interest, the interest of the higher idealism made it the duty of the working class to combat imperialism and to help the nationalist movement of oppressed countries. For what kind of socialism will it be, if it is based on the exploitation of other countries".[17] On the other hand, the nationalist movements could ill afford to be de-linked from the socialist movement. For as Nehru put it, "the nationalist movement under foreign domination may succeed in getting independence without the support of labour ... but it will result in creating a new capitalist state, nominally independent but with little freedom for the worker. That will not bring peace any nearer nor solve any of our problems".[18]

It was for this reason that he looked upon the League Against Imperialism as an important platform. The LAI would fulfil an essential need. The LAI for the first time, saw the common factors in the two movements and wisely sought to bring them together. "It tried to bring home to the European workers the need for national independence of all countries and it placed a new vision of social equality and freedom before the somewhat narrow nationalist movements of various countries".[19] And gradually even nationalist movement led by the like of Indian National Congress, conservative in their social outlook, would begin to look towards the socialist ideal of society. To this last hope and desire Nehru dedicated all his efforts from 1929 till the late thirties.

Nehru, thus absorbed the concept as well as the orientation of this alliance of world significance, the alliance that Lenin had put forward in 1920. But necessarily he absorbed it within his own perspective as a revolutionary democrat participating in the leadership of the anti-imperialistic forces in his country.

How would he, as the representative of the anti-imperialist forces in India, link himself with the new order envisaged by socialism ? He concentrated on the link between socialism and nationalism epitomised in the LAI, and advanced this new vision of an organic relationship between the two within the framework of the national movement in India. He wrote,"In oppressed countries. . . nationalism automatically and rightly takes precedence of all other sentiments. This is recognised even by socialists. But they point out that in such countries nationalism might be given a broader basis more in consonance with the tendencies of the age; that it might derive its strength from and work specially for the masses, the peasants and other workers. Personally, I accept in its fundamentals the socialsist theory of the state".[20]

At the same time he was one of the first leaders of the anti-colonist movement to make it quite clear that the movement towards socialism was a specific need for developing countries, and an objectively predetermined road to progress for states liberated from imperialist rule, including India. In this thesis he accepted many arguments later put forward by other politicians in Africa and Asia.[21] He clearly stated the unacceptability of capitalism for developing countries as they had no time to achieve progress by same methods, or at the same rate, as the western world once used, "Are we to follow the English, French and the American way?" he asked, "Have we time of 100 to 150 years to reach our destination ? This is impossible. We will perish in the process". The idea that only socialism could allow the former colonial people to wrench themselves out of their backwardnes was also put forward in his well-known article 'The Basic Approach'. He wrote, "In a poorly developed country, the capitalist method offers no chance. It is only through a planned approach on socialistic lines that steady progress can be attained, though even that will take time''.[22]

Nehru's revolutionary nationalism was consonant with the appeal made by the leader of the proletarian movement, Lenin, for collaboration and joint efforts in the fight against imperialism. Lenin was quick to perceive that there was a close identity of interests between the socialists in Europe and the nationalists in Asia, including India, and that the two ought to march together in their common struggle against the capitalist powers of Europe. It was this feeling of solidarity with Asian countries based on an awareness of identity of interests between the socialists in Europe and the nationalists in Asia, that determined Soviet attitude and policy towards India after the October Revolution. Lenin's policy was aimed at the formation of a united front of all anti-imperialist and anti-feudal forces in the countries oppressed by imperialism, at the building up of an alliance between the national liberation movement and Soviet Russia, the first country to practice Socialism.

Corresponding to Lenin's view Nehru also held that, ''Socialism in the West and the rising nationalism of the Eastern and other dependent countries opposed this combination of fascism and imperialism . . . Inevitably we take our stand with the progressive forces of the world which are ranged against fascism and imperialism''.[23]

Moreover, the Soviet example of rapid industrialization of a predominantly agricultural country through planned economic development and without any significant foreign assistance, fired the imagination of the leaders of the anti-colonial national movements. It not only gave a socio-economic content to their struggle for freedom but made them actually aware of the possibility of attaining not only political but also economic independence from the West. Finally, while, the rejection of the West by the national elite of Asia and Africa on ideological grounds was total, the rejection of the Soviet ideology was only partial, mainly relating to its political aspects. Most Afro-Asian leaders believe that capitalism not only leads inevitably to inequality and exploitation, but, what is more important from their point of view and more relevant, to imperialism. Almost all of them accepted in theory the economic aspects of socialism, with serious reservations about the Soviet political structure.

Endowed with an uncanny insight into the forces of history, Nehru could perceive the underlying urges of the world forces and the turn that the future would take. He took upon himself the task to educate and inform the peoples of all the subject countries as well as the rest of the world, that the place of all such countries under foreign rule was with socialist forces. A new analysis of imperialism had led him to believe that, the countries fighting for independence could never unite witth imperialists, their grave-diggers.

Nehru was remarkable clear when he affirmed his support to the rising Soviet state and its policy of co-operating with the national liberation forces. In fact, he was convinced that close collaboration and friendship with the Soviet Union-leader of the Socialist forces and the national liberation forces inspired him and convinced him that the fate of the two were enjoined.

The impact of Nehru's ideological progress on national thought and life was quite considerable. It was directly connected with the lessons he drew from his Marxian contacts. He discovered two shortcomings in his own nationalism and that of his copatriots and strove to remove them. The first was an insular outlook. The reaction against the stubborn faith of the pre-Gandhian nationalists, in British progressives, the over-confidence in Gandhian technique had promoted parochialism among the young nationalists, includingNehru, in the early twenties. As a result of his contacts abroad Nehru, realised the necessity of a close alliance between Indian nationalism and the world progressive forces. Marxism brought home this realisation intellectually, and Brussels, emotionally. He took upon himself the task to get the Indian National Congress committed to this alliance. Nehru's nationalism paved the way for socialism, and the latter, for internationalism.

Scientific Socialism and Nehru

The years 1917 to 1939 were a decisive period for Nehru. A prolonged stay in Europe including a trip to the Soviet Union in 1929 brought him closer to the principle of Scientific Socialism. During the months in the West he made the jump from a liberal nationalist to a Marxist and for a decade, under the influence of the Leninist variety. This was the greatest period and it was then that he become Nehru, the leader of Left India. It can safely be said that what he wrote and did from

1928 to 1939 was vitally alive than even his seventeen years of premiership.

The Glimpses, Autobiography, Whither India?, The presidential Address at Lahore (1929), Lucknow (1936) and Faizpur (late 1936) the Karachi Charter, the Faizpur Agrarian Programme, the ringing calls for Spain, for China, for Abyssinia, for a world front against fascism and imperialism -- all these saw Nehru at his best. This was the time he undertook whirlwind tours of India, accepted the presidentship of the All India Trade Union Congress, appealed for the collective affiliation of trade union and Kisan Sabha to the Congress and roused the entire student community to a knowledge of socialism. This too was the time when he openly opposed Gandhiji on the basis of complete independence as against Dominian Status, on the propogation of socialism (facing even the resignation of majority of the working committee) the drawing in of states peoples movement and defence of the Congress socialists.

Above all, there was a complete clarity about his ideas and his analysis of the world and the Indian scene. Time and again he referred to Marxism as the scientific method which alone could give one the correct approach to reality and to the Soviet Union as the prototype of new civilization of the future, despite much that he could not understand or like.[24]

Nehru was greatly enamoured by the Marxist interpretation of history. It must be remembered that it was not merely romantic idolation that led him to believe in socialism, but a rational, concrete and analytical study of history and the forces which were shaping the future course of the world. He believed that dialectical materialism, the historic contribution made by Marx represented a scientific methodology for understanding, the history, historic forces, historic development and various economic and social forces that shaped the course of history. He had used dialectical materialism for the purpose of understanding history, he analysed Indian history, world history and tried to understand, how the forces of fascism could grow in Spain, in Italy and in Germany, and even long before some of the Socialist parties and Communist parties in Europe could envisage the growth of this phenomenon. Summing up the Marxian impact on him, Nehru wrote: "A study of Marx and Lenin produced a powerful effect on my mind and helped me to see history and current affairs in a new light. The long chain of history and of social development appeared to have some meaning, some sequence and the future lost some of its obscurity''.[25]

The study of Marx convinced him of the inevitability of socialism. According to Marxian theory of materialistic interpretation of history, the progress of history and institution through development of economic system, one system replacing another which had turned obsolete would inevitably lead to the advent of socialism. Capitalism when it had run its full course would be a dead weight on the existing society and it would be replaced by another, which was more scientific and more rationally solve the problem of society. The Marxian economic interpretation of history by emphasising the inevitability of class-struggle paved the way for Nehru's socialistic thought. It provided the rationale for justifying the advent of socialism.

It is remarkable to note that though Nehru admired Marxism, he did not follow it in its entirety; but presented his own theory of the class-struggle but particularly in the later years, preceded from the thesis that class contradictions could be solved through class-cooperation in a cooperative way, rather then threatening or through the concept of war. Growth of democracy, franchise , working class-movement, comprehensive social security measures and extension of the power of the Trade Union, made Marx's violent solution redundant.[26] His philosophy is based on the consideration that in these nuclear times war big or small, hot or cold and ideological clashes including the Marxist concept of class-struggle with its violent solutions, had become fatal and therefore obsolete.

Nehru time and again said that Marxism should be studied in a new light so that it could catch up with the advancing world. Marx's reasoning was logical and correct but he did not and in fact, could not take into account new factors like advance of democracy and technological revolution as these conditions did not exist during his time. Marxism had to be reviewed in this context in order to offer new solutions to new problems.[27]

Thus, Nehru agreed with many principles of scientific socialism and the practical testimony of the Soviet Union with its successful existence against many odds, yet he can never be categorised a Marxist, in the real sense of the term. Once he remarked that the Marxian philosophy appealed to him in a broad sense and helped him to understand the process of history, but he hastened to add, "I am far from being an orthodox Marxist".[28] Then regarding the social structure of Russia, he said that he believed in the economic theory which served as the basis of the social structure of Russia, and he felt that Russia had made most remarkable progress, culturally, educationally and industrially. " But nevertheless, I do not accept or oppose every thing that has taken place in Russia and I do not follow blindfold the example of Russia. Therefore, I prefer to use the word socialism rather than communism because the latter has come to signify Soviet Russia".[29]

From these views of Nehru it is clear that though he turned to Marxist philosophy to understand the process of history, and accepted the important theme of social justice from Marxism and the basic economic theory of the Russian social structure, he did not accept Marxism in its totality, nor he insisted on emulating Russia completely to bring about the structural changes in the social and economic fields. Thus, his concept of socialism or socialist state cannot reasonably be quoted with Marxism in the strict sense, nor it can be callously subsumed to communism in the Russian way of life.

It was precisely for the this reason that he never exactly defined socialism. When he talked of socialism, it may be remembered that he had used various expressions both in his speeches as well as in his writings like economic democracy, socialist democracy, socialist state and socialistic pattern of society. When he used these expressions, he used them as synonymous to one another and not as some distinct expressions, nevertheless, he deliberately refrained from giving a dogmatic definition. When R.K. Karanjia, interviewing Nehru, asked for a definition of the new socialism' adopted to suit our country, Nehru unhesitatingly replied, " I am afraid I have no definition to give you. Definitions tend to become dogmas and slogans which prevent clear thinking in term of a rapidly changing world".[30].

Socialism and Democracy

Apart from nationalism, socialism and democracy are the two most important tenets of Nehru's political thought. Acharya Narendra Deva, the Marxian inspired thinker of Indian socialism in attempting to give a garb to Nehru's philosphy said in 1946 : "If I were to be asked to sum up his social philosophy in a neat phrase, I would say that it is democratic socialism''. Acharya Vinoba Bhave the Gandhian philosopher in an equally unweavouring tone in his obituary recollected in 1964, ''Jawaharlal's special legacy to us is the way of democratic-socialism.''[31]

Nehru had acquired and maintained thoughout his life, a half liberal, half Marxiststance, though Marxists claim that half Marxism is no Marxism. But this did not worry him, he did not borrow an ideology but built up one for himself. He saw himself as a libertarian Marxist and his idea of socialism encompassed at every stage a large and his irreducible measure of civil liberty. One could have neither democracy nor socialism wihtout the other; in fact each thrived on the other in a symbiotic relationship. Socialism is inherent in Democracy and Democracy is the womb of Socialism.[32]

A frequent criticism of socialism is made on the point that it allows little individual freedom and is antithetical to democracy. It is pointed out that they are diametrically opposite but Nehru did not subscribe to this view. According to him there is no dichotomy between democracy and socialism, they are two sides of the same coin, each gaining fulfilment in the other. He declared, ''I do not see why under socialism there should not be a great deal of freedom for the individual; indeed far greater freedom than the present system gives. He can have freedom of conscience and mind, freedom of enterprise, and even the possession of private property on a restricted scale. Above all, he will have the freedom which comes from economic security which only a small number possess today''.[33]

Nehru defined democracy in terms of a structure ot society in which economic and social equality would gradually be attained. Political, economic and social freedom could not be separated. It was an integrated conception, and there could be neither political nor economic democracy without social freedom. Writing in 1933, Nehru seemed to feel that the most important challenges ot democracy lay in existing economic structure of society. One obvious problem was that the ideology of nineteenth century democracy considered the question of economic inequality, which was made more acute by the tremendous production of new wealth, as completely outside its province. Formal democracy thus isolated itself from some of the most pressing and vital issues. Yet ''democracy means equality, and democracy can only flourish in an equal society".[34]

A second problem as Nehru viewed it within the framework of his socialism, was that in the nineteenth century democracy, political power had become the monopoly of the upper classes. The political structure was supposedly built upon the principle of equality, but it was never effected in practice. Far from granting some measure of economic equality, formal democracy did not even produce true political equality, the machinery of democracy had been exploited to maintain a class government which existed to further its own interests.[35] In other words, Nehru saw capitalism as the most basic reality of the twentieth century. He saw an essential contradiction between capitalism and democracy, and thus the capitalist system itself constituted the most serious problem confronting democracy. " The conflict between capitalism and democracy is inherent and continuous; it is often hidden by misleading propaganda and by the outward forms of democracy, such as parliaments, and the sops that the owning classes throw to the other classes to keep them more or less contented."[36] True democracy could be attained only through the elimination of capitalism.

Nehru's later speeches and writings indicated that he had greatly modified this oversimplified analysis of the problems confronting the modern democratic state. But he never abandoned the idea that democracy must be understood in terms of social and economic equality. Almost twenty years later he held that the whole purpose of the Indian constitution, as conceived in the Directive Principles, was to move towards 'a casteless and classless society'. Furthermore, anything that perpetuates the present social and economic equalities is bad.[37] Nehru asserted that the spirit of the age is for equality, although it reamain unfulfilled in practice almost everywhere.[38] And it was precisely to remove this discrepancy between theory and practice that Nehru chanelised all his efforts.

A programme for all-round democracy Nehru placed before the people in gereral in all speeches, with exclusive *concentration* in his addresses to the youth as early as and in the programme he drafted for the Independence for India League. It is also manifest in the positions he took vis-a-vis various classes in Indian society. However, in an attempt to extend and widen this necessary struggle for democracy he strove to give his programme socialist orientation.

Linking the struggle for democracy with a perspective that would open itself towards socialism, Nehru approached the question in a manner very similar to Mao-Tse-Tung's exposition of 'New Democracy', despite the total absence of orthodox Marxist categories in Nehru's vocabulary. Just as Mao had defined the first stage of the struggle in China as a struggle for "democracy of a new type", Nehru began with the proposition that it was essential for nationalists in India to take a principled stand on the struggle for Republicanism or democracy.[39] Nehru emphasised that the new Indian Republic could not be based on the exploitation of one group by another. The Russian Revolution had changed the face of the world and it was imperative that India understood the changing times and adapt itself accordingly.[40] Thus the conception of Swaraj or Republic had to be clarified, the new type of organisation that was needed in the country was precisely to establish this new ideal of Democracy or Republicanism interpreted as: a Republic wedded to a non-exploitative society.[41]

Curiously, the perspective put forward by the West European communist parties today, the Italian communists in particular is almost identical to many of the formulations of Nehru. Recalling Togliatti's elaboration of the prospect of a "democracy of a new type", Napolitano, a leading spokesman of the Italian Communist Party, holds that this was the most important concept in dissolving the false dilemma of whether the objective of the struggle against fascism was to restore bourgeois democracy or to establish the dictatorship of the proletariat. This false dilemma had paralysed all efforts to unify ... especially the left'. The Democracy of a new type, which transcended this dilemma that is "to create a democratic regime of a new type. which overcomes the demerits and the fundamental defects of "bourgeois democracy" and which is open to the possibility of successive developments and profound transformation in a socialist sense... What Toligatti called "a regime of progressive democracy".[42] When Nehru insisted that the relationship between socialism and democracy was organic, and that 'the rejection of democracy does not or should not come from the socialist side but from the other', he was not very far from Togalitti's declaration : "From democracy we want to take nothing; we want to add to it many things"[43]

India had to aim at a new type of society whose chief purpose would be the welfare of the people. Such a society would require not only a new social and economic set up, but a fundamental reorientation of human motivation. " We have to aim deliberately at a social philosophy which seeks a fundamental transformation of the structure, a society which is not dominated by the urge of private profit and individual greed and where there is a distribution of political and economic power. We must aim at a classless society based on cooperative effort where there is opportunity for all'.[44] This objective towards which society should move has been variously described by Nehru as a 'classless society', 'economic democracy', or a socialist pattern of society'.

The ideal or real democracy envisaged by Nehru may aptly be called a "politico-economic democracy". Its salient features, as he explained are the economic equality of the people, creation in the minds of the people a feeling of partnership not only in the governance of the country but also in various other activities with which they were directly connected and the free exercise of the people of their right to elect governments and to control them effectively. The politico-economic democracy of Nehru has been described by him, rightly so, as 'social and human democracy'obviously, therefore, this brand of democracy as its essential features reveal, would be irreconcilable with the capitalist system, but on the other hand it would be necessary, inevitable and natural ally of the new social order visualized by him, which would be socialistic.[45]

The task was made more difficult by Nehru's unwillingness to swerve from democratic path even though it might mean a slower pace, for to him this was the only way of strengthening the roots of socialism. The Indian 'caravan of crores' should advance towards socialism by democratic and peaceful methods. To Nehru the ends and the means were inextricably linked; socialism would endure only if the approach were democratic, and there was increasing conflict between the idea of parliamentary government and full blooded private enterprise, what India required was not merely an economic programme but a recasting of society and a revolution in thought; and if there were to endure they needed to be a popular acceptance and would take time to achieve. "We are not building a house with bricks and mortar, our materials are human beings, only with their willing cooperation can we build our society" [46]

Long years of hard thinking had enabled him to reach firm conclusion as to the path along which free India would march. The ideological shape of the nationalist struggle, the influence of western liberal thought and the more recent attraction of Indian philosophy, all mixed in him a form of granite core of intellectual and moral commitment to democratic values. For him democracy was an end in itself and not just a means. He disliked any form of forced conformation and attached supreme importance to the human personality. "Nothing can be worse for the world I think than a deprivation of human freedom of the individual".[47] Also though he professed no belief in Hindu faith, he felt the appeal of the Hindu idea that, if there be a divine essence in the world, every individual was endowed with a part of it.

According to Nehru, democracy is the most acceptable form of government because, in the first analysis, it promotes the balanced growth of individual and of society. The new social order of Nehru's conception assigned an active role to the individual. In other words, the individual is not rendered a non-entity, nor is he allowed to be submerged in the name of social good. For Nehru democracy and socialism are means to an end not the end in itself. [48]The end or the goal, as far as he is concerned, is good life of the people based on social justice. In his characteristic way he posed a question whether the good of the society was something apart from and transcending the good of the individual. His answer to his self-imposed question was that ,"If the individual was ignored and sacrificed for what was considered the good of the society, it would be a wrong objective". [49] Proceeding further he said that,"the real social progress will come only where opportunity is given to the individual to develop, provided the individual is not a selected group but comprises the whole community."

Thus, Nehru made the individual the basic entity of the society of his conception, considered the individual as a cooperative being contributing to the good of the society and laid stress on the duty of the individual. Nehru takes an organic view of society and stresses that the individual is the basic entity of the social process and responsible member of community, and inter-relation between individual good and social good is necessary phenomenon of a sound social system.This view of Nehru regarding individual, corresponds to Gandhiji's view of individual, who is at the centre of his concept of community, and to J.P.Narayan's view of man who is an organic entity and living cell of his "communitarian society".[50]

BASIC POSTULATES OF DEMOCRACY

Parliamentary System

As the type of democracy, there was really little discussion. There was as no political planning before 1947 as there had been no organised thinking on economic matters. Gandhiji had not favoured parliamentary democracy and his mind had run along lines of village administration and trusteeship. Nehru in the thirties had criticised Gandhi in the terms of Marx and contended that there was a structural violence bulit-in into capitalist society, just as he had rejected, from the Gandhian view -point, the coercion innate in Marxism. But parliamentary democracy did not appear to him to be inseparable from capitalism and seemed more acceptable than communism and fascism, which in those days appeared as alternatives. So Nehru made no effort to reverse the trend of constitutional thinking before 1947 or to resist British influence.

For Nehru parliamentary system held a special meaning. Only in a parliamentary system could democracy prosper and remain unadulterated. It was suited to India and was rooted in traditions of Indian history. Speaking in the Lok Sabha on March, 28, 1957, he explained, "We chose this system of parliamentary democracy deliberately; we chose it not only because, to some extent,we had always thought on these lines previously, but because we thought that it was in keeping with our old traditions..."[51]

Also the system held a special connotation for Nehru. . . It meant a specific condition of mind and involved many virtues like devotion to work, a cooperative spirit and a tolerant approach, "Parliamentary democracy naturally involves peaceful methods of action, peaceful acceptance of decision taken and attempts to change them through peaceful ways again. . . the quest of peace and the quest of democracy can only be made through method of peace and not through any other method."[52]

For Nehru parliamentary democracy symbolised change and continuity.[53] A balancing of the two had to be made for the smooth functioning of society, especially Indian society which had always revealed the unfoldment of these two forces. According to Nehru, parliamentary democracy was in tune with the Indian temper of continuity and change.

Ignoring all conventional wisdom Nehru gave adult suffrage to a people, the large majority of whom were illiterate. The people grew accustomed to political participation and learnt that they had a mind. Nehru taught them to apply that mind. All his public speeches, both before and after 1947, were part of a sustained programme of adult education. Over the years he helped to transform the political value structure of the Indian people. It was an unseen revolution.

Community Development

Decentralisation was, in Nehru's eyes, the foundation of parliamentary democracy; 'It is not good enough to work for the people and go ahead, and to give them a sense of working for themselves.'[54] His hopes lay in community development programmes and the national extension service. Nehru saw in these twin programmes the possibility of a great revolutionary change carried out peacefuly and without conflict. It was the forward movement of a whole people, a sense of participation not just in political activity but in economic and social development as well. Democracy in its fullest sense was the chance given to the people to decide for themselves. In all basic issues rather than merely securing the assent in decisions taken by others.[55]

Modernisation could be, imposed from above but to Nehru participation was the integral part of modernisation and that which vested it with endurance. It was because the community development programme involved the masses and gave them considerable initiative and responsibility that it evoked in Nehru the crusador's zeal. A self-reliant peasantry, persuaded to adopt new ways of thought and action without forsaking its traditinal culture, taking voluntarily to improved methods of cultivation and cooperative farming and governing itself through Panchayats, as well as social cohesion and create a democratic and socialist structure in India was Nehru's vision.

Planning

Nehru's aim was to build a free and democratic state in which the fundamental rights of the individual and the group--political, economic, social and cultural would be guaranteed. The state would be progressive and would utilise all scientific and other knowledge for the advancement of the people as a whole, and for the promotion of their happiness and their material as well as their cultural and spiritual well-being . It would not permit the exploitation of the community by individuals or group to the disadvantage of the former and to the injury of the nation as a whole. To realise the social objective the state must follow and co-ordinate the various activities of the nation as to avoid waste and conflict and attain the maximum results.

Immediately after Independence the A.I.C.C.stated in a resolution: "Politicalindependence having been achieved, the Congress must address itself to the next great task, namely, the establishment of real democracy in the country and a society based on social justice and equality. Such a society must provide every man and woman with equality of opportunity and freedom to work for the unfettered development of his or her personality. This can be realised only when democracy extends from the political to the social and economic spheres. Democracy in the modern age necessitates planned central a direction as well as decentralisation of political and economic powers in so far as this is compatible with the safety of the community as a whole. Our aim should be to evolve a political system which would combine efficiency of administration with individual liberty, and an economic structure which will yield maximum production without the operation of private monopolies and the concentration of wealth, and which will create a proper balance between urban and rural economies. Such a social structure can provide an alternative to the acquisitive economy of private capitalism and the regimentation of a totalitarian state." The statement reflects the entire approach policy and programming which Nehru had for independent India--a clear commitment to socialism and democracy.

The Nehru approach to planning may, perhaps, he called the middle way. It was an attempt to achieve rapid economic progress in manner in which political and economic democracy would be reconciled. He had great faith in persuasion which stems from his sense of democracy. In his speeches on planning, one can continually feel how he was trying to present the whole case, both for and against.

Under the leadership of Nehru, India made big advances. He initiated the thinking on planning in India. Through his speeches and through planning committees and the planning commission, he exercised a profound educative influence and made India conscious of the need for national planning. Through the Congress party and the Government, he made planning an instrument of national policy on the biggest scale outside the communist countries, and persuaded India to accept socialism as her goal. He brought to Indian planning a full appreciation of the scientific revolution which is transforming the world, a sensitive awareness of human values and cultural traditions, an inherent sense of democracy and an international outlook.[56]

Mixed Economy

As such, the tenets of socialism and democracy in practice, Nehru believed, would emerge more rapidly, and with less violence and conflict, from the accommodating ethos of a mixed economy than from a rigid and dogmatic adherence to orthodox socialist doctrines. He even accepted that a mixed economy was based on a 'mixed ideology'. [57] To Nehru the mixed economy was, in the context of Indian underdevelopment, an indirect approach towards the fact of socialism. A capitalist economy with considerable state control and a public sector directly under the state would gradually transform itself into a socialist economy. He envisaged that the private sector would help in increasing the national wealth even when the public sector gradually transformed itself even into a socialist economy. The private sector would help in increasing the national wealth even while the public sector gradually expanded, overlapped and finally overwhelmed the private sector.

So long as the state controlled the basic industries Nehru was willing to leave private enterprise in the background seeing no inherent conflict between the public and the private sectors and depreciating 'grousing, nibbling and squabbling' about priorities between them.[58] He did not think that this in itself would hinder the movement towards socialist objectives. For socialism was to him not a code of dogma but a pragmatic endeavour leading to higher production, more even distribution and greater equality of opportunity. His socialism encompassed sufficiency of means, equality of opportunity and poverty, not wealth as the evil to attack and abolish. Thus the system of mixed economy would involve private initiative, in keeping with the democratic spirit as well as promote a socialistic society.

Conclusion

Jawaharlal Nehru was clear in his mind as to what kind of socialism he wanted to introduce in India. The resolution of the plenary session of the Congress at Bhubaneshwar had mentioned the words Socialism and Democracy.[59] It was drafted under the stewardship of Nehru and he was aware of the fact that giving precise definition to India's path towards socialism, one has to know the perspective of history and the experience gained from the people's struggle for socialism. Socialism is the logical extension of democracy and democracy finds its true fulfilment in socialism. He taught that there are certain ingredients of socialism which are universal. Whether they are applied in Soviet Union or China, or in G.D.R.or U.A.R. or in any part of the world, they are universal and nowhere could socialism be built minus these universal ingredients which is that the state belongs to the exploited people, that the state, takes over the means of production, and function in the interest of the majority of the people, for which the legislative measures or parliamentary measures, peaceful measures had to be taken to deprive the small minority, otherwise socialism could not be built.

It is therefore, Nehru who taught that the ingredients of socialism are universal but in a vast country like India, of large complexities, with its distinctive and ancient civilization and own heritage, socialism could not be copied either from the Soviet Union or China or from any other socialist country. Socialism had to grow in the soil of india. Therefore, Indian conditions, Indian traditions and Indian problems had to be taken into consideration. Keeping this perspective in view, Nehru put forward the idea of 'Democratic Socialism' in consonance with the Indian mind and 'Indian genius'.

References

1. *Selected Works*, vol.4, p.205.
2. Bhagwan Josh ,"Nationalism, Third International and Indian Communists; Communist Party and the United National Front",(1934-39)in Bipan Chandra (ed), *The Indian Left: Critical Approach*, p.149.
3. *Ibid.*, The conception of nation-in the making is the central conception of the historiographical framework which Dr. Bipan Chandra has over the years, developed to understand the various aspects of the Indian National Movement.
4. Hans Kohn,' Nationalism', *International Encyclopedia of Social Sciences*, London Macmillan Company and the Free Press, 1968, vol.II, pp.63-69.
5. V.T. Patil, *Nehru And The Freedom Movement*, pp. 44-45.

6. J. Nehru, *The Discovery of India*, p. 332.
7. *Ibid.*, p.53.
8. *Ibid.*
9. Speech at the Lucknow Congress, J.S. Bright, *Important Speeches of Jawaharlal Nehru,* Lahore, The Indian Printing Works, 1945, pp.3-4.
10. *Ibid.*, pp. 3-4.
11. J. Nehru, *An Autobiography*, p. 426.
12. Speech at Kingsway Hall London, Form *The Bombay Chronicle* 16 July, 1938, in *Selected Works*, vol. 9, p. 72.
13. J.Nehru : *The Unity of India* - Collected Writings, 1937-1940 London, Lindsay Drummond, 1938, p.335.
14. Ganesh Prasad, *Nehru: A Study in Colonial Liberalism*, pp. 186.
15. *Selected Works*, vol.8, p. 102.
16. Dorothy Norman, *"Nehru : The First Sixty Years"*, vol.1,p. 119.
17. *Selected Works*, vol.3, p.152.
18. *Ibid.*
19. *Ibid.*
20. Report on the Brussels Congress, *Selected works*, Vol.2.p.287.
21. Rostislav Ulyanovysky, *Present day problems in Asia and Africa* Moscow, Progress, 1975, p. 202.
22. J. Nehru, *Congressmen's Primer for Socialism*, A Socialist Congressman Publication, New Delhi, 1963, p.50.
23. Dorothy Norman, *Jawaharlal Nehru, The First Sixty Years*, vol.1,p.427.
24. J.Nehru, *An Autobiography*, p. 166.
25. J. Nehru, *The Discovery of India*, p. 15.
26. J. Nehru, *An Autobiography*, p. 31.
27. *J.Nehru's Speeches*, vol.4, p. 120.
28. *Ibid.*
29. Dorothy Norman, *Nehru: The First Sixty Years, vol.1*, p. 450.
30. R.K.Karanjia, *The Mind of Nehru*, p. 37.
31. Benudhar Pradhan, *The Socialist Thought of Jawaharlal Nehru*, p. 171.
32. Dorothy Norman, *Nehru: The First Sixty Years*, vol. 1,p. 451.
33. *Ibid.*, p. 626.
34. Jawharlal Nehru, *Glimpses of World History*, p. 825.
35. *Ibid*, p. 935.
36. *Ibid.*, p. 825.
37. Speech in the House of the People, June 1, 1951, Parliamentary Debates, 1951, vol. 12, part II, vol. 9831.
38. J.Nehru, *The Discovery of India*, p. 532.
39. Sashi Joshi, ' Nehru and the Emergence of the Left Bloc, 1927-29' in Bipan Chandra, (ed.) *The Indian Left : Critical Appraisals*, pp. 74-75.
40. *Selected Works*, vol.3, p. 8.
41 *Ibid.*
42. Sashi Joshi, Nehru and the Emergence of Left Block 1927-29, Bipan chandra (ed.) *The Indian Left : Critical Approach*, p. 75.
43. *Ibid.*, p. 76.
44. Broadcast Speech, December 13,1952. *Building New India*, A.I.C.C., New Delhi, 1954, p. 53.
45. Dorothy Norman, *Nehru: The First Sixty Years*, vol.1,p. 625.
46. Speech at the A.I.C..C., 4 Jan. *The Hindu*, 5 January, 1957.
47. Nehru in the United States, 1949, *Visit to America*, New York, 1950, p. 136.

48. *J.Nehru's Speeches*, vol.4, p. 118.
49. *Ibid.*, p.119.
50. J.P.Narayan, *Communitarian Society and Panchayati Raj*, Varanasi, Navchitra Prakashan, 1970, pp. 122-125.
51. *J.Nehru's Speeches*. vol.3, pp. 155-56.
52. *Ibid.*, p. 158.
53. *Ibid.*, p. 157.
54. S. Gopal, *The Mind of Jawaharlal Nehru*, (Madras, Sangam Books, 1980), p. 26.
55. Speech at the Community Conference, New Delhi, May 7, 1952 in *J.Nehru's Speeches*, 1949-53, p. 84.
56. Address to the Associated Chambers of Commerce, Calcutta, Dec. 14, 1953, in *J.Nehru's Speeches*, vol.3, pp. 59-60.
57. S. Gopal, *Jawaharlal Nehru: A Biography*, vol, III, p. 290.
58. J. Nehru's Speeches at the A.I.C.C., Nagpur, 8 January, *The Hindu*, 9, Jan. 1959.
59. *J. Nehru's Speeches*, vol.III,

CHAPTER 7

CONCLUSION

Much has been said about Jawaharlal Nehru as a nation-builder, a democrat, a world statesman, a planner and a socialist, even after so many years of his death, Nehru is the topic of researching study, for he had both world-view of thought and thought of world-view, which holds relevance till today. He had immense faith in socialism and appreciation for the 'new-civilization' that it promised to achieve on a world-wide scale. He admired the socialism, being carried out in other countries like Russia and China but was very much sure about the type of socialism that would have to be adopted in India. Socialism to be meaningful to India would have to speak the language of India. Nehru's whole life was devoted towards achievement of this goal. The principles of socialism had a dominant impression, which was evident in the various ideas he formulated and the activities that he took up till his death.

Nehru was born to rich and aristocratic parents and was accustomed to a life confined to a microscopic minority even in the higher echelons of society. His English system of education starting from early childhood with the English governess till its ultimate fulfilment through Harrow, Cambridge and London, fitted him to be an English aristocrat of the Victorian era. Yet his desire that on his death, instead of being laid to rest at Rajghat, his ashes be scattered from the air over the fields where the peasants toil, sound comparatively strange and add a socialistic overtone to his life and mission.

Nehru's socialism has been enriched by five different streams of thought, i.e., Humanist liberalism, Fabianism, Gandhism, Vedanta and Marxism. Each stream carrying its own alluvial soil added to the fertility of Nehru's socialist concept and by such a mixture distinguished it from other brands of the same name. Nehru's socialism is unique. It has drawn from five different sources and therefore, combines five different fragrance. Like Marx he advocates inevitability of socialism, and views the forces of history through the Marxist mirror. Further, the scientific non-dogmatic and pragmatic nature of his socialism is Marxian in origin. Purity of means and acceptance of non-violent technique for the attainment of a socialistic society, as well as the agrarian bias and sympathy for the underdog is Gandhian in inspiration. Nehru's indebtedness to Fabianism is evident from his emphasis on reformism, constitutionalism and gradualism. Respect for freedom, dignity and creativity of the individual, belief in reason, faith in democracy and democratic institutions stems from the humanist liberal tradition. The ancient Indian culture and epics also had a profound impact on his thought process and mental make-up. He saw intense individualism, exclusiveness and metaphysical democracy in the Indo-Aryan civilization. The perception of the Universe as an organic whole and spurning of the profit motive as a value which ranked very low in the scale of Indian social system, as well as the spirit of social service emanated after a study of the Vedanta. This was indeed, the result of the quest for an Indian expression of socialist thought.

Thus, Nehru has brought about a synthesis between Fabianism, Gandhism, Liberalism, Marxism and the Vedanta. By a strange alchemy and uncommon genius he has made Marx and Gandhi great in their own ways. He has borrowed from Fabians, Marx, Liberalism and Gandhi, yet in reconciling all these elements he has forged his own brand of socialism. Nehru's socialism is thus three dimensional. It is founded on Gandhian ethics, Marxian economics and democratic politics.

Thus, he imbibed the tradition of ancient Indian culture and the rich history of the Indian national liberation movement, especially the philosophy and practice of Gandhism. He assimilated all that West European liberalism had to offer receiving his education in its cradle. Great Britain, and turned in his disappointment to the socialist idea, at first in their Fabian vision. But having ideas of equality and social justice, Nehru was bound to perceive by force of his critical, searching mind many of the premises of scientific socialism, Nehru did not resist the process. He repeatedly underlined the positive influence of the idea of scientific socialism on his world outlook.

With his sensitivity, keen perception and sharp intellect, Nehru's mind remained open to various influences. Yet, it is remarkable to note that, he did not adhere to any theory or principle as dogma. Indeed, the key to his thinking was scepticism about all claims to absolute truth and virtue. He did not borrow an ideology, but built one for himself and therein this uniqueness. Threfore, it is not possible to categorise Nehru. Resilience was the hallmark of his personality. He turned every influence, also every experience to suit the Indian condition.

Nehru had a distinctive philosophy of history, which prodded him into action and sustained all through the years of his premiership. He was a man with a gift for history, which made him out to be a politician with a difference. What distinguished him from others was his historical mindedness. In India, he brought thought to bear on politics. In other words he saturated politics with thought, with tne result that every action, policy or ideology that he contemplated for India or the world was judged in the historical perspective.

For him, historical and philosophical meditations was not an end in itself, but a search for an answer to the most important problems of concern to his homeland and the world. *The Discovery of India* and *Glimpses of World History*, are efforts in this direction. The past engages Nehru's interest primarily as a "pointer to the future". For him history is a school of life, experience and struggle, the source of the origin of his world-view. Nehru thought in concrete terms, with an eye to the tasks of the day but, simultaneously he sought to gain an insight into the future.

Similarly, he was much impressed by the rationalism and objectivity of the Marxist interpretation of materialistic conception of history. He considered it different from the prior theories regarding history, as none had given due importance to the concept of class-struggle which was present at all times. Nehru agreed with Marx in this respect and attributed fundamental importance to class-conflict and material changes as the forces of history. Moreover, Marxism presented a rationale for the advent of socialism. This is not surprising since Nehru himself saw in this science the ineluctable logic of historical development, the imperative demand of time--the epoch of transition to socialism. He repeatedly emphasised the favourable impact of scientific-socialism on his world outlook.

However, Nehru's conception of class-antagonism as the dominant urge behind historical change, is less dogmatic than that of Marx. While, accepting the inevitability of class-conflict Nehru does not view history as a story of class-struggle alone. Materialistic dialectics fail to recognize the higher human ideal of love and cooperation in human relations. To him, therefore, the reality of mutuality is as important and determining a factor as the reality of class-conflict in the development of human society. Throughout his search into history, it has been his endeavour to establish that man has a mind which is universal, cooperative and good, thereby having faith in the essential goodness of man.

Nehru dreamt of a better humanity, a greater wisdom of a finer cultural mantle for its body, than the bloody rags of a robot civilization. He was searching an all comprehensive philosophy that would maintain an equilibrium between Man's internal and external life and help him ascertain a purpose of life. He viewed man in totality. He derived inspiration from the Vedanta, and accordingly believed that the universe is an organic whole wherein every individual as an entity possesses a spark of the energy of the greater whole. As a result Nehru examines history with the temper and approach of science, allied with philosophy.

A deep historical perspective is the source of Jawaharlal Nehru's world -view which is value based, objective, progressive and humanistic. Having rejected abstract and fruitless quest of the meaning of history outside it as such, he gradually discovered and later recognized the internal laws of historical development. A recognition of objective laws led him to a comprehension of the upward spiralwise direction of the historical process, not without occasional regression. This led him to make an elaborate analysis of the forces influencing the course of the world. He came to realise that capitalism with its twin brother fascism, was the root cause of social and political evil and must be uprooted to be replaced by socialism. It must be remembered that it was not merely romantic idolation that led him to believe in socialism, but a rational, concrete and analytical study of history and the forces which were shaping the future course of the world. The study of Marx convinced him of the inevitability of socialism. The Marxian theory of materialistic interpretation of history, the progress of history and institutions through development of economic system, one system replacing another which had turned obsolete inevitably led to the advent of socialism. Capitalism when it had run its full course would be a dead weight on the existing society and it would be replaced by another, more scientific and which more rationally solved the problems of society. The Marxian economic interpretation of history paved the way for Nehru's socialistic thought. It provided the rationale for justifying the advent of socialism.

Jawaharlal Nehru's world-view rests on the pillars of internationalism which had its root in nationalism in which both are supplementary to each other. The approach was aided by Nehru's capacity to see beyond India and to place the national problem in world context. His internationalism did not question the basics of nationalism, nor did it deny the validity of national self-consciousness. He was an internationalist *par excellence*, a world citizen in the truest sense of the word, though he fought with all his might to support worthy national causes.

It was with this view that he urged for an integrated history and disapproved of historians who wrote history with a singular vision of the particular and lost sight of the unity of mankind, making history an immense aggregate of particular facts related to a man or group of men, nations or religion, without reference to larger context of human mind, family of nations and transcendent ideas. Even while writing about India and himself, he tries to keep up this integrated world-view.

Nehru was like the conscience-keeper of the world who passionately and boldly reiterated that the alternative to cooperation was world disaster. He used every opportunity to warn the world of the nuclear catastrophe and suggested ways to circumvent it. Emphasising on the commonness of purpose which could unite nations towards a stable order and new world, he tried to convince the people that common needs leading to progress of science and technology would bring the nations closer, as was in the case of Russia and America. Nehru rose much higher than the contemporary statesmen when he transcended the difference of ideology and system to propagate a 'new- world order' based on peace, justice and equality.

A study of Nehru from his numerous writings, his long struggle for the liberation of the Indian and other subjugated peoples, reveals that he had great ability to mould the ideal, for which he had always stood, into the framework of everyday, political, social and international life. He was perhaps, one of those rare historical figures who mastered the art of turning their philosophical concepts into social, economic and political institutions. This may have been the outcome of intrinsic harmony between his realistic world outlook and his philosophical approach to existence. Because he was endowed with an alert and profound mind, Nehru was able to absorb the spirit which moves the world at large both materially and spiritually. He was able, in other words, to grasp clearly the working of the main forces which join human history to the cosmic existence. Within such a philosophical framework he was able to follow a policy which helped India emerge peacefully from her long and ancient history into the modern stage of existence.

The concept of class-struggle is a central one in the study of scientific socialism. The first postulate of socialism is acceptance of the fact that in all types of societies mentioned hitherto in history, including the capitalist society at present, there have been inherent conflicts of class interest.

Nehru acknowledged the scientific accuracy of Marx's interpretation of history, based on the idea of class-antagonism. The materialistic interpretation of history stirred his intellect and for the first time he could get an insight into the forces of history. Marx's interpretation of history differed from the existing theories. It was logical, scientific and rational and explained history in a much more realistic manner holding material forces as the catalyst of history rather than vague utopian ideals. Nehru's writings and speeches of the thirties vibrate with frequent references to class-struggle as the basic tenet of the existing social system. He declared that class-struggles are inherent in society and could not be shirked.

A study of the functioning of colonialism-imperialism in the light of Marxian scholarship enabled him to understand the operation of the British imperialism in India and the world over. Nehru declared that the interests of the two nations could never converge and there was bound to be intensive struggle. The system of capitalism was based on exploitation, thus making class-struggle inevitable. Capitalism would have to be uprooted to pave the way for the transformation of an exploitive society into a socialist society. Nehru went ahead and formulated a precise programme of intensive struggle with the British and its cronies--the landed and the rich of India. Nehru's struggle was, therefore, two dimensional - on the one hand with the aliens and on the other with the feudal and capitalists of his own country.

In this regard, he repudiated the theory of trusteeship put forward by Gandhi. Nehru declared in unequivocal terms that the interests of the exploiter and the exploited could never be the same and to expect a change of heart on the part of the capitalists in favour of the labour and peasantry was not only absurd but impossible. He was convinced that the sole trusteeship could only be that of the entire nation. For this he advocated socialisation of land and nationalization of key industries.

It is instructive to note that during this period Nehru unhesitatingly advocated the use of violence to remove any obstacle that came in the way of achievement of such a purpose of social and political change in India. According to him Non-violence was also a form of coercion and the principal moral argument in favour of socialism was that it reduced the element of coercion. He inspired the youth for whole-hearted combat with the British and capitalists.

The first theoretical premise embedded in Nehru's paradigm was the premise of anti-imperialism being the primary contradiction in the colonial countries. Thus, it was only through the prism of anti-imperialist nationalism that Nehru viewed and discussed the role of various classes in society. For this purpose he formed a united front which comprised the peasants, workers and the middle-class intelligentsia. He put particular emphasis on the participation of the peasants and the industrial workers who would form the backbone of the national movement and without whom, achievement of freedom would be inconceivable. Nehru realized that the Indian labour was disorganized and in infant stage of development and it was possible that freedom could be achieved without their active participation, but he warned that, this would result in establishment of another capitalist state nominally independent but with little freedom for the worker, thereby creating a new problem instead of solving the old one.

Nehru further attacked the Princes and the Zamindars, considering them to be the off-shoot of capitalism. They were embodiments of feudalism and had to be uprooted if a non-exploitative society was to be built. He, therefore, formulated a programme for whole-hearted combat. The declaration of the Karachi Congress session was a testimony. He invited the youth to participate actively in the movement and educated them to combat capitalism - imperialism as a system. His intense concentration on the youth movement and middle-class intelligentsia during the years 1927-33 was precisely his attempt to cultivate a revolutionary outlook.

It is instructive to remember that, though Nehru admired Marxism, he did not follow it in its entirety; but presented his own theory of the class-struggle. He recognized the existence of class-struggle but particularly in the later years proceeded from the thesis that class contradictions could be solved through class-cooperation, by trying to win over people in a cooperative way, rather than threatening them or through the concept of war. After the Second World War, Nehru thought that it was a changed world.

Committed even from the early 1930s to fundamental changes in the economic and social structure of India, Nehru was by 1947 confident as well as determined that these changes should be brought about by peaceful means. In 1938, he had believed that a measure of coercion was necessary. In the mind 1940s he was on the horn of a dilemma, if conflicts were inevitable it would have to be faced, but it would be benefiting to minimize it. As a Prime Minister, he had no doubt that persuasion was the only possible way. Too much of a democrat by now to consider any other means and almost unawares', a vague idealist approach would creep in mind, something rather akin to the Vedanta approach. Nor did he think that armed struggle was indispensable for the recasting of society. His forecast was that in India where the princely states had been integrated and the Zamindari system abolished without any revolt, the propertied classes would accept the unavoidable as production increased, so that there was enough for all and distribution became more equitable without hardship to anybody. Socialism not rigidified by definition and adopted to the Indian context was the logical consequence of democracy. Discarding ideological slots, the people of India would move peacefully in their own way towards a social pattern where equality of opportunity would be provided and the economic power of classes and individuals controlled, with the hope that some day socialism would be fully realized. The benefits of higher technological and industrial experience could be obtained without going through a phase of capitalism or extreme regimentation inherent in the communism.

Nehru's perception of Indian society, the forces--economic, social and political working behind it, its traditions, culture and legacy of a great civilization led him to view the class-struggle and in turn the dictatorship of the proletariat in a different perspective. It was also anachronistic, for the industrial proletariat, the vanguard of the dictatorship, was absent in India. Socialism would be brought about with the help of the educated youth, peasantry and the labour, under the leadership of the middle-class intelligentsia.

Moreover, Nehru had great faith in the efficacy of the institution of parliament and parliamentary democracy. He felt that what could not be achieved through force and violence could be attained through consensus and persuasion. All his efforts were directed towards a revolution by participation and agreement, for the fundamental question before him was how would it be possible to devise a system which ensures domestic peace, invites popular participation and simultaneously creates conditions for an assault on intolerable poverty.

Nehru adhered to the theory of constructive gradualism, which meant that change is necessary but continuity is also to be maintained. Society could not be suddenly plunged into sudden changes, creating stunned perplexity and a sense of shock. Moreover, he was very sceptical about sudden changes leading to meaningless destruction of values. The Industrial revolution and its aftermath, and consequences arising out of the change was not acceptable to him. Likewise, Nehru admired the socio-economic changes taking place in Soviet Russia but was at the same time categorically against the way the revolution had taken place. He lamented that the modern world was getting out of these, with what he called, "Life of Mind".

In this context, he even accepted the Basic Approach of the Vedanta which makes his effort unique in that he tries to synthesise materialism with spiritualism adopting the middle path for solving the problems of India and the world. A note written on 13 July, 1958, has a curious ending: "In considering the economic aspects of our problems, we have always to remember the basic approach of peaceful means; and perhaps we might keep in view the old Vedantic ideal of the life force which is the inner base of everything that exists''. And in one of the very last things he wrote before he died, on 25 May, 1964, he observed that, in India it was important to profit by modern technical process and increase production, but in doing so we must not forget that the essential objective to be aimed at is the quality of the individual and the concept of *dharma* underlying it''.

Therefore, Nehru's socialism as well as his approach to class-struggle is evolutionary. As a law student of twenty-one he was vaguely attracted to Fabianism and socialistic ideas in general. These ideas gradually receded into the background as the national movement claimed an increasing measure of his attention and loyalty. Later, during the 1930s, influenced by the thoughts of Marx and Lenin he gave scant attention to Fabianism. Prof. S. Gopal, has described Nehru of 1927-28 as a self-conscious, revolutionary, radical; but during 1933-36 he was on the verge of becoming a Marxist revolutionary, anti-imperialist. This was his greatest Marxist phase, ''The Indian summer of his Leftism''. It is instructive to compare Nehru's ideas of 1936 with his ideas twenty years later. This comparison clearly reveals the very considerable changes that had developed in his political philosophy. The years 1935-36 and 1955-56 represent two rather distinct periods in Nehru's political thinking. The radical Nehru of 1930s who regarded socialism as a 'vital creed' was a mellowed man in 1955 when he said, ''the mere adoption of the term capitalism or socialism does not solve any economic problem, but simply indicates a certain approach in understanding and in trying to find a solution to that problem''. Thus we see that Nehru's socialism is evolutionary, changing with the current and need of the times, particularly to suit Indian conditions, as he perceived them. In contrast to his ringing declaration in 1929 that he was a scientific socialist, Nehru now conceded the attractions of a utopian socialism with no attachment to any particular doctrine but a broad commitment to everyone in society being well-off and equal. The nearest definition he would give of socialism was the creation of equal opportunity for all of India's population, leading on to the raising of the level of progress equally for all.

Nehru had a clear vision of the future society of India which would be a mixture of modernity and tradition. He visulised a society which would be free of any type of exploitation, injustice and above all purged of poverty. A society is truly free if it consists of free people, and the people can be said to be truely free, if they achieve both political and economic freedom. Whenever there is oppression be it political, economical or social in nature the society can hardly be described as just. Nehru pondered deeply over the ills deep rooted in society and attributed this phenomenon to the present social structure. He identified the present social-structure with capitalism and its consequences, that had divided society into rich and poor, the exploiter and the exploited. According to him the system perpetuated by capitalism was a negation of justice.

Nehru's whole approach to human misery was not intellectual but emotional, probably of the same variety that moved, great men to reform the world. While he thought and pondered over the doctrines of Marx and Hegel, what stirred and inspired him into action was a dream to secure a fair deal to his countrymen, was this tender emotion. It was, therefore, Nehru's aim to establish a just state by just means or social justice by not merely "justifiable" but just means.

In short, the new social order of Nehru's conception is the socialist, unitary or classless society, wherein the law of life becomes one of cooperation and not competition or acquisitiveness, the distributive justice taking such shapes and forms as equitable distribution of wealth, grant of basic necessities of life to all, equality of opportunity assured to all, the humanistic approach or attitude to all problems in all spheres of activities becoming the way of life and wherein every individual enjoys the freedom coming from his release from economic and cultural bondage.

Nehru did not only believe in socialism but took positive step to bring social justice and equality in India. Since the ethical and humanitarian approach persisted throughout his life, he justified socialism not only on the ground of its inevitability, but on the ground of social justice and egalitarian society.

The tools he used to usher India into the modern age and achieve social justice or the dynamics of social change that he contemplated are - science and technology, planning, industrialization, nationalisation, community development, land reforms and various social legislations like Hindu Code Bill, abolition of Zamindari, change in property relations, reforms in education and drive against untouchability, to mention only a few.

Nehru will be remembered in history as a planner for the country owes to him the progress it is making towards self-reliance and self-growth in industry and in the activities associated with vital industries like power, fuel, transport and technical skill. He laid stress on heavy industries for more employment and greater production. Nehru concentrated on planning, formulating five-year plans as Chairman of the Planning Commission, trying to get them implemented as Head of the Government, and popularising them with the people and seeking cooperation in the development process by explanations and exhortations. Nehru had found his mooring. He clearly saw what had to be done in free India. The doctrine of socialism now ceased to be a subject of barren ideological polemics or academic bone of contention, for it was through the apparatus of planning that he endeavoured to render flesh and blood to his socialist ideas. For Nehru the plan had a deep significance, it was the dynamic through which the development of a particular structure of society was to be achieved. Nehru always emphasised on the 'human factor' involved in planning. Through the apparatus of planning he sought not merely material advancement but an advancement in the minds of human beings, leading to a transformation of society. This is a unique contribution and a new content infused into the concept of planning.

The community development and Panchayati Raj programme evoked in him a crusador's zeal because it involved the masses directly and gave them considerable initiative and responsibility. By 1956 it covered over a quarter of rural India and was spreading fast. The organization was well-knit and Nehru thought that the scheme could be extended from the development of amenities like roads, schools and wells to intensive agricultural production.

Similarly, Nehru held land reforms as one of the first priority in his plan of action towards achievement of social justice. He made an enduring contribution in terms of evolving an approach to this problem, a programme for tackling it and in terms of using state power for implementing the programme. Central to this agrarian programme of the Indian National Congress adopted under Nehru's leadership was concept of land to the tiller, land to the working peasant, who is the backbone of Indian agriculture and of India's economy and society. The first dimension of land reform in Nehru's conception therefore, involved a restructuring of property relations relating to land. It was in this vein of speedy reforms that emphasis was placed on land ceilings. The second dimension of land reform which concerned him was that of very low productivity of land. Land reform, therefore, should involve not only restructuring of the land ownership pattern but also such redesigning of the land operative pattern as was by the necessity of modernising the productive techniques. Nehru was led towards considering consolidation of holdings and cooperative farming as indispensable for agricultural modernisation. The entire idea behind cooperation and cooperative farming was genuine participation of people. Decentralization, diminution of bureaucratic control, lack of compulsion and voluntary collaboration would be the distinctive marks of the Indian model of socialism in the countryside. The third dimension of the land problems that concerned him was the social and cultural backwardness of the man behind the plough. The social reform of the peasant was essential part of Nehru's conception of agrarian reorganisation. The fourth dimension of the problem which concerned him was the tremendous and growing population pressure on land, an index of India's backwardness. His views encompassed a gradual transfer of population from agriculture to non-agricultural occupations such as cottage industries and small-scale industries as an outlet to relieve excessive pressure on land. In this background land reforms were basic to Nehru's perspective of economic development with social justice within the framework of political democracy for India.

Nehru introduced a number of social legislations towards amelioration of various discrepancies that abounded in the Indian society. Foremost was his effort to restructure the property relations. He was convinced that property relations had to be amended to suit the needs of the country. The amendment proposed by Nehru and accomplished by his government is a fundamental step towards the socio-economic emancipation of the country.

An important goal which Nehru achieved through legislation is the improvement in the status of women through the passage of various tedious bills like The Hindu Code Bill, Hindu Marriage Act, The Hindu Succession Act, The Hindu Minority and Guardianship Act etc. Nehru put all his weight behind these legislations and through personal effort, and prodding tutored the parliament and the public in the principles underlying the bills. The bills brought in a long overdue social change in India–the emancipation of women. Similarly, his emphasis on basic education as the means of eradicating ignorance and superstition and to endow the people with a scientific temper and approach, is laudable.

Throughout his premiership Nehru strove hard to bring about social justice through just means. All the methods which he advocated and the reforms that his government accomplished were in keeping with the temper and mind of the country i.e. social - justice through democratic means. Though there is still much to be desired, yet to Nehru goes the credit of modernising India, for making a breakthrough amidst various challenges and hurdles that were present in India since millennia.

For well over four decades, preceding the transfer of power, the Indian political scene was stormed by a galaxy of leaders and illustrious personalities. Jawaharlal Nehru was one of those who played a crucial role in the political and constitutional evolution of India, emerging as an outstanding leader of the national movement.

The role of Nehru in the national movement is multi-dimensional. He performed various important roles simultaneously and therein lies his uniqueness. At once, he was the leader of the youth, guiding them, educating them in lessons of nationalism and socialism and channelising their energies towards achievement of freedom, at another, he was the mediator who by his ceaseless efforts saved the Congress and thereby the movement from breaking point.

Gandhi, transformed the struggle into a mass movement but gradually the responsibility of consolidating the multifarious forces and guiding them amidst the stormy period of post world-war, towards independence, fell on Nehru. He imparted to the national movement a content and a substance and thereby made it a national movement. By linking politics and economics in the context of freedom he rendered to the movement a scientific temper and a socialist orientation. He visualised the changing role of India in a changing world for he saw her a part of the greater whole. In this context his effort to bring India closer to the socialist and progressive forces of the world is remarkable. The phenomenal roles which Nehru played in modernising the movement will be remembered in history with reverence. It goes to his credit that despite the Mahatma's charismatic presence and powerful impact, Nehru did manage to lift the movement out of its medieval and obscurantist garb and bring it parallel to the similar movements taking part in the world. In other words, Nehru in this decade fused the elements of radicalism or modernity into the mass movement. There is some truth in the otherwise facile contention that the representatives of the modernist trend tended to be somewhat aloof from the problems of the masses, particularly their poverty and their political subjectivity. It was frequently described as a movement of the snobs by the snobs and for the snobs. In contrast, whatever may be their antediluvian concepts and their reactionary outlook, the traditionalists could speak to the masses in a language they understood, give them an approachable image and restore their self-respect as a nation. Nehru's abiding achievement will always be his burning repudiation of this thesis. No national leader was more scientific, more modern, more radical and yet in tune with the masses. Thus, he made the movement at once anti-medieval, modern, anti-imperialist and anti-capitalist.

The quintessence of Jawaharlal Nehru's thought is Nationalism, Socialism and Democracy. His uniqueness lies in the fact that he integrated the three concepts to formulate a comprehensive philosophy. He did not view one apart from the other, and brought about a synthesis, which was otherwise considered opposing and contradictory in political thought.

Nehru was aware of the negativity of nationalism, its abuse and the consequences which arose out of unbridled nationalism. Yet at the same time due to a study of the forces of history he understood that nationalism had also a constructive side and was inevitable and unavoidable especially in Asia and the developing countries. Thus, the nationalism of Nehru as opposed to the traditional concept was a definite ideal, and a positive norm. With this view he incorporated socialism with nationalism, thereby making nationalism a creative urge, a natural phenomenon and a progressive movement. This is one of Nehru's unique contribution.

A regular criticism levelled against socialism is that it allows little individual freedom and is totally incompatible with democracy. But Nehru did not subscribe to this view, he went ahead and amalgamated the two. For him socialism and democracy are not incompatible but supplementary to each other. He linked the struggle for democracy with a perspective that would open itself towards socialism. The new type of organization that was needed in the country was precisely to establish this ideal of democracy or republicanism interpreted as a Republic wedded to non-exploitive society.

It is not easy to make an exact and precise evaluation of Jawaharlal Nehru because there is no aspect of India which remains unifluenced by the Nehru phenomenon. Any statement made about him is bound to do his complex personality little justice. He is not only a statesman and an ardent admirer of freedom and democracy, but a historian, a philosopher, a distinguished literary figure, a social architect and an internationalist.

By the end of 1956, Nehru was recognized as one of the few living men who made an impression on the world. "The man who", in the words of Harpers Magazine 'since the era of the Churchill - Stalin, Roosvelt era, is the most arresting figure on the world political stage.'

One of the greatest contributions of Nehru to India was the air of modernism he brought in without destroying the strong edifice which enabled Indian culture, which was not moving, was too submerged and crushed under the burden of the past, and in a coma, Nehru gave a gentle push forward and took her to the new realms of modernism the life of the west, and he sought to blend western materialism with the eastern spiritualism. He ceaselessly strived to find a synthesis between the world of fact and the world of spirit for it was increasingly obvious that the overemphasis on the former was the spirit of man while excessive reliance on the latter made India's people despicable. He endeavoured to wedge the India of the past with that of the present with an agile mind - a mind governed by practical idealism dedicated towards social betterment. By his profound leadership he moulded and inspired a whole generation of Indians kindling them through a loyalty of principles and keeping the country and her people glued together as he gave them a sense of purposeful direction. The problems created by diverse languages would have created conflicts in the country. But during the Nehru era the problems created with it very rarely threatened national unity. Whenever it threatened to do so he was in a position to ease the situation.

The tools Nehru used to usher India into the modern age were science and technology, industrialization and national planning. He upheld science as the greatest revolutionary force of the modern times and among the greatest of the services to his motherland, was to ceaselessly inculcate the scientific outlook and temper among his countrymen. The essential aspect of his science was to teach man to think and act in a rational way. It is the scientific approach–the search for truth and new knowledge, the refusal to accept anything without testing and trial, reliance on observed fact and not on preconceived theory--all this is necessary for the application of science but for life itself and the solution of many of its problems, he ridiculed uncontrolled use of science but believed in Scientific Humanism. Nehru was the man who went for rapid industrialization with the primary purpose of absolving labour and not for creating fresh unemployment. To raise his countrymen from the shackles of poverty and unemployment to better standards of living but to relieve the pressure on land, he felt rapid industrialisation was necessary. A comprehensive scheme of national planning embracing every activity for national development was formulated.

According to Nehru, a "proper approach" to socialism, based primarily on European experience, would not help. The doctrine of socialism should be adopted to the facts of the Indian situation and the historical background of her people, the tremendous achievement in science and technology should be utilized, but brought in line with the experience of India. If socialism were to succeed in India, it could not be a carbon copy of European socialism but should fit in with the basic Indian philosophic outlook.

Nehru's grand vision of a modern democratic, socialist India, achieved with as much importance attached to the means as to the end. Nehru's hope was for a society where decisions would be made on the basis of popular will and rational discourse by education and social progress promoted by general consent. He could not be convinced that socialism required the discarding of liberal values. His strategies, both political and economic arose coherently out of his fundamental belief in liberty. Nehru had a harmonic conception of society, of an India finding her own peaceful path to modernity without suppressing her individuality. He tried to evolve a modern state within the Indian culture, which he came to call the 'Indian genius'.

In essence, Nehru sought to give India a dynamic, secular outlook, a social fluidity, utilisation of vast national resources, discarding beliefs of the medieval ages, faith in science and its application and widespread education, opportunities and social justice for all its people. Above all, his greater contribution to the world at large is that through his very own interpretation of socialism, which may also, be called 'Humanistic

Socialism' he made socialism popular, a household word. It was due to his staunch faith in socialism, its practice in India through stages, its achievements that socialism came to be acceptable. Thus the socialist thought of the contemporary world is indebted to Jawaharlal Nehru for this monumental contribution.

A humane democratic-socialism is Jawaharlal Nehru's specific brand of socialism. It is above, all, a humanistic creed, placing its major emphasis on the fulfilment of the individual. But unlike the European radicals, who looked down on revolutionary change it could inspire authority to coherent activity and sustain popular initiative as a liberating force. Moreover, by linking socialism with democracy, Nehru made socialism a more respectable creed, thereby liberating it from dogma and rigidity.

Today, over three decades later, the Basic Approach continues to be classic diagnosis and thereby for ensuring social progress and economic justice without the loss of political freedom in the chaotic conditions of a developing society. Attempts at one party dictatorship devised to accelerate socialism have failed in most cases. Even the more institutionalised, more principled socialist systems like those in China and Eastern Europe have learnt the need for democracy in the party, in the state apparatus, in industry and in agriculture, that is, on the plant floor and in the collective farm, for genuine improvement. The new thinking and the attempt at restructuring and openness which is now sweeping through the Soviet Union, and hopefully in Eastern Europe represents an acknowledgement of the continuing relevance of these concerns of Nehru of thirty years ago.

The experience of Indian democracy in practice demonstrates that Jawaharlal Nehru was fundamentally correct in his analysis, his prescriptions were provisional, based upon the technological and economic environment in the fifties and rooted in the ideas he had absorbed during a long and sustained period of self-education. All that has happened since then, both in the world and in India, the electronic revolution with its impact both on national economies and their international links and also on the conditioning of the human mind in the mass have only served to underline the essential appositeness of democratic socialism in our large, still imperfectly organized nation state.

Socialism without democracy has also been tried and found wanting, it leads to political oppression, economic stragnation and nothing less than the alienation of the individual in condition of anomy. Many of the alternative prescriptions for social action and economic organization have failed. Jawaharlal Nehru's patient, serious search for a viable solution to the problems of twentieth century society in the nuclear age has to be continued by his successors with the same sincerity and firmness of purpose. In doing so, we should never forget that the ineluctable pre-condition for such creative action is a democratic culture and not merely democratic institutions coupled with a socialist way of thinking.

BIBLIOGRAPHY

PRIVATE PAPERS

Jawaharlal Nehru Papers : (1920-1945), (N.M.M.L.)
The Files of All India
Congress Committee : (1920-1946), (N.M.M.L.)

OFFICIAL RECORDS

Home Political Files	: (1920-1928),(National Archives, New Delhi)
Indian Foreign Affairs	: (1956-1959), (I.C.W.A)
Foreign Affairs Record	: (1956-1963), (I.C.W.A)
Speeches in Parliament	: (1956-1959), (N.M.M.L)
Constituent Assembly Debates	: (1947-1949)
Parliamentary Debates, House of Peoples Official Record	: (1952-1955)
Prime Minister's Press Conferences, (P.M.'s Secretariat, (P.I.B)	: (1950-1963)
Nehru Clippings	: (1956-1959), (N.M.M.L)
Progress of Land Reforms (Planning Commission)	: (1950-64) N.M.M.L.
Five Year Plan (First And Second (Planning Commission)	: N.M.M.L

ENCYCLOPAEDIAS

International Encyclopaedia of Social Sciences, vol. II, Kohn, Hans, (ed), (London, Macmillan and Free Press, 1963)

Encyclopaedia Britannica, vol. 6,8,10, (Chicago, Encyclopaedia, Britannica, INC.)

Marxism, Communism And Western Society : A Comparative Encyclopaedia, vol. IV, (New York, Herder and Herder, 1972)

The Encyclopaedia of the Indian National Congress, vol. 9, 11, Zaidi, A.M; Zaidi, S.G; (ed), (Delhi, S. Chand & Co., 1980)

BOOKS WRITTEN BY JAWAHARLAL NEHRU

Nehru, J. *Readings in Indian History Politics and Philosophy*, , (ed.), K. Sachidanannda Murty, (Bombay, Allied, 1967).

Nehru, J. *An Autobiography*, (New York, John Day, 1936)

Nehru, J. *Discovery of India*, (Meridian Books, 1956)

Nehru, J. *Glimpses of World History*, (New York, John Day, 1942)

Nehru, J. *On Community Development, Panchayati Raj and Cooperation*, (Delhi, Publication Division, 1965)

Nehru, J. *Soviet Russia*, (Law Journal Press, 1928)

Nehru, J. *China, Spain and the War*, (Kitabistan, 1940)

Nehru, J. *India and the World*, (London, George Allen &Unwin, 1936)

Nehru, J. *A Bunch of Old Letters*, (Bombay, Asia Publishing House, 1958)

Nehru, J. *Unity of India*, (London, Durmond, 1941)

Nehru, J. *Whither India ?*, (Allahabad, Kitabistan, 1958)

Nehru, J. *Recent Essays and Writings*, (Allahabad, Kitabistan, 1934)

Nehru, J. Congresssman's Primer for Socialism, (A compilation) by Malviya, H.D. (Delhi, A.I.C.C., 1976)

Nehru, J. *India And the World,* (London, George Allen & Unwin, 1936)

Nehru, J. *India on the March,* (New Delhi, I.N.C., 1957)

Nehru, J. *Before and After Independence,* (ed.), Bright T.S. (New Delhi, Printworks, 1952)

SPEECHES OF JAWAHARLAL NEHRU

Jawaharlal Nehru's Speeches, Vol. I to IV, (Delhi, The Publication Division.)

Nehru On Socialism: Selected Speeches And Writings, (New Delhi, Perspective Publication, 1964)

Bright, J.S; (ed.) *Important Speeches of Jawaharlal Nehru,* 1922. to 1945, (Lahore. The Indian Printing Works, 1945)

Gopal, S; (ed.), *Selected Works of Jawaharlal Nehru,* vols. 1 to 15, (Orient Longman, A Project of the Jawaharlal Nehru Memorial Fund, 1972)

Gopal, S; (ed.) *Nehru : an Anthology,* (Bombay, Oxford University Press, 1980)

BOOKS WRITTEN ON JAWAHARLAL NEHRU

Audichya, J; *The Economic Ideas of Nehru,* (Jodhpur, Jain Brothers, 1977)

Ahuja, B.N; *Jawaharlal Nehru: The Leader of East And West,* (Lahore, Varma Publishing Company, 1947)

Afanasyev, V.G; *Marxist Philosophy,* (Moscow, Progress Publishers, 1980)

Ahluwalia, B.K; (ed.) *Jawaharlal Nehru: India's Man of Destiny,* (New Delhi, Newman Group, 1978)

A Souvenir; Nehru and India, Essay Competition, 1981, (New Delhi, Journalists Welfare Foundation, 1981)

Bhatia, Vinod; *Jawaharlal Nehru and the Making of Indo-Soviet Relations,* 1917-1947, (New Delhi, Panchsheel Publishers, 1982)

Bandopadhyay, J. *The Making of India's Foreign Policy,* (New Delhi, Asian Publishers, 1982)

Bloomfield. J; (ed.) *Class, Hegemony and Party* (London, Lawrence and Wishart, 1977)

Beer. M; *Fifty Years of International Socialism,* (London, George Allen & Unwin, 1937)

Brecher, Michael : *Nehru: A Political Biography,* Bombay, Oxford University Press, 1959)

Chandra, Bipan; (edt.), *The Indian Left:Critical Appraisals,* New Delhi, Vikas, 1983)

Chandra, Bipan; *Nationalism And Colonialism in Modern India,* (New Delhi, Orient Longman, 1984)

Chopra, V.D; *India and the Socialist World,* (New Delhi, Allied Publishers, 1983)

Crossland, C.A.K; *The Future of Socialism,* (London, Jonathan Cape, 1963)

Crocker, Walter, Nehru: *A Contemporary's Estimate,* (London, Allen & Unwin, 1966)

Cousins, Norman, *Profiles of Nehru: America Remembers A World Leader,* (New Delhi, India Book Company,1966)

Dass, M. N : *The Political Philosophy of Nehru,* (New York, 1961)

Desfosses, Levesque, *Socialism in the Third World,* (New York, Praeger Publishers, 1975)

Deva, N.A; *Socialism And The Revolution,* (Bombay, Padma Publications, 1949)

Dahiya, B.N; *Jawaharlal Nehru: India's Man of Destiny,* (New Delhi, Newman Group of Publishers, 1971)

Dutt, R.C; *Socialism of Nehru,* (New Delhi, Abhinav Publications,1981)

Hutheesing, Krishna, *We Nehrus,* (Bombay, Pearl Publications, 1967)

Entinger, Y; and M. Melikyan, O; *The Policy of Non-Alignment,* (Moscow, Progress Publishers)

Edwards, M; *Nehru: Political Biography,* (Allen Lane, the Penguin Press, 1971)

Imam, Zafar; *Towards a Model Relationship* (New Delhi, ABC Publishing House, 1983)

Gopal, S, *Jawaharlal Nehru: A Biography*, vol. I, II and III, (Bombay, Oxford University Press)

Gopal, S; *The Mind of Jawaharlal Nehru,* (Madras, Sangam Books, 1980)

Gopal, S; *"The Formative Ideology of Jawharlal Nehru"* in K.N. Pannikar, *National and Left Movement in India,* (New Delhi, Vikas, 1980)

Gandhi And Nehru . A Symposium, New Delhi, NMML, 1979)

Jayate, Satyameva, *Nehru Discovered,* (Madras, Aiyar, 1961)

Jawaharlal Nehru in Soviet Perspective: A Symposium, (New Delhi, Sterling Publishers, 1980)

Joshi, P.C; *Gandhi and Nehru (ed.),* (Bombay, Oxford University Press, 1979)

Karanjia, R.K.; The Philosophy of Nehru, (London, George Allen & Unwin, 1966)

Karanjia, R.K; *The Mind of Mr. Nehru,* (London, George Allen & Unwin, 1960)

Kanwarlal, *Jawaharlal Nehru: Promise And Performance,* (New Delhi, Arts & Letters, 1970)

Karka, D.F; *Nehru: The Lotus Eater From Kashmir,* (Richard Clay and Co., Ltd., London, 1953)

Karl Marx and Our Time, Articles and Speeches, (Moscow, Progress, 1983)

Karunakaran, K.P; *The Phenomenon of Nehru,* (New Delhi, Gitanjali Prakashan, 1979)

Khan, Rasheedudin, (ed.) *Perspectives of Non-Alignment,* (New Delhi, Kamlakar Prakashan, 1981)

Kaushik, P.D; *The Congress Ideology and Programme,* 1920-1947, (Bombay, Allied, 1964)

Laski, H.J; *Liberty in the Modern State,* (1948)

Mahajan, V.S; *Socialistic Pattern in India,* (New Delhi, S. Chand & Co., 1974)

Malviya, H.D; Land Reforms in India, (New Delhi, I.N.C., 1954)

Mathur, M.V; and Narain Iqbal, (ed.), *Panchayati Raj, Planning And Democracy,* (Bombay, Asia Publishing House, 1969)

Marx and Engels, *Manifesto of the Communist Party,* (Moscow, Progress, 1952)

Mecellan, David, *Marxism After Marx,* (London, Macmillan, 1979)

Mansingh, Heinisath, *Diplomatic History of Modern India,* (Bombay, Allied Publishers, 1971)

Mathai, M.O; *Reminiscences of Nehru Age,*(New Delhi, Vikas, 1978)

Moraes, Frank, *Jawaharlal Nehru: A Biography,* (New York, Macmillan., 1956)

Mende, Tibor; *Conversations With Mr. Nehru,* (London, Secker & Warburg, 1956)

Menon, K.P.S; *The Flying Troika,* (Nehru in Soviet Union), (Bombay, Oxford University Press, 1963)

Mehta, A; *Democratic Socialism,* (Bombay, Bhartiya Vidya Bhavan, 1959)

Mishra, D.P.; *Living an Era: The Nehru Epoch,* vol.II, (Delhi, Vikas, 1978)

Moraes, Frank; *Witness to an Era,* (Delhi, Vikas, 1973)

Mukherjee, Hiren, *The Gentle Colossus: A Study of Jawaharlal Nehru,* (Calcutta, Manisha Granthalya, 1964)

Mukerjee, G.K; *Nehru: The Humanist,* (New Delhi Trimurti Publication, 1972)

Myrdal, Gunnar, *The Challenges of World Poverty,* (Penguin International, 1970)

Namboodripad, E.M.S; *Economic And Politics of India's Socialist Pattern,* (Delhi, P.P.H., 1966)

Naik, *Soviet Policy Towards India,* (Delhi, Vikas, 1970)

Naraiyan, Jayprakash, *Socialism, Sarvodaya and Democracy;* Selected Works, (ed.) by Prasad, Bimal, (Bombay, Asia, 1964)

Narayan, J.P; *Communitarian Society and Panchayati Raj,* (Varanasi, Navchitra Prakashan, 1978)

Nanda, B.R. (ed.) *Socialism in India,* (New Delhi, Vikas 1972)

Nanda, B.R; *The Nehrus: Motilal And Jawaharlal,* (London, George Allen & Unwin, 1962)

Nanda, B.R; (ed.) *Indian Foreign Policy; The Nehru Years,* (New Delhi, Vikas, 1976)

Narsimhachari, K.J; *The Quintessance of Nehru,* (London, George Allen & Unwin, 1961)

Narasamiha, C.D. (ed.) *Nehru: Jawaharlal India's Spokesman,* from speeches and addresses by Pandit Jawaharlal Nehru, (Madras, Macmillan, 1960)

Nehru Legacy: A Symposium,(New Delhi, National Book Club, 1966)

Nehru And The Modern World, International Round Table On Jawaharlal Nehru, New Delhi September, 1966, (New Delhi, UNESCO; 1967)

Neeraj, *Nehru And Democracy in India.* (Delhi, Metropolitan Book Company, 1972)

New Statesman:Profiles, (Bombay, Wilco Publishing House, 1958)

Norman, D; *Nehru: The First Sixty Years.* vol,I and II, (Bombay, Asia Publisahing House, 1965)

Pandey, B.N; *Nehru* (London, Macmillan, 1976)

Patil, V.J; *Nehru And The Freedom Movement,* (New Delhi, Sterling Publishers, 1979)

Prasad, B; "Jawaharlal Nehru as Prime Minister" in B.N. Pandey(ed.), *Leadership in South-East Asia* (New Delhi, Vikas, 1977)

Prasad, Bimal, (ed.); *India's Foreign Policy,* (New Delhi, Vikas, 1979)

Ponlantzas, N; *State, Power, Socialism,* (Presses Universitaires de France, 1978)

Range, Willard, *Jawaharlal Nehru's World View: A Theory of International Relation,* (Athens, University of Georgia Press, 1961)

Rao, B.G; and, Rao Amiya, *Six Thousand Days: Jawaharlal Nehru, Prime Minister* (New Delhi, Sterling Publishers, 1974)

Rao, M.B; *Documents of the History of the Communist Party of India,* vol.II, (New Delhi, Peoples Publishing House, 1976)

Rao, V.K.R.V; *The Nehru Legacy,* (Bombay, Popular Prakashan, 1971)

Rao, *Indian Socialism,* (New Delhi, Concept Publishing Company, 1982)

Rana, A.P; *The Imperatives of Non-Alignment,* (Delhi Macmillan, 1976)

Radhakrishnan, S (ed.) ; *On Nehru,* (New Delhi, Publication Division, 1965)

Roy, M.N; *"Jawaharlal Nehru: An Enigma or a Tragedy"?* in A.B. Shah (ed.); *Jawaharlal Nehru: A Critical Tribute,* (Bombay,1965)

Rader, M; *Marx's Interpretation of History,* New Delhi, (Oxford University Press, 1979)

Ralhan, O.P; *Jawaharal Nehru: A Broad Chronological Study,* (Delhi, S.S. Publications, 1983)

Ravindran, K; *Nehru's Idea of History,* (Delhi, Light and Life, 1980)

Rajan, M.R;(ed.) *India's Foreign Relations During the Nehru Era,* (Bombay, Asia Publishing House, 1976)

Raghavachari, S.S.; *The Unfolding Purpose,* (Madras, University of Madras, 1969)

Reid, Escot, *Envoy to Nehru* (Delhi, Oxford University Press, 1981)

Sarkar, Sumit; *Modern India,* (Delhi, Macmillan India,1983)

Sarin, L.N; *Jawaharlal Nehru* (Delhi, S.Chand & Co. 1968)

Scientific Communism: A Text Book, (Moscow, Progress Publishers,1975)

Shean, V; *Nehru: The Years Of Power,* (New york, Random House, 1960)

Shetty, Krishna, K.P; *Fundamental Rights and Socio-Economic Justice*, (Allahabad, Chaitanya Publishing House, 1969)

Sen, N.B. (ed); *Glorious Thought Of Nehru,* (New Delhi, New Book Society of India, 1964)

Seton, M; *Panditjee: A Portrait of Jawaharla Nehru* Seminar on Nehru: (Madras, The Centre or Social Research, 1974)

Sinha, *The Red Rebel In India,* (New Delhi, Associated 1968)

Sinha, B.K; *Co-Operatives In India,* (New Delhi, National Co-Operative Union of India)

Smith, D.E; *Nehru and Democracy: The Political Thought of An Asian Democrat,*(Bombay, Orient Longman, 1958)

Tarachand; *History of the Freedom Movement in India,* vol. 1 to 4, (Publication Division,1961)

The Basics of Marxist-Leninist Theory,; (Moscow, Progress, 1979)

Thompson, George; *From Marx to Mao-Tse-Tung: A Study in Revolutionary Dialectics* (G. Britain, The London City Press, 1977)

The Seminar on Nehru,;(Madras, The Centre for Social Reserch, 1974)

Tandon, P.J (ed.); *Nehru: Your Neighbour,* (Calcutta, Signett Press, 1946)

Tyson, Geoggrey, R; *Nehru:TheYears of Power,* (Bombay, Jaico, 1970)

Ulyanovysky, R; *National Liberation: Easays in Theory and Practice,* vol. I and II, (Moscow, Progress, 1978)

Ulyanovysky, R; *Present-Day Problems in Asia* and *Africa,* (Moscow, Progress, 1980)

Ulyanovysky, R; *Socialism and the Newly Independent Nations,* (New Delhi, PPH, 1970)

Vaizey, John; *Revolutions of Our Time:Social Democracy,* (London, Weidenfield and Nicholson, 1971)

Verma, D.C; *The Unfinished Revolution,* (New Delhi, National Publishing House,1981)

V. Zimayanin; *Jawaharlal Nehru* (Moscow, Progress Publishers, 1982)

Zakaria, R (ed.), *A Study of Nehru,* (Bombay, Bennet Coleman, 1966)

ARTICLES, PERIODICALS AND JOURNALS

Bahuguna, H; (ed.); *Socialist India, Weekly of the* INC, (New Delhi, National Herald Press),May, 1970 to Nov., 1970 vol. VI

Chatterjee, Partha, "Jawaharlal Nehru And the Decade After Freedom", *Indian Historical Review.*

Dietmar Rothermung, "Nehru and Early Years of Socialism In India", *Socialist India,* Independence November, 1970.

Dubey, Suman, "A Troubled Legacy", *India Today,* June 15, May, 1984.

Inderjeet, Badhwar; "A Dynamic View", *India Today*, 31st May, 1984.

Joshi, P.C; " Nehru and the Land Problem", *Mainstream* vol. XXI, No. 12 Nov. 20, 1982.

Prasad, Ganesh; "Shaping of Nehru's World-View", *Mainstream,* (New Delhi) vol.XX, No. 39, 29, 1982.

Singh, M.H.K; "Jawaharlal Nehru and Economic Change", *Economic and Political Weekly,* (New Delhi, vol.X, No.33, Aug., 1975.

Sarkar, Sumit; "Popular Movement and National Leadership, 1945-47, *Economic and Political Weekly,* vol. XVII, Annual Number, 1982.

Sen, Mohit; "The Social Democrat", *Mainstream*, No-63, Nov., 1964

Tausing (ed.); *Eastern World* (London) vol. 18, 1964-68 *Gandhi Marg*.

The Indian Journal Of Political Science. A Quarterly (New Delhi) The Indian Political Science Association, vols. XXX 35, No, 1 to 4, 1974

Nehru, Birthday Special, *Mainstream*, vol. XXIII, No. 12, 1984.

NEWSPAPERS

1. *Amrit Bazar Patrika* : 1947-1950
2. *The Hindu* : 1947-1956
3. *The Hindustan Times* : 1956-1958
4. *The Independent* : 1925-1926
5. *The National Herald* : 1956-1958
6. *The Statesman* : 1953-1964
7. *The Bombay Chronicle* : 1947-1958
8. *The New York Times* : 1956
9. *Washington Post* : 1955
10. *The Leader* : 1917-1928

Index